AUGUSTINE

The Arguments of the Philosophers

EDITOR: TED HONDERICH

Grote Professor of the Philosophy of Mind and Logic
University College, London

The purpose of this series is to provide a contemporary assessment and history of the entire course of philosophical thought. Each book constitutes a detailed, critical introduction to the work of a philosopher of major influence and significance.

Already published in the series:

*J. L. Austin	Geoffrey Warnock
Ayer	John Foster
*Bentham	Ross Harrison
*Berkeley	George Pitcher
Bergson	A. R. Lacey
Butler	Terence Penelhum
*Descartes	Margaret Dauler Wilson
*Dewey	J. E. Tiles
Gottlob Frege	Hans Sluga
Hegel	M. J. Inwood
Hobbes	Tom Sorell
Husserl	David Bell
William James	Graham Bird
*Kant	Ralph C. S. Walker
Kierkegaard	Alastair Hannay
Locke	Michael Ayres
*Karl Marx	Allen Wood
Meinong	Reinhart Grossman
*John Stuart Mill	John Skorupski
G. E. Moore	Tom Baldwin
*Nietzsche	Richard Schacht
Peirce	Christopher Hookway
*Plato	J. C. B. Gosling
*Karl Popper	Anthony O'Hear
*The Presocratic Philosophers	Jonathan Barnes
*Thomas Reid	Keith Lehrer
*Russell	R. M. Sainsbury
Santayana	Timothy Sprigge
*Sartre	Peter Caws
*Schopenhauer	D. W. Hamlyn
*Socrates	Gerasimos Xenophon Santas
Spinoza	R. J. Delahunty
*Wittgenstein	Robert J. Fogelin

*available in paperback

AUGUSTINE

Christopher Kirwan

London and New York

First published in 1989
First published in paperback in 1991 by Routledge
11 New Fetter Lane, London EC4P 4EE

Simultaneously published in the USA and Canada
by Routledge
a division of Routledge, Chapman and Hall, Inc.
29 West 35th Street, New York, NY 10001

Printed in Great Britain by
T. J. Press (Padstow) Ltd
Padstow, Cornwall

British Library Cataloguing in Publication Data
Kirwan, Christopher
Augustine.
1. Christian church. Augustine, Saint,
Bishop of Hippo
I. Title II. Series
270.2092

Library of Congress Cataloging in Publication Data
Kirwan, Christopher.
p. cm. – (The Arguments of the philosophers)
Bibliography: p.
Includes index.
1. Augustine, Saint, Bishop of Hippo. I. Title. II. Series.
B655.Z7K5 1991
189'.2–dc20 91–27216

ISBN 0–415–06364–7

s.

Contents

Preface

In the library of the monastery at Seville where St Isidore was a monk at the end of the sixth century, the case containing the works of St Augustine bore a superscription (I quote from memory), 'Anyone who says he has read all this is a liar'. My own reading of Augustine, confined to the last eleven years, has been far from complete. For that and other reasons I am conscious that the book here presented about his philosophy is in some ways only a sketch. Not that what I have written is likely to break new ground: such a vast literature of commentary on this Doctor of the Church exists, continuous from his day to ours, and he has helped to shape the thought of so many great thinkers, that anyone who had time to absorb the tradition would probably find most of his own critical ideas anticipated, in one way or another. The excuse for this book is rather that it observes Augustine from a stance outside that Christian theological tradition, the stance of an analytic philosopher, who happens also to be an atheist (though that should make little difference), and who knows something of Augustine's Greek predecessors in philosophy but not much of his medieval or renaissance successors.

Having Augustine's *philosophy* as my subject has meant that large stretches of his thought – on baptism and the sacraments, for example – could reasonably be passed by in silence. In fact I have been pretty selective even within the areas now conventionally assigned to my discipline. Free will and time occupy the centre of the stage. By a decision which was deliberate at the time but now seems to me somewhat perverse, Augustine's philosophy of mind gets no attention; let me merely plead that to do it justice would have made the book that I have written too long. Other topics covered either spring from the major theme of free will – the problem of evil, original sin – or have seemed likely to interest the general votary of philosophy who is historically minded – scepticism, language, morals, and politics. The full list in my bibliography of Augustine's works and English translations of them known to me will help to guide further into his thought; and every chapter ends with some suggestions for reading among the moderns.

I am anxious to thank many kind friends and acquaintances for help great and small, the extent of which I cannot now always remember. Among them are: Bill Anglin, Catherine Atherton, David Bakhurst, Lesley Brown, Myles Burnyeat, Nicholas Denyer, John Foster, Justin Gosling, Dewey Hoitenga, Anthony Long, Howard Robinson, Mark Sainsbury, Andreas Schubert, Graham Shaw, Richard Sorabji, Christopher Stead, Michael Woods. Drafts of several chapters were given as talks in Oxford, Cambridge, Nottingham, and Prague, to audiences who made me think hard and change much, I hope for the better. A period of leave from my College helped a good deal to move things along, as did my welcome at the Institute for Advanced Study at Princeton where I was privileged to spend a term of that leave. Finally I wish to record very special thanks to my friend and colleague John Lucas, who jointly with me ran three graduate classes on aspects of Augustine's philosophy. In those enlivening sessions – some of them among the early summer flowers of Merton College garden – I learned to value even more than before the range and fecundity of his mind, and to feel myself the beneficiary of a generous spirit.

The translation of the *Confessions* that I took into the army as a conscript soldier remained unread in my locker. Had Pine-Coffin's delightful version been available then, I might have persisted. I am happy to acknowledge the permission of Penguin Books Ltd to reproduce two passages from Saint Augustine, *Confessions*, translated by R. S. Pine-Coffin, Harmondsworth, Penguin, 1961. (The other quotations from Augustine and other writers are nearly always in my own translation.) I also acknowledge permission to reprint in revised form my article 'Augustine against the Skeptics', from *The Skeptical Tradition*, edited by Myles Burnyeat, Berkeley, University of California Press, 1983. The copyrights in those works are owned respectively by R. S. Pine-Coffin and the Regents of the University of California.

Christopher Kirwan
Exeter College, Oxford
April 1988

I

Life and works

At the time of Jesus, Judaism was gaining converts throughout the romanized Mediterranean. Christianity inherited this proselytizing habit, through Paul; and gradually the new religion, imbued with Jewish culture and morality but disowned by the nation of its founders, established churches in every part of the Roman Empire. Within a couple of hundred years systematic Christian thinkers had appeared, Clement and Origen at Alexandria, Irenaeus – also a Greek – at Lyons, Tertullian at Carthage. Growth in numbers made Christianity visible enough by the middle of the third century to attract centrally directed persecution under the emperor Decius in 250–1, revived more fiercely in the Great Persecution of Diocletian and his successors in 303–312. But then, in an instant, came triumph, with the conversion in 312 of Constantine the Great (c.274–337) and his defeat of the rival western emperor Maxentius later in the same year. From that turning point there was to be no lasting retreat, and 'the religion of Constantine achieved, in less than a century, the final conquest of the Roman empire' (Gibbon, *Decline and Fall*, vol. 3, p. 215).*

Aurelius Augustinus (354–430) was born during this conquering century, the fourth of the Christian era, the first of Christian government. His birthplace was Thagaste, a hill town in the north African province of Numidia, now Souk-Aras in Algeria, about fifty miles inland and south of Hippo Regius (later Bône, now Annaba in Algeria), where, as bishop, he was to spend the second half of his life. In the year of his birth Constantius II, sole survivor of Constantine's three sons, ruled an increasingly turbulent empire. Alamans and Franks were ranging unchecked in Gaul; from the east the emperor's cousin Gallus, fresh from suppressing a variety of disturbances – revolt in Galilee, Isaurian

* References are explained in the Bibliography, p. 225.

1

pirates, food riots in the great metropolis of Antioch – was recalled to court and executed. The north African provinces themselves – that is, the northern seaboard now comprising Tunisia, Algeria, and Morocco – had for long been prey to bands of Circumcellions, dispossessed brigands who were suspected of being employed by the schismatic Donatist church there against the minority Catholics. Yet people did not think of these various troubles as terminal. The empire had always been a melting pot of races and cultures. In Africa Berber-speaking country people, some still worshipping the grim local god who went under the Latinized name of Saturn, mixed uneasily with Greeks on the coast (among them Valerius, Augustine's predecessor as bishop) and with scattered upper-class Latin-speakers. Everyone knew that civilization was only skin-deep.

Augustine's family was of the romanized sort, poor but respectable, beholden to the patronage of a neighbouring grandee, Romanianus, who was to help pay for Augustine's education. His parents Patricius and Monica had at least two other children, a boy Navigius and a girl of whom we hear later as head of a nunnery attached to her brother's cathedral (*Ep.* 211.4). In his childhood, Augustine wrote, 'I was already a believer; so was she [Monica], and the whole household except my father' (*Conf.* 1.11.17). The influence of this famous mother, flamboyant, devout, exigent, and inflexible, is daringly portrayed in her son's *Confessions*; she was, as Rebecca West wrote, 'a smooth cliff on whom the breakers of a man's virility would dash in vain' (West 1933:27). When at last he returned to his childhood religion in Milan at the age of 33, she was there to enjoy her triumph; and it was in her son's company the next year, 387, that she died at Ostia near Rome, her reward the lovely posthumous tribute in *Confessions* book 9.

Before this time the young Augustine had found a wider stage than small-town Thagaste. His workmanlike early education there, designed in the traditional Roman manner to make a boy familiar with the Latin classics and competent to succeed in public life by tongue and pen, had been followed by a year at the neighbouring university of Madaura, and then an idle year back at home while his father – soon to die – sought more funds. In 371, at the age of 17, he was sent to university at Carthage, metropolis of Roman Africa, where he was chiefly to remain until 383 and which he was to revisit often later for councils and other church business. At first he made the most of student life: he was top of his class, enjoyed the bawdy theatre, used sex in search of love, and consorted guiltily with a student group who called themselves the Smashers ('eversores'). But within two years the style had changed completely: he was living with a woman, in the then accepted arrange-ment which would end with her dismissal as soon as he attained wealth and status enough to undertake the public and family duties of a legal marriage; he had a son by her, Adeodatus (who died in his teens); and his reading of Cicero's now lost dialogue *Hortensius* had put into his head the ambition of an intellectual life in which he should abandon power and pleasure in order to devote himself, preferably in a kind of monastic community of kindred spirits, to the pursuit of truth.

In this new mood he came upon the Manichees, self-styled Christians of whose teaching we shall hear more in chapter 4. Peter Brown has compared their appeal in Carthaginian student circles to that of communists in 1930s England (Brown 1967:54). They were trendy, cliquish, intellectually dashing, and illegal; they promised emancipation, not indeed to the whole of society, but to choice minds who would join the life of their 'elect' – vegetarian, celibate, contemplative. Augustine became a 'hearer' – corresponding to the Catholic status of catechumen – and remained so for nine years. In 375 he returned briefly to Thagaste with the intention of teaching literature, where he converted his patron Romanianus and his patron's young relative Alypius, who was later to follow Augustine into the Catholic church and the episcopate and to remain a lifelong friend and ally. But Monica, scandalized, was minded to shut him out of the house. Back in Carthage, and now a teacher of rhetoric, his enthusiasm for the Manichees eventually waned, and the sense of freedom at first engendered by them gave way to sceptical doubts.

In 383, aged 28, Augustine moved to Rome, preceded by Alypius and encouraged by powerful friends to seek a better class of pupil and colleague than provincial Carthage could supply. His mother, hoping to dissuade or accompany him, was given the slip on the quayside. But in Rome things began to go wrong. His health was bad, his spirits low, and his pupils would not pay their fees. A professorship fell vacant at Milan, residence of the imperial court; Augustine was offered it and went north again in 384. There Monica joined him, and also his brother Navigius, Licentius the son of Romanianus, the 13-year-old Adeodatus, and Adeodatus' mother (whom Augustine never names). Alypius was among them too, and another lifelong African friend Evodius, who would become bishop of Uzala near Carthage. With marriage now in prospect the nameless concubine of the last thirteen years was sent home to Africa; but Augustine to his own disgust took up with another mistress. A circle of Platonists, led by an elderly Christian called Simplicianus, drew him into their number, rescued him from the Ciceronian scepticism which his stay at Rome had nurtured, and exposed him apparently for the first time to the serious – and of course basically Greek – traditions of ancient philosophy. This Platonism, which we call Neoplatonism, had been instituted a century before by Plotinus (205–70) and disseminated by his pupil and editor Porphyry (*c.*232–304); both wrote Greek, both taught in Rome, both were pagan – Porphyry an anti-Christian polemicist. The combination which they found, or thought they found, in Plato of ascetic high-mindedness and systematic metaphysics appealed to the visionary spirit of the times. Augustine was impressed.

It would not be easy to conjoin marriage with Platonism. A philosopher, as Augustine's contemporaries saw things, could flourish only in a semi-monastic setting surrounded by other males and free from the then very real cares of domestic and public life. Marriage went with the professorial and even political ambitions that had drawn him northwards from Africa. Yet marriage, he now felt, actually defiled those ambitions, for it would perpetuate his enslavement to sexual pleasure. Augustine was ill and deeply wretched, even (his mind on a projected speech in praise of the emperor) envying the boisterousness of a drunken beggar whom he encountered in the streets of Milan. Alypius urged the case for philosophy; but Augustine felt need of a 'medicine' against lust, fearing that he 'would be too miserable unless folded in a woman's arms' (*Conf.* 6.11.20).

The medicine was dispensed through another part of Milan's dowry to him, acquaintance with its bishop Ambrose. Ambrose was the first of western Christendom's scholar-statesmen, a former provincial governor raised to bishop from layman – indeed unbaptized layman – by popular demand. It was during Augustine's stay in the city that Ambrose successfully resisted pressure from Justina, Arian mother of the emperor Valentinian II, to surrender one of his churches to the use of her sect; and sixteen years later he was to exact penance from another emperor, Theodosius I, for a massacre at Thessalonica. Besides those notable assertions of ecclesiastical power, bishop Ambrose used sermons and tracts to transmit the subtleties of contemporary east Christian theology to the Latin-speaking west, and was the author of several surviving hymns (and even, according to some, of the so called Athanasian creed). Augustine heard the bishop's sermons and was enthralled. It occurred to him to study the Bible. They met – once at least in Monica's presence – and we can imagine Augustine's feeling that in this man his mother's piety was fused with an intellect worthy of his own and his friends' philosophical aspirations.

Through these or whatever means Augustine came to his conversion: to the moment in a Milanese garden in August 386 when, as he recounts in the *Confessions*, he heard a child's voice from a house nearby chanting, 'Pick it up and read it, pick it up and read it.' He walked over to where Alypius was sitting, took a copy of St Paul, opened it and read silently where his eye fell: 'No revelling or drunkenness, no debauchery or vice, no quarrels or jealousies! Let Christ Jesus himself be the armour that you wear; give no more thought to satisfying the bodily appetites' (Rom. 13:13 NEB). Thus he gained the self-command (continentia, *enkrateia*

4

LXX) which, so the Wisdom of Solomon told him (8:21 Vg, *Conf.* 6.11.20), could not be had except by God's gift.

He resigned his professorship and retired to a friend's villa at Cassiciacum (perhaps Cassago near Como), accompanied by Monica, Adeodatus, Alypius, and the others of his African circle who had congregated in Milan. To that winter belong the first of his extant writings, a group of hardly Christianized dialogues on philosophical themes. Next spring, 387, Augustine, Alypius, and Adeodatus were baptized. The plan now was to establish a lay monastic community back in Thagaste, and there they all returned in the autumn of 388, Monica dying on the way at Ostia, the port of embarkation near Rome.

Although the community came into existence at Thagaste, its life was cut short little over two years later by an event which, surprising though it appears to us, was of a kind commonplace at the time: on a visit to the coast at Hippo early in 391 Augustine was seized by the congregation during a service in the Catholic cathedral, presented to their bishop Valerius, and forced to accept ordination as a presbyter (*Serm.* 355.2). What did the Hipponese Catholics want him for? They might have set their eyes on his wealth (it had only been 'a few small fields', *Ep.* 126.7), had he not already bestowed it on the church at Thagaste; they will have desired an administrator to manage such things as poor relief, to arbitrate in disputes, and to be spokesman with the civil authorities, for in the newly Christian empire churches were acquiring the functions of a social services department; more especially they needed him as their champion in controversy with the schismatic Donatist church, then much the more powerful Christian community in the town (see chapter 11). Bishop Valerius was elderly, foreign, and conscious of his inadequacy; he would willingly coach Augustine to succeed, as duly happened in 396 after an intervening stage when, against the rules, they held episcopal office jointly. (Alypius became bishop of Thagaste, where he seems to have been still in post at Augustine's death.)

However much Augustine may have pined for the lost life of contemplation (*Op. Mon.* 28.37) there is no doubt that he grew into a first-rate pastor. We can savour his qualities still in various letters he wrote to simple and troubled people: to Sapida, a consecrated virgin, consoling her on her brother's death (*Ep.* 263); to a nuisance called Audax, delivering a kindly rebuff (*Ep.* 261); to an Arian general Pascentius, expounding the *homoousion* with controlled irritation (*Ep.* 238); or patient in answer to footling questions from a fellow bishop Hesychius about the Second Coming (*Ep.* 197, 199). On a wider scene, we have his own report that he persuaded the citizens of Mauretanian Caesarea (Cherchel, Algeria) to abandon the custom of their murderous annual town-battles (*Doct. Christ.* 4.24.53). These pastoral virtues shine out too in the only contemporary *Life* of Augustine, written by another simple soul Possidius, who

5

in Augustine's early episcopate had lived under him as a presbyter in the clergy-house at Hippo, and was afterwards bishop of nearby Calama. Seemingly unaware of Augustine's empire-wide fame and influence – of, for example, the rancorous pamphleteering about original guilt with Julian of Eclanum which occupied Augustine's last years – Possidius portrays the older man as an austere but fatherly table-companion.

The fame had come rapidly, in Africa at least; for in addition to his ordinary pastoral duties Augustine found himself appropriated by his fellow African bishops as their spokesman in controversy. There were Manichees as well as Donatists in Hippo, whom Augustine sought to confront in public debates; when those became too noisy for the speakers to be heard, he turned to treatises, much like open letters written for the edification of friends and the discomfiture of enemies (even private letters would often be read and disseminated by their bearers, and might be composed with that eventuality in mind). It was such controversy, in which his skill was redoubtable and his relish unbounded, that evoked much of the philosophy with which I shall be concerned in this book; for when Augustine wrote he usually wrote 'contra', against someone: on evil against the Manichees, on toleration against the Donatists, on grace and freedom against Pelagius and his followers (and the same holds good of his purely doctrinal writing – on the sacraments against the Donatists, on the Trinity still touched by the fading Arian controversy). Church politics appealed to him much less strongly, although with the arrival of the fifth century he was drawn progressively into a leading role in the series of councils at Carthage which strove to tighten the noose around the Donatists.

He was presbyter and bishop at Hippo for over thirty-nine years, often travelling up country or to Carthage on church business but never again leaving north Africa. In 410, aged 55, he shared the universal shock at the sack of Rome by Alaric the Goth. In his own north Africa revolts by Gildo in 398 and Heraclian in 413, two of the local military commanders-in-chief, called counts, needed imperial intervention. A year before Augustine's death the Vandals under Gaiseric crossed from Spain, devastated the seaboard, and laid siege to Hippo. Some months before the city fell, amid reports of ruin and atrocity in the country around, Augustine died there in 430 at the age of 75.

Works

Augustine modestly declared that his eloquence did not match his loquacity ('ego quidem parum eloquor, etsi multum loquor', *Ep.* 231). Near the end of his life he wrote to another correspondent of the amazement with which he discovered that he had produced 232 works (*Ep.* 224); as Possidius ingenuously but justly put it, 'there is hardly a scholar with the capacity to read and know them all' (*Vita*, ch. 18). This output was achieved by the use of secretaries, sometimes more than one at a time; but in spite of the temptation we may feel to regret the lavishness of their help, which induced in Augustine the habit of repeating old points in full detail to each new audience, we have to remember in his justification that he could rarely be sure that what he had already published was widely known. In 426 or 427 he surveyed his writings in a book called *Retractationes*, really a catalogue with comments and some retractions. From it we know that little he then possessed or remembered has since been lost; and what survives is immense, a greater bulk according to Chadwick (1986:1) than is extant from any other ancient author. It falls mainly into three genres – sermons, treatises, and letters; but here it will be more useful to divide it by subject matter.

First is a group of purely philosophical works, addressed to intellectuals such as those he collected at Cassiciacum in 386 and later in the short-lived Thagaste community. The style is Cicero's, itself modelled on the dialogues of Plato and Aristotle. The main works in this group (with dates) are *Contra Academicos* (386), *De Beata Vita* (386), *Soliloquia* (386–7), *De Dialectica* (387, authenticity disputed), *De Libero Arbitrio* (388, finished in the 390s), *De Musica* (387–90), *De Mendacio* (?396), *De Magistro* (389), and *De Diversis Quaestionibus* (388 and later).

Augustine's first major production as a presbyter (391 on) is the record of a public debate, *Contra Fortunatum Manichaeum* (392). Other Manichees felt his lash in *Contra Felicem Manichaeum* (398) and the mammoth *Contra Faustum Manichaeum* (?400); *Contra Epistolam Manichaeorum quam Vocant Fundamenti* (397) examines the Manichee credo; and there are other attacks in *De Moribus Ecclesiae Catholicae* and *De Moribus Manichaeorum* (both c.388), *De Duabus Animabus contra Manichaeos* (392–3) and *De Natura Boni contra Manichaeos* (399). As time passed he wrote also against the Donatists, in tracts such as *Contra Epistolam Parmeniani* (400), *Contra Litteras Petiliani* (401–5), *De Baptismo contra Donatistas* (400–1), and *Contra Cresconium Grammaticum* (405–6). This onslaught culminates in the grand conference between nearly 300 Catholic and as many Donatist bishops held in Carthage in 411, summarized by Augustine in his *Breviculus Collationis contra Donatistas* (413) (see chapter 11).

Only three works written during his episcopate (394 on), other than commentaries, give the impression of having been conceived as something more than urgent responses to the pressure of events and correspondents, but two of those three are his masterpieces. The *Confessions*, begun about 397, the year of Ambrose's death when Augustine was 42, and finished some four years later, is mainly an account of his life and emotional progress up to the death of Monica in 387, cast as an address to the God for whose peace he now saw himself as having yearned in vain until his conversion. The *City of God against the Pagans*, that 'huge work' as he called it, was written in the intervals of other business over most of the last seventeen years of his life between 413, shortly after the Donatist conference, and 426. In it he presents the history of the world as a preparation for the kingdom of heaven, in which the 'city' or community of saints, still in his age scattered dead and alive among the more numerous damned, would be separated from that mass and come together into everlasting life. The sack of Rome, ancient head of a mighty empire, in 410, is used as a lesson to pagans of the emptiness of worldly success. *De Trinitate*, third of this trio, also occupied Augustine over a long period, 399 to 419. It has in recent times been valued less by theologians as a defence of Nicene orthodoxy (Augustine was somewhat out of touch with the still uproarious trinitarian controversies in the east) than by certain philosophers for its elaborate analogies between the triune deity and the human mind.

The *Confessions* ends with an examination of the account of creation in Genesis 1–3. This subject and the problems about time which it suggested held a peculiar fascination for Augustine, perhaps because of his consciousness of the scorn felt for the Genesis story by both Manichees and pagan Platonists. Besides these concluding books of the *Confessions* he attempted three full-scale commentaries on Genesis: *De Genesi contra Manichaeos* (388–9), *De Genesi ad Litteram Imperfectus Liber* (393) and *De Genesi ad Litteram* (401–14). He wrote other biblical commentaries as well, though not to a grand plan like his contemporary Jerome. The main ones are: *De Sermone Domini in Monte* (394), *Enarrationes in Psalmos* (a large collection of expositions, some preached, 392–420), *Annotationes in Job* (399), *Tractatus in Johannem Evangelistam* (c.407–c.416), *Tractatus in Epistolam Johannis ad Parthos* (i.e. the first epistle of John, same dates), *Locutiones in Heptateuchum* (419–20), and short works on Paul's epistles to the Romans and Galatians. The collection of some 500 *Sermons* is, of course, mainly exposition of scripture too.

Old Simplicianus, the Christian Platonist who in Milan had introduced Augustine to the writings of Plotinus and Porphyry, succeeded Ambrose as bishop there in 397. A little before that, having kept in touch with his protégé back in Africa, he sent Augustine some questions on biblical exegesis to which Augustine replied in *Ad Simplicianum de Diversis Quaestionibus* (395). One question, 'Why did God hate Esau?', set Augustine thinking about the dependence of the human will on divine grace. Fifteen years later the sack of Rome brought refugees from Italy to Africa; and among them was Pelagius, a provincial from Britain (the first native of these islands from whom literary works survive) who had at much the same time as Augustine sought his fortune in Rome. Unlike Augustine Pelagius, who seems to have been a Christian already,

8

remained in the old capital, and remained a layman. Among upper-class Christian ascetics he made his mark as a teacher; his message, as Brown quoting Portalié has put it, 'was simple and terrifying: "since perfection is possible for man, it is obligatory" ' (Brown 1967:342). After a brief stay in Africa Pelagius moved on to Palestine; he and Augustine never met. But a disciple and fellow refugee Celestius scandalized Carthage in 411 by questioning the transmission of Adam's guilt and the need for infant baptism, and was denounced. When the matter came to Augustine's ears in Hippo his alarm was instant. It did not take him long to trace the origin of Celestius' views to Pelagius. Then began the campaign in defence of grace which above all else has stamped Augustine's name on the history of Christian theology; a campaign which he conducted with scant good will but passionate conviction, his opponent at first Pelagius and later, after Pelagius' death, the sharp but merciless Julian of Eclanum. The most important of Augustine's anti-Pelagian writings, many of them short, are: *De Peccatorum Meritis* (411), *De Spiritu et Littera* (412), *De Natura et Gratia* (413–15), *De Gratia Christi et de Peccato Originali* (418), *Contra Duas Epistolas Pelagianorum* (422–3), *Contra Julianum* (423), *De Gratia et Libero Arbitrio* (426), *De Correptione et Gratia* (426), *De Praedestinatione Sanctorum* (429), *Contra Secundam Juliani Responsionem Opus Imperfectum* (unfinished at Augustine's death).

There also survive a great number of letters to and from Augustine, 270 in the seventeenth-century Maurist edition of his works (more have been discovered since). Almost every year between his conversion and death is represented. The variety of subject matter suggests that the collection is unselective. Some few of the correspondents – for example, Jerome, Prosper, Marcellinus – will appear in these pages.

The Bible: text

Ambrose persuaded Augustine that the Bible was worth studying, and in particular that the Old Testament did not merit the Manichees' dismissal of it as old-fashioned rubbish. He recommended Isaiah, but Augustine's favourite books were to be Genesis and Psalms, besides of course the letters of Paul, second founder of Christianity, whose peevish exhortations to charity, and chastity, appealed so strongly to fourth-century Christian intellectuals. His older contemporary Jerome once promised in a dream never again to peruse the pagan authors, on whom like Augustine he had been raised (he broke the promise, and there was dispute whether, as made in dream, it was a real promise). Augustine adopted no such self-denial – the *City of God* in particular is peppered with classical allusions, and his fine prose style never lost the influence of Cicero and Virgil. Although he opposed lewdness implacably (e.g.

9

Conf. 1.13.20–16.26), serious-minded pagans retained his respect, and the saying with which according to Possidius he faced death is a quotation from Plotinus (Brown 1967:426). Nevertheless his own reading, as a bishop, will have been almost exclusively Christian, and within Christian literature (if only because few Christians before him had written in Latin and he found Greek burdensome) mainly the Bible.

Augustine's Bible was a version now known as the Vetus Latina, probably made in the second century but by his day diffused into many and inaccurate sub-versions (Augustine speaks of an 'infinita varietas', *Doct. Christ.* 2.11.16); no complete manuscript of it survives. It had been translated as to the New Testament (henceforward 'NT') from the original Greek, and as to the Old Testament ('OT') from the Greek Septuagint version ('LXX'), so called from a tradition that a part of it, the Pentateuch (first five books), was itself translated from the Hebrew in Alexandria by seventy or seventy-two Jewish scholars on the orders of King Ptolemy II Philadelphus (285–246 BC) – though as a whole the LXX in fact includes some works composed (in Greek) as late as AD 100.

The LXX, and hence Augustine's text of the OT, is in various ways unsatisfactory and in various ways unfamiliar to modern readers of the Bible. It quite often mistranslates (e.g. notoriously Is. 7:14 *'parthenos'*, 'virgin', for *''almah'*, 'nubile woman'); it fails to respect the traditional arrangement of books into Law (*Torah*, the Pentateuch), Prophets (*Nebilim*, including history down to the Babylonian exile in 587 BC) and Writings (*Ketubim*, Hagiographa); and within some books the content and arrangement are also markedly unlike what we are used to. The most conspicuous difference is that the LXX contains a group of books, first collectively dubbed 'Apocrypha' by Jerome, which seem to have found favour only among hellenizing Jews and were excluded from the Jewish canon when that came to be fixed, probably in the main at a Jewish synod at Jamnia (south of Jaffa) about AD 100. From that time onwards the Hebrew Bible stabilized into a form considerably different from the OT used by Augustine. Not only did it omit the apocryphal books, and order the remainder into Law, Prophets and Writings, but a purified Hebrew – or in a few places Aramaic – text was gradually established which, from the later scholarly labours of 'Massoretes' in the second half of the first millennium, has come to be called Massoretic.

Christian revision was more tardy than Jewish, but took place within Augustine's own lifetime as a result of a commission about 384 from pope Damasus to his secretary Jerome to correct the gospels. Jerome (Eusebius Hieronymus, ?331–419) was a north Italian who after a conventional upper-class education in Rome had adopted the life of ascetic scholar and made himself fluent in both Greek and Hebrew. When in 386 he returned to the east (where he had earlier spent almost a decade, some of it as a hermit in the Syrian desert) and founded his own monastery at Bethlehem, he set about the greater task of translating the whole OT into Latin direct from Hebrew. Nearly all Jerome's translations are incorporated into the Vulgate version ('Vg') which soon came into standard use in the Latin west.

From about 400 Augustine used Jerome's gospels in his cathedral at Hippo and quoted them in his writings. But the much greater divergences between Jerome's Hebrew-based and Augustine's LXX-based OT proved more than the latter could adapt to. His first letter to Jerome (*Ep.* 28 = Jerome, *Ep.* 56, 394–5) had deprecated the whole project. Although this letter took nine years to reach Bethlehem, news of its contents preceding it provoked a tetchy response from the pugnacious Jerome to his unknown African correspondent. Augustine did not give way, and later wrote describing the uproar in a church at Oea (Libyan Tripoli) which greeted Jerome's translation 'ivy' for 'gourd' at Jonah 4:6. (Nevertheless the two Doctors of the Church later became allies against the Pelagians.) Augustine was not alone in defending Christian tradition against what Jerome called the 'hebraica veritas': two centuries earlier even such a relentless exegete as Origen, anxious though he was to avoid the ridicule of learned Jews, had championed the LXX, asking:

> Are we to suppose that providence which has provided for the edification of all the churches of Christ through the medium of the holy scriptures has not taken proper care of the needs of those for whom Christ died? (*Ep. ad Afric.* 4, quoted by M. F. Wiles in Ackroyd and Evans (1970:456); cf. Augustine, *Doct. Christ.* 2.15.22, *City* 18.43)

The Jewish philosopher Philo (*c.*20 BC–AD *c.*50) had shared the same attitude, four centuries before Augustine.

Since Augustine's day the form in which the OT is received by Christians has shifted gradually, though incompletely, from that of the LXX towards that of the modern Massoretic Hebrew canon. Jerome's OT was based on a Hebrew text hardly inferior to the Massoretic. Although he favoured exclusion of the Apocrypha, some of which he did not retranslate, the Vulgate which derives from his work refused to make that break with Christian tradition (and even added, as 4 Esdras, an apocalypse not surviving in either Hebrew or Greek); but it is an effect of the coincidence of the Reformation with the north European Renaissance that Protestant translations, including the Authorized ('King James') Version in English ('AV'), conform to the Hebrew canon; while the Eastern Church has adopted an intermediate position since 1672. The order of OT books remains, however, broadly as in the LXX in all Christian versions. The NT canon has not changed since Augustine's time (he ascribed Hebrews to Paul, *Doct. Christ.* 2.8.13).

One particular disturbance to the OT tradition affects references within the book of Psalms. Although all traditions include the same material in the same order, and all divide it so as to make a total of 150 psalms, the divisions differ between the Hebrew Bible (to which conform the AV, the Book of Common Prayer ('BCP') which 'followeth the Division of the Hebrews', and other Protestant usage) and the LXX (followed by Augustine, the Vulgate, and Roman Catholic usage). Pss 1–8 and 148–50 are the same in both numerations. Pss 9 and 10 in the Hebrew (= BCP) are combined into one by Augustine (= Vg), so that his numerations run one behind the Hebrew in Pss 10–112 (= Heb.Bib. 11–113). At Augustine's Ps 113 the Hebrew divides again (= Heb.Bib. 114–115), but it then combines his 114 and 115 (= Heb.Bib. 116), so that Augustine remains one behind in Pss 116–45 (= Heb.Bib. 117–46). Finally, the Hebrew combines Augustine's 146 and 147 (= Heb.Bib. 147). Wherever the numbers diverge I shall give a double reference, in the form 'Ps 118 [Heb.Bib. 119]'. Those using Protestant Bibles must remember to be guided by the Hebrew references.

The Bible: interpretation

A great deal of the Bible, especially the OT, is obscure and allusive, so that every hearer and reader since well before Augustine's day has needed help in clarifying the meaning and supplying the context. But more than that was required by Jews: for to religious Jews the OT contained not just history and homily but the Law, *Torah*, which guided their lives, and in order to preserve respect for the *Torah* it had long been seen to be necessary to employ a style of purifying or laundering interpretation. This was midrash, whose origins go back to the time the OT canon was closed, probably in the third century BC. 'Midrash ensured that scripture remained an active and living force in Israel' (G. Vermes in Ackroyd and Evans 1970:220; alongside it was a distinct, non-rabbinic, tradition of interpretation current among hellenized Jews and notably exemplified by Philo, who had some influence on Augustine through Ambrose).

Jewish midrash, being liable to beget extravagance, soon collected its own rules. Two styles of interpretation were distinguished, literal and allegorical. Although both appear in Augustine, he quickly came to disfavour the allegorical, his title *De Genesi ad Litteram* marking what was to be a permanent shift from the manner he had earlier used in *De Genesi ad Manichaeos*. Modern readers will smile at Augustine's claim to interpret literally, and the verdict that his standards were depressingly low cannot, I fear, be avoided. However, it is vital to notice on his behalf that the literal does not exclude the *figurative*, for whereas 'literal' is an epithet of interpretations, 'figurative', in Augustine's acceptation, is an epithet of texts. When he declares that 'no Christian will venture to deny that they are to be understood figuratively' (*Gen. Lit.* 1.1.1), 'they' refers to *res gestae*, events. A literal interpreter of the Bible will, in Augustine's view, *find* figures there.

We need a further distinction, for there are two ways in which a text itself can be figurative. On the one hand its author may have written figuratively, intending his words not, or not only, to record the event or convey the advice which would be understood from their ordinary meaning but to allude to a different event or give advice which bears on a different context; on the other hand, events themselves may be figurative, significant of something beyond themselves. Augustine explains this further distinction with reference to Paul's words at 1 Cor. 10:6: 'For he does not say, These things were said, or were written, in a figure; but, he says, They happened in a figure' (*Enarr. Ps* 77.3). A text will be said to *pre*figure if the further event or context alluded to is future relative to the event primarily recorded or the date of the author's recording it; such texts are prophetic.

This prophetic mode of interpretation goes back to the OT canon itself (e.g. Dan. 9) and is prominent in the NT (e.g. Matthew). It pervades Augustine's writings. To give one example: that the people of Christ would be preferred over the Jewish people 'was prefigured', he says, when Jacob set Ephraim before Manasseh (*Enarr. Ps* 77.9, referring to Gen. 48:14). Throughout the Bible, Augustine holds, readers should expect to learn 'what is recorded as done, what is foretold as future, and what is prescribed or cautioned as to be done' (*Gen. Lit.* 1.1.1).

The recorded events really happened, he insists, even the upsetting ones like Sarah's treatment of the slave-girl Hagar (Gen. 16, see *City* 13.21). For the Bible never lies (and indeed must have divine authority because of its consistency! *City* 18.41): for example, since Jesus says that Ps 109 (Heb. Bib. 110) is by David, it is by David (*City* 17.14, referring to Mt. 22:43). Augustine nowhere suggests that all truth is to be found in the Bible – the sciences progress. But they progress by adding to what is revealed in holy scripture, never by correcting it: 'Whatever the [scientists] can demonstrate about the nature of things by reliable evidence, we can show not to be contrary to our writings' (*Gen. Lit.* 1.21.41). He is even willing to assert that the obscurities of the Bible have their value, being 'divinely arranged for the purpose of subduing arrogance by hard work and of protecting the mind, which often depreciates what it finds easy to explain, from feelings of disrespect' (*Doct. Christ.* 2.6.7). This attitude of utter submission to the authority of a certain body of texts has to be kept in mind by the student of Augustine's thought.

Suggestions for further reading

On Augustine consult the excellent biography by Brown (1967) or the short survey by Marrou (1957), or Chadwick's (1986) recent compact and scholarly account. On the background the most useful books are Armstrong (1967) for the philosophy, Frend (1984) for the Christianity, and for the Bible Ackroyd and Evans (1970). Mackie (1982) and Swinburne (1977), are good general treatments of philosophy of religion. For an account of Augustine's philosophy with a different emphasis from mine see the chapters by Markus in Armstrong (1967). Another study, thorough and judicious, is Bonner (1986). Cross and Livingstone (1974) is an invaluable aid on Christian history and doctrine.

II

Against the sceptics

The dialogue Contra Academicos

Augustine's attack on scepticism is largely confined to the *Contra Academicos*, his earliest surviving work, which he composed at the time of choosing between Christianity and pagan Neoplatonism. Fourteen years before, when he was an eighteen-year-old student at Carthage, Cicero's now lost protreptic *Hortensius* had attracted him to the pursuit of wisdom (*Conf.* 3.4.7, *Beata Vita* 1.4). He resolved, according to the account in the *Confessions*: 'To bend my mind to the holy scriptures, to see what they were like. . . . But they seemed to me unworthy of comparison with the dignity of Cicero' (*Conf.* 3.5.9). He was probably at that time already under the influence of the Carthaginian Manichees who, while honouring Jesus and Paul, derided the inconsistencies and crudities of the Bible, and especially the Old Testament. But the positive doctrines of Mani, which correspondingly claimed the authority of reason, gradually lost their hold on Augustine (*Conf.* 5.6.10–5.7.13) until, some ten years later: 'There began to arise in me the thought that those philosophers whom they call Academics were wiser than the rest, because they held that everything ought to be doubted, and they declared that no truth can be apprehended by man' (*Conf.* 5.10.19, cf. *C. Acad.* 3.20.43). That was in Rome in 383 or 384. There followed exposure to Neoplatonism (*C. Acad.* 2.2.5, *Conf.* 7.13.26) and, connectedly (cf. *Ep.* 6.1), conversion to Christianity in 386 at Milan. Shortly afterwards Augustine retired with his African friends to the country villa at Cassiciacum where the *Contra Academicos* was written. His conversion had had a strongly intellectual element. Confidence in reason reasserted itself, together with a new conviction, perhaps due to Ambrose (*Conf.* 6.4.6), that the Bible could be defended (*Conf.* 7.21.27). At the end of his life he wrote of the *Contra Academicos*: 'My purpose was to rid my mind, with the strongest reasoning I could, of the arguments [argumenta] of

15

those who cause many to despair of finding truth. . . . For these arguments were also influencing me' (*Retract*. 1.1.1, cf. *Ep*. 1.3, *Trin*. 15.12.21).

This influence on Augustine was the echo of an ancient rivalry between two of the main schools of hellenistic philosophy, the Garden (Academy) and the Porch (Stoa), called after their respective sites in Athens. The Academy had been founded by Plato (*c*.429–347 BC), and reverted to the nurture of Platonism in the last century of its long existence (it was suppressed in AD 529). For part of the intervening period, however – between 273 BC when Arcesilaus of Pitane (*c*.315–241/0 BC) became its head and about the time of Christ – it was the centre of ancient scepticism. Arcesilaus crossed swords with Zeno of Citium (335–263 BC), himself a former student at the Academy, who had meanwhile founded the Stoa and begun the development of an elaborate system of philosophy, laced with much technical terminology.

Among their manifold enterprises the Stoics proposed a test for knowledge, dubbing it a 'criterion of truth' (Augustine will refer to it as Zeno's 'definition') and dubbing judgements that pass it 'apprehensions' (*katalēpseis*) and those that fail it 'opinions' (*doxai*); they held that the wise man was better off without opinions. The Academics adopted – or at least conceded for the sake of argument – both the criterion of truth and the recommendation to shun opinion; but they differed from the Stoics in rejecting the possibility of arriving at judgements which satisfy the criterion (see Sedley 1983:12–14). From this combination of views two consequences flowed, which became the marks of scepticism in the ancient world: (a) *katalēpsis*, and so knowledge, is impossible, and (b) the wise man will abstain from judgements altogether, remaining in a state of suspension, *epochē* (we can see Augustine distinguishing the two elements in the passage from *Conf*. 5.10.19 quoted above).

The controversy thus begun by Arcesilaus and Zeno continued under various of their successors, notably the Stoics Cleanthes (331–242 BC) and Chrysippus (*c*.280–207 BC) and the Academic Carneades (214/13–149/148 BC), but was petering out by the time that Cicero (106–43 BC) studied as a young man in Athens under the Academic Philo of Larissa (160/159–80 BC). Thereafter the sceptical tradition was kept alive outside the Academy, for example in the still extant works of the Greek physician–philosopher Sextus Empiricus (fl. *c*. AD 180).

Augustine, ill at ease with Greek, knew neither Sextus's writings nor those of the hellenistic thinkers which, though now lost, must have been available still in his day. His evidence for the sceptical philosophy was drawn mainly, perhaps only, from Cicero, and therefore mainly from the defence of scepticism in Cicero's *Academica* (though evidently also the *Hortensius*, *C. Acad*. 3.14.31). It is not possible to tell which of the two editions of Cicero's dialogue was known to him, whether the first from which our book 2 or 'Lucullus' or *Prior Academics* survives, or the second incorporating our book 1 or 'Varro' or *Posterior Academics* (*C. Acad.*, ACW 12, p. 156 n. 57). The plan of Augustine's response to Cicero in the *Contra Academicos* is loose. His book 1 premises that the wise man alone is happy (cf. *Beata Vita* 4.26, *City* 22.22) and asks whether wisdom consists in finding truth or in seeking it. Book 2 expounds the doctrine of the Academy that 'philosophical' knowledge is impossible: 'Nor is it possible for a man to achieve knowledge, at any rate of those things that pertain to philosophy' (*C. Acad.* 2.5.11), and that the wise man will assent to nothing (ibid.). Some objections are brought, but the main reply is reserved to a long discourse which Augustine puts into his own mouth and which occupies most of the final book 3 (*C. Acad.* 3.7.15–3.20.43).

In spite of being so ill-read in the rich tradition of ancient scepticism, Augustine offers several arguments in the *Contra Academicos* that are well worth examining. I shall look at three of them. The third will lead eventually beyond that dialogue into regions where he appears to be a remarkable pioneer.

The argument from beatitude

In book 1 of the *Contra Academicos* Licentius, who takes the sceptic's side, asserts that the search for truth, if conducted in the best possible way, will suffice to produce the only happiness that is proper to man: 'The end of a man is to seek the truth perfectly' (*C. Acad.* 1.3.9).

> In that case [responds Trygetius], a man cannot be happy. For how could he be, since he cannot attain [assequi] what he greatly desires? Yet a man can [potest] live happily. . . . Therefore he can find the truth [verum]. Otherwise he must get a grip on himself and not desire the truth, to avoid the necessity of being miserable because he has not been able to attain it. (*C. Acad.* 1.3.9)

Both parties agree that this last alternative will not work: a man who abandons his desire for the truth will not be happy either. So it is a premise of the argument that:

(1) Every happy man greatly desires the truth.

The other premises are:

(2) Men can be happy;
(3) No man can be happy if there is something he greatly desires but cannot attain.

Let us state the conclusion as weakly as possible:

Therefore some men can attain some truth.

Is the argument a good one? A crude defence might go as follows. Suppose the conclusion's contradictory, that no man can attain any truth. Then by (3) all who greatly desire any truth will be unhappy. Hence by (1) all who are happy will be unhappy, that is, no one will be happy, contrary to (2). One objection to this defence is that its outcome is *not* contrary to (2), which only says that some men, perhaps all men, have a capacity for happiness. Even with the stronger of these two readings it seems that the argument will not go through. For if we construe (2) as 'All men have a capacity for happiness' and (3) as

> (3a) No man has a capacity for happiness if any of his strong desires are unfulfillable,

it will follow only that every *happy* man can attain some truth: the possibility will not be excluded that no men are happy. One way of meeting the objection is to read into (2) the stronger sense 'Some men are happy', taking its 'potest' for 'some'. Then the argument is valid. But is (3a) true? It is tempting to suppose that Augustine would have supported it with the thesis that

> (T) No man is happy if any of his strong desires are unfulfilled.

But this support is illusory. For suppose none of us happy with any strong desires unfulfilled; we still might be capable of happiness though some of our strong desires are incapable of fulfilment, since we might still have the recourse of abandoning the unfulfillable desires. Just so it might be that in a perfect sports meeting everyone who jumps four feet jumps five feet, even though there is a sports meeting that could be perfect (by Billy Bunter's withdrawal from it) at which not everyone who does jump four feet can jump five feet – Bunter does and can't. So (T) does not entail (3a).

This prompts the suggestion that premise (3) of the argument should be understood differently, as

> (3b) Happiness is incompatible with the presence of unfulfillable desires.

(3b) does not entail (3a); the desires in (3a) would have to be, in addition, ineliminable. But this does not matter, because (3b) itself validates the argument, and could easily be the intended meaning of (3): we merely have to take its 'can' with wide scope, so that (3) proposes unhappiness as a necessary consequence rather than necessary unhappiness as a consequence. Moreover, (2) can now be weakened to 'Some men are capable of happiness' without forfeiting validity, provided that (1) and (3b) are taken as necessary truths, and 'it can be' is cancellable from 'it can be that some men can attain some truth'.

But is even (3b) true? I suppose that Augustine, with his keen sense of the affinity between love of truth and love of women, might well have thought so (cf. *Lib.Arb.* 2.13.35, and *Sol.* 1.13.22, '‹Wisdom› which . . . you desire to see and hold as it were naked, without any veil intervening'): there is no joy in a hopeless passion. Unfortunately such a line of thought is still not cogent, unless it presupposes (T). If we count it no bar to happiness that an object of passion is unattained, there will still be no bar, surely, if the object is unattainable, so long as the lover thinks otherwise. This last is not enough for (3b); or if we imagine that it is enough, then the argument from it is no longer valid: we may only infer, unexcitingly, that some men think they can attain some truth.

However, if (T) itself were asserted as a premise, the argument would go through; and (T) is asserted in a version of the argument from *De Beata Vita*, a dialogue whose setting and composition belong to the same months as the *Contra Academicos*. There the Academics are offered a choice of three consequences if they deny the attainability of truth. They must either give up desire for the truth, or allow that a wise man need not be happy, or treat as happy the man who lacks what he most ardently wishes to have (*Beata Vita* 2.15). The premises thus become:

Every happy man greatly desires the truth;
Some men can be wise, and all the wise are happy;
(T) All who are happy and greatly desire something have attained it.

As before, it does follow that truth is attainable by some men, provided that all these premises are taken as necessary.

An earlier section of the *De Beata Vita* is plausibly read as asserting (T) while denying its converse:

So is this agreed between us, I said, that no one can be happy who does not have what he wants, though not everyone who has what he wants is happy? They granted it. (*Beata Vita* 2.10)

Denial of the converse is later retracted, on the ground that what makes fulfilled desire for something unsatisfactory is nothing but fear of its loss (2.11), and the fear is itself a kind of unfulfilled desire (4.27). But (T) itself has meanwhile been questioned, with the suggestion that he who seeks the truth has God on his side, which is enough for happiness even without possession of the truth that is sought (3.20). Augustine's response is to reject the claim that all who have God on their side are happy (3.21).

Plainly, the little argument of *Contra Academicos* 1.3.9 needs some such assistance as is offered by the sister dialogue in defence of (T). And it is perhaps an innovation that Augustine sees the need of such assistance, since earlier thinkers, in the Aristotelian, Stoic, and sceptical traditions alike, had tended to assume that the only profitable response to the discovery of obstacles in the way of getting what one desires is to trim the desires. Nevertheless I find the assistance inadequate. We may admit that God's favour is not enough on its own: the important thing for happiness is to feel that you have that favour, or in some similar way to feel supported or self-confident, and hopeful. But it is wrong, as Tolstoy and Russell saw, to think that a happy man must have achieved his major goals (Russell 1930:23; cf. Kenny 1965–6:45).

Later in book 1 we find the suggestion that wisdom is the knowledge of those human and divine things that pertain to a happy life (*C. Acad.* 1.7.23). Perhaps this stems from the thought that you cannot be happy without the security of knowing that your projects really do conduce to happiness, a thought which makes the intellectual project of discovering wherein happiness consists special among a man's projects in needing to be accomplished before the man can be happy. I do not claim to have blocked that interesting route to the thesis that the attainment of some truth is necessary for happiness, but only the route from the premise that *desire* for some truth is necessary for it.

The argument from verisimilitude

Two arguments in the *Contra Academicos* concern credibility. In the second, Alypius puts forward the view that wise men have possession of things they have found approvable or credible ('inventorum probabilium habitus', *C. Acad.* 3.3.5), but do not know anything. Augustine gets him to retract this on the ground that wise men must know wisdom ('si inveniri . . . sapiens . . . queat, potest . . . scire sapientiam', *C. Acad.* 3.4.9, cf. Cicero, *Academica* 2.24). The argument is confused and unconvincing, and its conclusion, that if there is no knowledge there is no wisdom, does no more than dent the bodywork of the Academic bulldozer.

The earlier of the two arguments is more interesting. Academics describe the credible as 'like a truth' ('probabile . . . scisne ab ipsis etiam verisimile nominari?', *C. Acad.* 2.7.16; the Latin idiom 'verisimile' is due to Cicero, *Academica* 2.32). If someone who had never seen your father asserted, on seeing your brother, that he was like your father, you would take him for a madman or a fool (*C. Acad.* 2.7.16). In the same way the Academics make themselves ridiculous when they say that in life they follow the likeness of a truth ('veri similitudinem sequi') although they do not know what the truth itself is ('ipsum verum quid sit ignorent', *C. Acad.* 2.7.19). To this the Academics are made to reply with an alternative, ostensive definition of 'credible': we expect a fine day after a bright night, and credible things are 'like that' (*C. Acad,* 2.11.26). But Licentius suggests that even the new definition can be applied only by comparison with instances of knowledge (*C. Acad.* 2.12.27, cf. Cicero

Academica 2.32–4); and although the suggestion is received with scorn (*C. Acad.* 2.12.28), Augustine continues to be attracted by the thesis it supports (*C. Acad.* 3.18.40, and cf. *Sol.* 1.2.7).

The thesis comes from Plato:

> Whenever someone on seeing a thing thinks, 'This that I now see wants to be like some other thing there is, but falls short of it and cannot be like it, but is inferior,' is it not necessary that he who thinks this should have known beforehand that thing which he says this one resembles but falls short of? (Plato, *Phaedo* 74d9–e4)

If the thought on seeing x, 'x falls short of y', requires previous knowledge of y, then so, clearly, does the implied thought, 'but x does (somewhat) resemble y'. It is the latter requirement that Augustine takes over from Plato, and illustrates by the case of Licentius' father. I begin by examining the illustration.

'So that's Licentius' brother. How like Romanianus!' Augustine cannot have meant to say that no sane man would make this remark unless he had *met* Romanianus. The thesis is that he must already know him, and in particular know how he looks. Moreover it is not asserted that the only way of getting to know that two people look alike is from knowledge of the looks of both. Augustine, like Plato, stresses that the route to knowledge of similarity requires knowledge of one of the similars *when* it is through knowledge of the other ('fratrem tuum visum', *C. Acad.* 2.7.16). Yet Licentius was right to deny (*C. Acad* 2.7.16) even this restricted claim, for there are cases of telling from how just one thing looks that it is part of a matching pair, or that something else, with whose looks one is not yet acquainted, matches it. For example, previous inspection of the outside of your garage block may allow me to infer, on entering your left garage, that the inside of your right garage is the same size and shape. The more natural expression of the knowledge so acquired would be, 'So your other garage must be just like this one inside'; but you would hardly mark me down as a madman if I chose instead to say, 'So this garage must be just like your other one inside.'

In addition to this objection, there are problems about applying Plato's thesis to Augustine's purpose. Absurdity is supposed to arise from the Academic proposal to follow the verisimile while not knowing the verum ('ipsum verum ignorare', *C. Acad.* 2.6.15; 'verum . . . non novimus', 2.9.20) or not knowing what the verum is ('quid sit', *C. Acad*, 2.7.19, 2.12.27). A complicated ambiguity lurks here, for we need to distinguish three possible conditions under which the Academic will assent to a proposition P:

(a) he finds P like some truth or other;
(b) he finds P like some particular truth; or

(c) there exists some particular truth that he finds *P* like (cf. Grice 1969:145; Ackrill 1974:194–5).

(b) and (c) are genuinely analogous to the Romanianus illustration, where there is or is thought to be some particular person Romanianus to whom the young man present is found similar. But only (a) imputes a sensible procedure to the Academic. If we now consider the ignorance of verum which is supposed incompatible with that procedure, it follows that the ignorance cannot be of *that* true proposition whose likeness it is proposed to follow, since no such proposition is identifiable. Nor, in spite of the 'quid sit', does it seem likely that Augustine means ignorance of what truth is. For one thing, that would be 'ignorare veritatem', and Augustine is careful elsewhere to distinguish veritas from verum (*Sol.* 1.15.27). For another, no defence is offered, or available, for the tacit inference that would then be required from 'you know what truth is' to 'you know some truths'. Nothing remains then, against the Academic who opts for policy (a), but to construe his vaunted ignorance of verum, on Augustine's behalf, as ignorance of all true propositions: in fact, ignorance.

In view of this, a better analogy with the Academic claim would be, not regarding someone as like Romanianus while not knowing Romanianus, but regarding something as like, say, a bell while not knowing *any* bells. Why should that be thought impossible? We might try, forlornly, to help Augustine as follows. No one finds things alike without finding them alike in some, perhaps inarticulable, respect, such as shape or pitch, or more generally looks or sound. Suppose I am woken by what sounds to me like a bell. If that is to be a true description, I do not need, admittedly, to be acquainted with any bells, for no bells need exist or even be thought by me to exist. But I do need to know how a bell sounds, that is, how at least some bells would sound if there were any. If we now ask the Academic in what respect the propositions he assents to are required to be like a truth, he will answer merely that they must seem or appear true (cf. Cicero, *Academica* 2.23.4). Then what follows is that he needs to know how a truth would seem if there were any. But this, unfortunately for Augustine, he can do without having knowledge of truths, indeed without there being any truths for him to know.

Withholding assent

We now come to Augustine's main attack on scepticism, in which he separates its two traditional elements of denying knowledge and prescribing *epochē*, suspension of judgement. The long speech in book 3 of *Contra Academicos* attends to these elements successively, drawing sometimes on material from earlier chapters. Since my comments on the second element can be brief, I shall start with it.

The prescription of *epochē* is put forward in the dialogue as a consequence of the thesis about knowledge:

> If ‹one› assented to uncertain things, one would necessarily be in error [erret necesse est], which is forbidden to the wise man. (*C. Acad.* 2.5.11, cf. 1.3.7)

Since not all assent to the uncertain leads into error, this looks to be at best an argument against habitual assent (cf. Cicero, *Academica* 2.67). Probably Augustine, who was in some confusion about the nature of error (*C. Acad.* 1.4.10–12; contrast *Ep.* 199.52 of AD 419, which nearly gets it right), means 'errare' here in the sense of 'risk error' (cf. Cicero *Academica* 2.66, Plutarch, *Adversus Colotem* 1122b). If so, the argument for *epochē* he has in mind runs as follows:

(4) it is unwise to risk error;
(5) he who assents to what he does not know risks error;
(6) no one knows anything;
therefore it is unwise for anyone to assent to anything.

The argument is valid. But Augustine rightly attacks its first premise, in a response which is none the less sound for being rhetorical and scornful. He points to Carneades' concession (Cicero, *Academica* 2.99, cf. ibid. 2.104) that without some surrogate for assent – such as following the credible (*C. Acad.* 3.15.34) – it is possible neither to act (e.g. to journey past a road junction, *C. Acad.* 3.15.33–4) nor to settle disputes (e.g. in litigation, *C. Acad.* 3.16.35–6). Action risks error, and so does judgement by imputing it. But abstention from action is impossible, and from judgement absurd. So the risk of error is unavoidable, and cannot be forbidden to the wise man. In sum, withholding assent fails to secure the very advantage that the argument urged in its favour.

So understood, this is a thoroughly successful rejoinder, demolishing the supposedly Academic premise that it is unwise to risk error. But it has to be noticed that Augustine assumes, what Descartes may have wished away, that the seeker after truth lives in the real world where he must act and judge; so he is not a Pure Enquirer in the sense introduced by Bernard Williams (1978:46ff.). It is also worth remark that there was another Academic argument for withholding assent apparently unknown to Augustine, namely 'from the conflict of arguments' (e.g. Diogenes Laertius, *Lives of the Philosophers* 4.28).

Knowledge: the agreed conditions

In the remainder of this chapter I shall examine Augustine's major argument against the Academic assertion that knowledge of interesting, 'philosophical', matters is unattainable. The argument rests on what Augustine calls Zeno's definition, i.e. the Stoic criterion of truth, and goes as follows:

(7) Zeno's definition gives a sufficient condition of knowledge;
(8) its definiens is satisfied by some things pertaining to philosophy;
therefore there is knowledge of some things pertaining to philosophy.

(7) is stated at *Contra Academicos* 3.9.21:

I for my part do not see how to refute [Zeno's definition], and I judge it to be entirely true.

(8) is supported by various instances put forward by Augustine as satisfying the definiens, which are of two types: necessary truths – for example, 'The world is either one or not one' (*C. Acad.* 3.10.23) – and subjective truths – for example, 'This smells delightful to me' (*C. Acad.* 3.11.26).

He rightly sees his argument as having a dual role: it purports not only to prove that there is knowledge but also to show what is wrong with a famous Academic proof that there is not. That proof, set out in *Contra Academicos* 2.5.11, relied on the denial of (8) and took Zeno's definition as a necessary condition of knowledge. Thus Augustine's assertion of (8) both rebuts the Academic proof and has a place in his own counterproof.

In Augustine's treatment, as in that of his predecessors, the question answered by Zeno's definition contains some obscurities, and the answer is variously formulated. I begin with two remarks about the question. First, in the modern philosophical sense of 'criterion' it asks for a criterion not of truth but of knowledge; for the definition offers not conditions, nor even recognizable conditions, for being true but rather conditions for recognizing or perceiving something to be true. 'Perceive' covers more than sense-perception (cf. *Sol.* 1.4.9, 'Do you perceive these things by the senses or the intellect?'). Like Cicero before him, Augustine uses 'perceptio' interchangeably with 'comprehensio' (apprehension), which is Cicero's translation of the Stoic '*katalēpsis*' (*Academica* 1.41, 2.18; cf. Jn 1:5, 'And the darkness comprehended it not', quoted by Augustine in a comparison with Neoplatonism at *Confessions* 7.9.13). He also ignores a further distinction which the Stoics had made between apprehension and understanding ('*epistēmē*'), allowing knowledge (scientia) to cover both even though Cicero had reserved 'scientia' for '*epistēmē*' (*Academica* 1.42, cf. *C. Acad.* 1.7.9; Cicero's actual treatment invites this conflation, see *Academica* 2.83, 'There are four heads which purport to prove that nothing can be known, perceived or apprehended'). Secondly, the objects of perception are not described as propositions, in spite of the expectation aroused by Augustine's mode of exemplifying them (e.g. 'This smells delightful to me', *C. Acad.* 3.11.26). Usually he leaves their nature unspecified; but two versions of the definition give them as visa, appearances or presentations (*C. Acad.* 3.9.18,21), following Cicero's translation of another Stoic technical term, *'phantasia'* (*Academica* 1.40, 2.18). In this, Augustine is once more following the main tradition: Cicero tells us that the Academics constructed, at no less length than the Stoics, an art of presentations ('artem quandam de iis quae visa dicimus') in which their force and kinds were defined, and especially the nature of that which can be perceived and apprehended (*Academica* 2.40). The tradition does not go back as far as Arcesilaus himself, who held that the criterion of truth was concerned with assent, which could be given only to propositions (*axiōmata*) and not *phantasiai* (Sextus, *Adversus Mathematicos* 7.154); but we shall see that Augustine can evade this objection.

So the question is: under what conditions will a presentation be perceived? Augustine in effect lays down two further conditions for perception – in addition to what is perceived being a presentation – the first of which is that the presentation is true. This is sufficiently obvious from his earliest formulation, where perception of a truth is defined as if no other kind of perception is thereby omitted (*C. Acad.* 2.5.11). He also directly asserts that there cannot be knowledge of falsehoods:

> Everyone is agreed that there cannot be knowledge of false things
> (*C. Acad.* 3.3.35, cf. 3.9.21).

But what is truth in presentations? A presentation is something impressed on the mind by a feature of the world, which is its source ('animo impressum ex eo unde esset', *C. Acad.* 2.5.11). Between the impression and the feature there is a *relation* of truth when the impression presents the feature as it is; and an impression has the *property* of truth when it stands in that relation to its source (cf. Sextus, *Adversus Mathematicos* 7.168). The relation was sometimes taken as symmetrical, so that Cicero can speak of a presentation 'impressed from a true source' ('impressum a vero', *Academica* 2.112). There is a tacit analogy here with such things as pictures, maps, and sentences. The representation on page 27 of my atlas might be true to Brazil, not at all true to Bulgaria; it will be true *simpliciter* if it is true to what it is a representation of. Of course the analogy is misleading in various ways. Information will flow from a map or a sentence, as from a witness, only if those sources are, so to speak, audible and intelligible as well as accurate. But a presentation is conceived as something that cannot fail to be 'read' correctly: although even a true

25

one can deceive a man, that must be because he distrusts its truth, not because he scans it incompetently or is ignorant of the mode (whether natural or conventional) in which it represents. In view of these peculiarities we may well wonder whether there are such things, as we may about sense-data. On the other hand it seems possible to interpret the project for an 'art of presentations' innocuously. Understand 'the presentation that *p* is true', sc. to its source, as meaning, 'it is presented that *p* because it is (from its being) true that *p*'; and understand 'it is presented' to mean 'it appears, or seems'. Both these interpretations may well have been assumed by Augustine: for the past participle 'visum' (unlike the Greek abstract noun '*phantasia*') naturally refers to features or states of the world, not of the mind; and its derivation (like that of '*phantasia*') from the common verb for 'seem' gives little positive encouragement to the idea of a representative medium or mental correlate of external things.

If this is right, we can see the function of visa in Augustine's Zenonian definition as follows. If I perceive or know something, it must appear to me, and appear because it is true. So much, according to Cicero, had been admitted by those Peripatetics who said we can perceive what is impressed from a true source (2.112). The something will be a state of affairs, which might be identified with a proposition as Arcesilaus wanted. But already in Plato's *Theaetetus* we find roughly these two conditions rejected as insufficient; for, so far as seeming can be identified with being believed, and in spite of the causal connexion they impute between seeming and being (which is absent from Plato), the two conditions fail to distinguish knowledge from certain kinds of lucky guess. We need, as Cicero says against his Peripatetics, some 'magna accessio', some important extra. It is the purpose of Zeno's definition to supply the extra.

Knowledge: Zeno's condition

Unfortunately the final, and controversial, condition of knowledge is expressed by Augustine in several different ways, all with precedents in the tradition. Initially he puts it like this:

> ⟨Zeno⟩ says that that truth can be perceived, which is so impressed on the mind from the source it is from that it could not be from a source it is not from [ait id verum percipi posse, quod ita esset animo impressum ex eo unde esset, ut esse non posset ex eo unde non esset]. (*C. Acad.* 2.5.11)

Suppose it appears to Socrates that the leaves are quivering. Could the appearance have been caused by anything else? Since it is doubtful whether any particular event could have had a different cause, let us take the question to ask about the *actual* cause of *similar* events ('could not' in its generalizing sense): are suchlike appearances ever caused by states of affairs that are not suchlike? Well, evidently they are; and since Augustine agrees with the Academics in understanding Zeno's definition to constitute also a necessary condition of knowledge ('it is manifest that nothing else comes to be perceived', *C. Acad.* 3.9.21), he would in this case have us deny to Socrates, I believe, the knowledge that the leaves are quivering. The reasoning that leads to such a denial seems to be as follows: *F*-type appearances come from sources that are not *F*-type if and only if those appearances are false (to their sources); and if an appearance, even a true one, belongs to a type with some false members, there's no knowing that it is not false itself. We find the reasoning in Cicero's comment on a formulation very close to this one of Augustine's:

> We claim that that definition of Zeno's is quite correct, for who can apprehend anything so as to make you fully confident that it is perceived and known, if it is such as even a false one could be? [quod est tale quale vel falsum esse possit?] *Academica* 2.18; cf. 'of the same kind' ibid. 2.77; also ibid. 2.40–1, 84, 112, Sextus, *Adversus Mathematicos* 7.248, 252)

The Zenonian objection against a claim to knowledge can be met if the truth perceived is unlike every falsehood:

> Let Carneades show that *that* opinion [that the number of worlds is finite or infinite] is like any false one! (*C. Acad.* 3.10.23, cf. 3.12.27, Cicero, *Academica* 2.83, Sextus, *Adversus Mathematicos* 7.164)

and the likeness is detectable:

> It is so true that it can be distinguished from the false by unlike marks. (*C. Acad.* 2.6.14; cf. 3.10.23, Cicero, *Academica* 2.90)

In order to detect unlikeness we need a sign (signum, nota), and that is what Sextus has in mind when he reports the Stoics as asserting that

> anyone who has an apprehensive presentation comes systematically in contact with the actual differences of things, since a presentation of that kind has some such peculiarity [*idiōma*] in comparison with others, like the horned snakes in comparison with other snakes. (Sextus, *Adversus Mathematicos* 7.252, cf. Cicero, *Academica* 2.84)

Augustine concurs in the same requirement, continuing his first formulation of Zeno's definition:

> Put more briefly and plainly, a truth can be apprehended by signs which cannot be possessed by anything false [his signis verum posse comprehendi, quae signa non potest habere quod falsum est]. (*C. Acad.* 2.5.11)

Since the efficacy of a sign depends on its being recognized as such, 'cannot' here, as often in Cicero too, needs to have an epistemic sense, 'manifestly are not'. I take Augustine to mean that the signs must be such that it is manifest that they belong to no falsehoods. This is the sense in which they must be distinguishing.

Does anything philosophical satisfy the conditions?

A full examination of Augustine's epistemology would next enquire whether such distinguishing signs are, as he supposes, necessary for knowledge. Doubtless they are not. On the other hand their sufficiency, when they are conjoined with the uncontroversial conditions, is plain enough, and that is all that Augustine need assert, in premise (7), for his argument against the Academics. I pass therefore to premise (8).

Augustine sets himself to find not just instances of knowledge but instances that 'pertain to philosophy' (C. Acad. 2.5.11). Although his own discussion often ignores the restriction, he revives it in book 3 chapters 10–13, where the Academic Carneades is once more cited as concerning himself only with what philosophers enquire into ('quae inter philosophos inquiruntur', C. Acad. 3.10.22). What is the force of this? In Carneades the restriction may have been dialectical, for the sake of argument. In Augustine's treatment it comes to little. He divides philosophy (much as the Stoics had) into physics, ethics, and dialectic, but allows subjective truths into the first two divisions and necessary truths into all three. Whether his instances would have passed muster with Carneades we cannot say, because the source of the ascription to Carneades is unknown. I shall give Augustine the benefit of this doubt, only remarking that subjective truths had not generally been cited on either side in earlier controversy about the existence of knowledge (Burnyeat 1982:37ff.).

On premise (8), and there alone, Augustine sees himself in contest with the Academics. He will win the contest if he finds a 'philosophical' truth which, when – at least sometimes when – presented, is presented in conjunction with *some* sign manifestly *not* shared by any falsehood. He doesn't win, because he doesn't keep his eye on the ball. To begin with, *Contra Academicos* 3.9.18 misreports Zeno's definition as requiring only 'is presented with *no* sign that *is* shared with any falsehood' ('quale cum falso non haberet signa communia'): love-fifteen. Then in one of several limping discussions of self-refutation he claims that the definition will itself be an instance, satisfying its own condition for perceptibility, provided that it cannot be *shown* to be capable of falsity ('ostendas eam etiam falsam esse posse', C. Acad. 3.9.21): love-thirty. He rallies at 3.10.23, claiming to have found 'disjunctions' that *have nothing* in common with a falsehood: fifteen–thirty. Better still, no one can *confuse* them with any likeness to the false ('nec similitudine aliqua falsi ea potest quisquam confundere', *C. Acad.* 3.10.23): thirty all. Now it might seem that once we are given some truth that cannot be confused with – that is, mistaken for – a falsehood, we have a truth that can be distinguished as true, and Augustine is well on the way to victory. But 'cannot be mistaken for a falsehood' is ambiguous as to the scope of both 'cannot' and 'mistaken' (cf. the Argument from Verisimilitude above). If Augustine means to say about each of his instances – for example, 'The world is either one or not one' – that there is no falsehood it can be mistaken for, he may be right; perhaps the proposition is not misidentifiable. Yet its truth value might still be inscrutable. Augustine is not entitled to infer, as the trend of his argument requires, that such a proposition cannot be *mistaken for false*. Moreover, 'cannot be mistaken for false' is still ambiguous, between 'cannot be taken for false (which would be an error)' and 'cannot be erroneously taken for false'. That is, we have to ask whether Augustine means that his propositions cannot both *be* true and be taken for false, or both *are* true and cannot be taken for false. For necessary truths these conditions are equivalent, but for contingent truths like 'This seems white to me' (*C. Acad.* 3.11.26) the former may hold without the latter. We find the latter, stronger condition in yet another of his formulations of Zeno's definition:

> That presentation can be apprehended which so appears that it cannot appear false. (*C. Acad.* 3.9.21; here 'cannot' means what it says.)

Let us pause for review. Augustine has begun unpropitiously by looking for propositions having no sign in common with any falsehood, or even for propositions not provably capable of falsehood. I take him to be correcting these lapses when he substitutes the condition 'unconfusable with any falsehood'; but the condition is still weaker than Zeno's. By a scope fallacy he then tacitly infers that what satisfies the condition will be incapable of being taken for false; with this fallacy the score moves to thirty–forty. Nevertheless we cannot be sure that the fallacy has led him yet into error. Since his specimen necessary truths are all simple (cf. Descartes, second *Replies*, Adam and Tannery (eds) 1985: VII, 125) and his specimen contingent truths are subjective, it is a defensible view that none of them can be taken for false – that is, disbelieved – or even doubted; they compel assent. What he needs, then, is a reason for treating indubitability, or unrejectability, as a sign of truth. But unlike Descartes, Augustine offers us no such reason; so the game goes to the Academics.

Does 'sum' satisfy the conditions?

In looking for propositions that compel assent and cannot be doubted, Augustine was following in the Stoic tradition (Sextus, *Adversus Mathematicos* 7.257). His well known adumbrations of Descartes' 'Cogito ergo sum' (see Gilson 1951:191–201) seem to be original. Even if Descartes thought it impossible to doubt one's own existence, it was not that feature that he exploited in the *Second Meditation* but rather the fact that a man's doubt of, or other mental attitude towards, the proposition that he exists ensures that the proposition is true:

> as often as it is mentally conceived by me it is necessarily true [quoties a me . . . mente concipitur necessario esse verum]. (Descartes, Adam and Tannery (eds) 1985: VII, 25)

Likewise when Augustine offers 'I am', 'I am alive', and 'I think' as instances of knowledge, he eschews mention of literal indubitability. These instances are absent from the *Contra Academicos* (perhaps as 'not pertaining to philosophy' – Carneades is made to concede knowledge that he is a man and not an ant, *C. Acad.* 3.10.22); but they occur, without argument, in works from the same period (*Beata Vita* 2.7, *Sol.* 2.1.1). An argument appears in the *De Trinitate*:

> Even if someone doubts, he is alive . . . if he doubts, he thinks . . . therefore whoever doubts on another matter ought to doubt about none of these things; if they were not ‹true›, he could not doubt about anything. (*Trin.* 10.10.14)

Such doubts ought to be dispelled, then, because it is a condition of their existence that they be unfounded. We must notice that this is presented as an argument against *epochē*, not as a proof of knowledge.

A passage in *De Vera Religione* has an even more limited purpose, aiming to establish not that there are some truths one ought not to doubt but that one ought not to doubt that there are some truths:

> Everyone who observes [intelligit] himself doubting observes a truth [verum], and about that which he observes he is certain; therefore he is certain about a truth. Everyone therefore who doubts whether truth exists [utrum sit veritas] has in himself a truth on which not to doubt. . . . Hence one who can doubt at all ought not to doubt about ‹the existence of› truth. (*Ver. Rel.* 39.73)

Let us call the man who doubts about the existence of truth, that is, whether there are truths, an *ephektikos* (suspender). The argument appears to rest on the assumption that one who is certain of anything ought not to be *ephektikos*. But this is admissible only if the 'ought' has wide scope, that is, as saying that it would be inconsistent, and so wrong, to be both certain of some truth and doubtful whether there are truths ('of some *truth*' is actually redundant). The assumption so understood, namely

(9) One ought not to be both certain of some truth and *ephektikos*,

will validate Augustine's argument if it is joined by two others:

(10) if someone is doubtful (about anything), it follows he is certain he is doubtful;

(11) what follows from something that ought to be, ought itself to be.

Since if someone is doubtful it follows trivially that it is true that he is doubtful, we can infer from (10) that if someone is doubtful it follows that he is certain of some truth. From that we can infer, by simple modal logic, that if he is not both certain of some truth and *ephektikos*, it follows that he is not both doubtful and *ephektikos*; and hence (because by the definition of '*ephektikos*' he cannot be *ephektikos* without being doubtful about something) that he is not *ephektikos* at all. Since by (9) one ought *not* to be both certain of some truth and *ephektikos*, we can finally infer by (11) that one ought *not* to be *ephektikos* at all. Unfortunately for Augustine's argument, (10) is a bad epistemological principle and (11) is a dubious deontic principle (though commended by Chellas (1980:190ff.), where it appears as 'ROM'); and I do not see ways of dispensing with them on Augustine's behalf.

In any case we are looking in these later treatises for more than an argument against *epochē*; and Augustine does not indicate a route of advance from 'ought not to be doubted' to 'is known'. The route which Descartes' 'ergo' formulations misleadingly suggest – to exhibit a proof of 'sum' in demonstration of its provability and so knowability – is not available from the starting point of doubt about 'sum'. For suppose a man follows the method apparently recommended by Descartes, and succeeds in doubting (and not believing) his own existence. At the time of doubting he does not know that he exists, for one of the conditions of knowledge, belief, is absent. But when the doubt is dispelled by recognition of its groundlessness, he no longer has the extra premise with which to pass by *modus ponens* from 'If I doubt my existence, I exist' to 'I exist'. Moreover, this Cartesian characteristic of 'sum' and 'vivo' and 'cogito' and 'dubito', that doubts about them ensure their truth, is not shared by two other propositions put into the same bag by Augustine, 'I want to be happy' and 'I do not want to err' (*Trin.* 15.12.21). What all these do have in common is that *belief* in them ensures their truth: they cannot be believed erroneously. Two passages directed explicitly against the Academics make use of this feature. In *De Trinitate* Augustine bids us say against the Academics not 'I know I'm not mad' but 'I know I'm alive'. So one who says he knows he is alive can never be deceived [falli] nor a liar [mentiri]. Therefore let a thousand kinds of deceptive presentation be urged against one who says, 'I know I'm alive'; none of them will frighten him, since even a man who is deceived is alive. (*Trin.* 15.12.21, cf. *Du. An.* 10.13)

The other, and well known, passage comes from the *City of God* and runs in part as follows:

Against these truths the arguments of the Academics are no terror, when they say, 'What if you are deceived?' For if I am deceived, I am. For one who is not, assuredly cannot be deceived; and because of this I am, if I am deceived. Because, therefore, I am if I am deceived, how am I deceived ‹in thinking› that I am, when it is certain that I am if I am deceived? Because, therefore, I who was deceived would be, even if I were deceived, it is beyond doubt that I am not deceived in that I know myself to be. (*City.* 11.26)

In these places, as G. B. Matthews has shown, Augustine is not 'using *modus ponens* to establish the conclusion that he exists' (Matthews 1972:163); the conclusion is that he cannot erroneously believe he exists (or is alive). The argument for that conclusion contains an explicit premise 'Si fallor, sum':

(12) If Augustine believes something erroneously, he exists

(cf. *Lib. Arb.* 2.3.7 for its contrapositive; both passages were alleged by Mersenne to anticipate Descartes, Gilson 1951:191–2); and a tacit premise:

(13) If Augustine exists, he does not believe erroneously that he exists.

From (12) and (13) it follows that if any of Augustine's beliefs are erroneous, belief that he exists is not; hence if that one is erroneous, it is not; hence it is not. The premises are generalizable and necessary. So the conclusion is generalizable and necessary: *no* one *can* believe erroneously that he exists (compare the similar reconstruction in Matthews 1972:162).

We may now finally ask, though Augustine does not ask, whether 'sum' and the other examples in these passages satisfy Zeno's condition for knowledge. Of course if a proposition has the features that (a) it is believed by someone and (b) it cannot be erroneously believed by that person, then it is true: the features are jointly possessed by no falsehood. The question we have to consider, though, is whether the features can be a 'distinguishing sign' of the truth of Augustine's examples. In order to be a sign, the features must be manifest in those examples; and in order to be a distinguishing sign in the required sense, it must be manifest that no falsehood possesses them. The former condition is fulfilled by anyone who recognizes the examples as (a) among his own beliefs, and sees the force of Augustine's proof that (b) he cannot believe them erroneously; and the latter condition is fulfilled by anyone who sees the force of the simple little proof just given that no falsehood can possess features (a) and (b) jointly. If anything can be manifest, these facts can be. Accordingly it would be unreasonable to deny that the examples can satisfy Zeno's condition for knowledge. I conclude that Augustine eventually succeeded in meeting the Academics' challenge, in the form in which he set it up for himself.

How much has been rescued?

When Augustine's 'Si fallor, sum' was brought to the attention of Descartes, Descartes commented that while each of them had proved the 'certainty' of his own existence, they put the proof to very different uses (letter to Colvius, 14 November 1640, in *Philosophical Letters*, 83–4). This is true of the two philosophers' answers to scepticism considered generally. Augustine claims in the *Contra Academicos* to have found a range of propositions that can be known. But unlike Descartes he does not seek to build any edifice on this foundation: in particular he does not seek to reinstate the multitudinous propositions which pass for known in scholarly circles, let alone in ordinary life. I suspect that the reason lies in the continuing influence on him of Neoplatonism. There is a passage in the *Retractationes* which takes a thoroughly Platonic line about ordinary claims to knowledge. In *De Utilitate Credendi* Augustine had written: 'What we understand, we owe to reason, what we believe, to authority' (*Util. Cred.* 1.11.25, cf. *Divers. Quaest.* 48). The *Retractationes* quote 'understand [intelligimus]' as 'know [scimus]' and go on:

> This is not to be taken in such a way as to make us frightened in
> ordinary speech of saying that we know what we believe on
> adequate testimony. It is true that when we speak properly, we are
> said to know only what we apprehend with the mind's firm reason.
> But when we speak in language which is better suited to common
> use – as even holy scripture speaks – we should not hesitate to say
> we know both what we have perceived by our bodily senses and
> what we believe of trustworthy witnesses, while understanding the
> distance between the latter ‹two› and the former. (*Retract.* 1.14.3)

We may wonder whether Augustine continued to think that satisfaction of Zeno's condition was necessary for 'apprehension by the mind's firm reason'. I do not know the answer (but see now Burnyeat 1987). But I think that he himself did not much care how extensive a title to knowledge he had acquired by 'ridding his mind' of the Academic argumenta. The important thing was to have rid his mind.

Further reading

On the *Contra Academicos* see O'Meara in *ACW* 12. On the anticipation of Descartes see Matthews 1972. For the earlier and later history of scepticism see especially Burnyeat 1983.

III

The nature of speech

Signs

Augustine's reflections about language can be found in three treatises, *De Doctrina Christiana* (AD 396–426) on interpreting the Bible, *De Magistro* (AD 389), a dialogue with his son Adeodatus on how and whether teaching is possible, and *De Dialectica* (? AD 387), a fragmentary schoolbook containing prolegomena to logic. The last of these, sometimes referred to as *Principium Dialecticae*, is of disputed authorship; if genuine – and there now seems no strong reason for doubting its authenticity (see B. D. Jackson's introduction to the Pinborg edition) – it will probably be one of the works about which Augustine wrote:

> Of the other five textbooks [disciplinae, courses of study] which I also started ‹at Milan›, on dialectic, rhetoric, geometry, arithmetic and philosophy, only the beginnings survived, and I lost even those, though I reckon that some people have them. (*Retract.* 1.5)

The characterization of language which we find in these three texts is neither original nor profound nor correct. Nevertheless it is appealing, it is bold, and it has had – partly through the wide currency of Augustine's writings – a lasting influence. Augustine's theory is that language is a system of signs:

> A word is a sign of any kind of thing [verbum est uniuscujusque rei signum], which can be understood by a hearer, and is uttered [prolatum] by a speaker. A thing is whatever is sensed [sentitur] or understood or is hidden [latet]. A sign is what shows [ostendit] both itself to the senses [sensui] and something beyond itself to the mind. To speak is to give a sign by an articulate utterance [voce]. By articulate I mean one that can be comprised [comprehendi] of letters. (*Dial.* 5.7)

A sign is a thing causing [faciens] something else, beyond the impression [speciem] which it presents to the senses, to come into thought from it. (*Doct. Christ.* 2.1.1)

All teaching [doctrina] is of things [res] or signs, but things are learnt through signs. I mean [appellari] here *things* in the proper sense, which are not employed for signifying anything [non ad significandum aliquid adhibentur]: for example, a log, a stone, a sheep, and the like. I do not mean the log which, as we read, Moses threw into the salt water to remove its salinity [Ex. 15:25] or the stone that Jacob placed at his head [Gen. 28:11] or the sheep that Abraham sacrificed in place of his son [Gen. 22:13] – these are things in such a way as also to be signs of other things. But there are other signs, such as words, whose sole use is in signifying. For no one uses words except for the purpose of signifying something. From this it can be understood what I mean [appellem] by signs, viz. things that are employed for signifying something. Hence every sign is also a thing of a kind – for what is not any kind of thing is nothing at all – but not every thing is also a sign. Accordingly in this distinction between things and signs, when we speak of things let us so speak that even if some of them *can* be employed for signifying, that fact is not to stand in the way of the division by which we shall deal first with things and then separately with signs. We must bear in mind that in the case of things we are to consider what they are, not what else they also signify beyond themselves. (*Doct. Christ.* 1.2.2)

One who speaks [loquitur] gives forth [foras dat] a sign of his will by means of articulate sound. (*Mag.* 1.2)

These texts invite us – more or less compellingly – to attribute to Augustine four key propositions:

(1) Speaking is giving signs;
(2) words are signs given in speech;
(3) a sign is a thing employed for signifying something;
(4) words are things whose sole employment is for signifying.

The texts leave it unclear so far whether in a passage of speech each separate word is a separate sign; they also leave it unclear whether in the employment of words for signifying the signifying is done *by* the words or only through them by those who speak them. Both these questions get answered in the second chapter of *De Magistro*:

AUGUSTINE: Are we agreed then that words are signs?
ADEODATUS: We are.
AUG: How can a sign be a sign unless it signifies something?

AD: It cannot.

AUG: How many words are there in this verse?

    Si nihil ex tanta superis placet urbe relinqui

[If it please the gods that nothing should be left from this great city, Virgil: *Aeneid* 2.659]

AD: Eight.

AUG: Then there are eight signs.

AD: Yes.   (*Mag.* 2.3)

So we can add:

(5) Every word is a sign;

(6) every sign signifies something.

In asserting (5) Augustine joins an ancient debate: mainline Stoicism had agreed with him (for the evidence see Atherton 1986:1.2.3.5), whereas Aristotle had earlier held that certain words, such as 'every' (*De Interpretatione* 10.20a 13), only consignify – contribute to the significance of a larger whole – and certain others, such as prepositions (*Poetics* 20.1456b 38ff.) do not signify at all.

Indicative and representative signs

The word 'signum' had two main senses in classical Latin, 'indication' and 'representation', both of them common. In the former sense Cicero can ask whether the gods give signs of future events (*De Divinatione* 1.82–3); in the latter Lucretius speaks of 'brazen signs' – statues – by the city gates, whose right hands are worn from the touch of passers by (*De Rerum Natura* 1.318). Although I shall call these indicative and representative signs, the distinction is of two senses of the word for 'sign', not two kinds of sign: for many things are signs in both senses, as with those roadsigns which indicate an approaching feature by depicting it.

    The thousand or so years of philosophy before Augustine had seen much theorizing and debate about indicative signs (see Sedley 1982), for which the Greek word was 'sēmeion'. 'Sēmeion' and its cognates such as 'sēmantikē' were not used in the other Latin sense 'representation' (nor, I think, was the Latin 'significare', unlike the English 'signify'). So it will not be surprising if Augustine's definition of 'signum', drawing on what he had learnt in the 'secular schools' (*Doct. Christ.* 4.1.2), should likewise ignore the sense 'representation'. And that is what we find in the passages quoted above, where there is nothing about representing: a sign, he says in his definitions, causes something beyond itself to come into thought (*Doct. Christ.* 2.1.1), and shows something beyond itself to the mind (*Dial.* 5.7). Let us call 'indication' the philosophical sense of the word. Indicative signs can be subdivided into evidence, e.g. of Napoleon's being dead, and reminders, e.g. of Napoleon; I have not found this subdivision in Augustine, but it may underlie the garbled account in Sextus (*Outlines of Pyrrhonism* 2.101–2, *Adversus Mathematicos* 8.152–3) of 'indicative' (*endeiktika*) and 'commemorative' (*hupomnēstika*) signs.

The definitions of 'signum' that we have found in *De Dialectica* 5.7 and *De Doctrina Christiana* 2.1.1 are actually wrong, for both of them ignore the existence of undetected signs. For example, a reddish discoloration of the hair called kwashiorkor is an indicative sign – evidence – of protein deficiency. If in some sufferer this sign goes unnoticed or, though noticed, the protein deficiency is not diagnosed from it, then the sign fails to 'cause' the deficiency to come into thought, and fails to 'show' it to anyone's mind. But it is a sign no less. I think that Augustine is not misled by the error he makes here; and I shall assume that when he speaks of 'signa' he normally means the word in its ordinary philosophical sense of 'indication'.

It is of prime importance to recognize, however, that Augustine's sign theory of speech does *not* employ the non-philosophical sense of the Latin word, 'representation'. The evidence for this has been deployed in the last few paragraphs, and seems to me decisive: the philosophical tradition which he inherited, being Greek, ignored that sense; and his own definitions are obviously intended to stand in the tradition. I do not need to deny, of course, that outside the theory of speech he may sometimes have intended the non-philosophical sense, as perhaps for example when he reminds his congregation that Christ's sign, the sign of the cross, is 'fixed' in the forehead of every baptized Christian (e.g. *Enarr. Ps* 30 [Heb. Bib. 31].4.7).

There are powerful twin temptations to read Augustine's sign theory anachronistically as asserting that words are representative signs: first, that would be the right way – the obvious way – to understand such an assertion in modern English (or, I dare say, modern Latin), and secondly, the theory so understood has much more initial plausibility. Indeed the proposition that words represent is not only plausible but true, provided that it is qualified doubly: both so as not to apply to all words and groups of words, but only to referring expressions and certain kinds of sentence; and also so as not to carry the implication which in *my* use I intend 'represent' to carry, that what is represented is modelled or pictured – that is, the structures contained within the represented thing are matched by structures within its representation. But then we are in a dilemma. On the one hand the implication, if it *is* present, delivers a false theory, the 'picture theory' of language once held, and later convincingly demolished, by Wittgenstein. Whereas alternatively, once the implication and the claim to generality are dropped, what remains is too weak to be interesting: 'represent' applied to speakers or to words comes to say no more than 'mean', leaving, as we shall see and as all modern discussions of language acknowledge, the serious work still to be done in explaining what meaning is. In any case, whether interesting or not the representation theory is not Augustine's, and we can conclude that for him:

(7) 'Sign' means 'indication'.

What is signified?

In order to complete the outline statement of Augustine's theory we need now to ask what kinds of thing words signify. Augustine gives divergent answers. On the one hand, his general remarks about signs in the passage already quoted from *De Doctrina Christiana* suggest that words will regularly signify external objects – the same kind of thing as Moses' log specially signified (in that case, Augustine thinks, the cross of Christ); and this is confirmed in a later passage of the *De Magistro* (4.8) when we learn that the nouns (nomina) 'Romulus', 'Roma' and 'virtus' signify respectively Romulus, Rome and virtue. On the other hand we have already found Augustine asserting that a speaker may give a sign of his *will* (*Mag.* 1.2); just so

> banners and standards impart [insinuant] through the eyes the
> military leaders' will, and all these things are, as it were, a sort of
> visible word. . . . Words ‹themselves› have acquired complete
> dominance among men for signifying anything conceived in the
> mind that anyone may wish to communicate [prodere]. (*Doct. Christ.*
> 2.3.4)

This rival suggestion that words signify thoughts and wills, not external objects, is a natural corollary of the view that thoughts are *conveyed* by words. Locke was to make the connection:

> The Comfort, and Advantage of Society, not being to be had without
> Communication of Thoughts, it was necessary, that Man should
> find out some external sensible Signs, whereby those invisible *Ideas*,
> which his thoughts are made up of, might be made known to
> others. For this purpose, nothing was so fit, either for Plenty or
> Quickness, as those articulate Sounds, which with so much Ease
> and Variety, he found himself able to make. Thus we may conceive
> how *Words*, which were by Nature so well adapted to that purpose,
> come to be made use of by Men, as *the Signs of* their *Ideas*; not by
> any natural connection, that there is between particular articulate
> Sounds and certain *Ideas*, for then there would be but one Language
> amongst all Men; but by a voluntary Imposition, whereby such a

Word is made arbitrarily the Mark of such an *Idea*. The use then of Words, is to be sensible Marks of *Ideas*; and the *Ideas* they stand for, are their proper and immediate Signification. (*Essay* 3.2.1, cf. Hobbes, *Leviathan* part 1 chapter 4)

We shall gradually discover that Augustine agrees with most of this. What is now relevant is that he agrees that words were instituted for bringing thoughts (cogitationes) to another's notice (*Ench.* 22.7, quoted on p. 45 below). Suppose that on some occasion you told me what you were thinking: then

> The sound of your syllables delivered [perduxit] your thought to my ear, and through my ear your thought [cogitationem tuam] descended into my heart (*Ev. Joh.* 8.37.4).

At one place Augustine even calls the transferred item a 'significatio', which is given by the speaker to his words and conveyed (deportaret) to the hearer through the hearer's ears (*Qu. An.* 32.66).

There is thus an important unclarity at the core of Augustine's theory of language, which we can record as follows:

(8) Words convey thoughts, but it is unclear whether Augustine means that words signify the thoughts they convey or the things which are the subject matter of those thoughts (or both).

We shall find that the former alternative more naturally fits groups of words, such as sentences, the latter single words, such as names.

Given signs

More needs now to be said about proposition (2), that words are signs given in speech.

Book 1 of *De Doctrina Christiana* has discussed the teaching of things; book 2 turns to the teaching of signs. Not all signs are to be considered, but only 'given signs'. Here is how these are differentiated:

> Among signs, some are natural, some given. The natural ones are those which, without a will or any kind of urge [appetitu] to signify, cause [faciunt] something else beyond themselves to be recognized [cognosci] from them. An example is smoke signifying fire, which it does [facit] without willing to signify; rather by observation of and attention to familiar phenomena [rerum expertarum] it is recognized that there is fire lurking, even if only smoke is apparent. The track of a passing animal belongs to this kind; and a face will signify the state of mind of someone who is angry or sad, even without any will on the part of the angry or sad person. . . . Given signs are those which living things give among themselves for demonstrating, so far

as they are able, the impulses of their mind, or whatever it may be that they have sensed or understood. There is no reason [causa] for our signifying – that is, giving a sign – except to express [depromendum] and transmit to someone else's mind what is going on in the mind of him who gives the sign. (*Doct. Christ.* 2.1.2–2.2.3)

This passage invites several criticisms, most but not all of which can readily enough be turned aside by a friendly interpretation. First, Augustine's labels 'natural' and 'given' are misleading in suggesting that he divides signs according to whether they originate from inanimate or animate things. The basis of his division is actually quite different, for a sign made by a living thing, as for example a footprint, even if made deliberately, as for example a campfire, will be natural in Augustine's sense if it is not intended as a sign of that of which it is a sign. Hence natural as opposed to artificial *origin* is not necessary for membership of Augustine's first class of signs. Conversely his given signs include less than the word 'given' suggests, and not only by excluding, as we have just seen, signs given but not meant to signify: they also exclude some things meant to signify, and so given *as* signs. For Augustine is simply wrong to assert that the only reason for anyone's giving a sign is to transmit the contents of his mind. I might shout as a sign of my presence, or walk along a chalked line as a sign of sobriety. Sundials and clocks give signs of the time without having minds to transmit the contents of. These cases do not fit under Augustine's definition of given signs. So the fact that a sign originates by being given, or even given as a sign, is not sufficient for membership of his second class.

Secondly, if we go by the letter of Augustine's definitions in *De Doctrina Christiana*, given signs do not need to be signs. For signs must succeed in 'causing' something further to come into thought (2.1.1, and compare the requirement on natural signs that they cause recognition), while given signs need only be meant to cause this. Even if we go, more reasonably, by the ordinary philosophical sense of 'signum' as 'indication', there is a gap between something's being meant to indicate and its doing so. Two conceptions of a given sign thus seem to contend in Augustine's text, that of an indication which is given and that of something which is given as an indication.

Thirdly, in defining a natural sign Augustine slides from the requirement that *there is no will* to signify to the weaker requirement that *it*, the sign, does not will to signify. The latter would allow a sign to be at the same time both natural and given. For example, if before leaving my burning bedroom I open the window in order to show neighbours by the issuing smoke that there is fire inside, then although the smoke does not will to signify fire, I do. Since I do, the smoke that issues from my window will apparently count for Augustine as a given sign – I give it to my neighbours for demonstrating something I have sensed – even though it also counts as a natural sign if it succeeds in the purpose I assign it of causing recognition of something beyond itself, without *its* willing to do so. By the same argument all words will be not only given but also natural signs whenever they succeed in the purpose which, as given signs, are allegedly assigned to them by their speakers. Here we should surely respond on Augustine's behalf by revising his definition of natural signs to exclude all signs intended as such.

Fourthly, Augustine makes a false – though only incidental – contrast ('rather', 'sed') between one thing's willing to signify another and one thing's causing recognition of another by 'attention to familiar phenomena', that is, by constituting inductive evidence. Given signs too are often inductive evidence: if I cough discreetly with the object of giving you a sign of my presence in a room where you think you are alone, your recognition of my sign depends no less on learnt correlations and experience of causal connections than it would do if, intending no sign but rather bent on concealment, I let slip an inadvertent hiccup. It is possible that Augustine is influenced at this point by the fact that *verbal* signs are non-natural in a different sense, noticed by Locke in the passage quoted above: viz. that their *being signs* – their constituting evidence of the things they are signs of – arises through 'arbitrary' imposition (sustained, in the normal case, as a convention). But aside from the fact that not all given signs are arbitrary in Locke's sense (or conventional) – something noticed by Jackson 1972:97 – even the arbitrary ones will be recognized only by people whose ability to recognize was learnt in ordinary inductive ways.

In spite of all these difficulties, I think there emerges from this passage of *De Doctrina Christiana* a fairly definite account of the way in which, according to Augustine, words are signs. They are given signs in the sense that a speaker gives them to demonstrate or reveal some further thing beyond themselves. In order to be so given they do not, in fact, need to be signs in Augustine's official sense of causing the further thing to come into thought; but they do need to be given *as* signs in that official sense. Unclarity remains over the ordinary philosophical sense of 'sign', viz. 'indication'. Augustine's given signs *need* not be signs even in that sense; but they normally will be so (you do not normally give as an indication what is not an indication), and it is hard to suppose, in view of his confident use of the word, that he thought they would ever not be. As to what they are signs of, the description 'impulses of the mind, or whatever it may be that ‹living things› have sensed or understood' still leaves us in the dark whether Augustine means to specify mental contents, or admits external objects too among the things signified by words.

Finally, the fact that at least some of the things signified by given signs are mental – 'impulses of the mind' – can be used to show that Augustine thought that given signs, at least when they qualify as signs in the philosophical sense, qualify by falling under the sub-head of evidence rather than that of reminders (they are *endeiktika*, not *hupomnēstika*). He says that living things give signs for demonstrating the impulses of the mind 'so far as they are able'. Minds, he generally assumes, are inner and opaque, difficult things to expose; and he would surely have agreed with Locke that if exposure is to be achieved it is 'necessary . . . to find out' devices for the purpose. If so, the role of those signs which someone gives of his mental impulses will be not to remind observers of them but to make them evident to observers. Given signs will be given as evidence – and, we are assuming Augustine infers, will therefore at least normally *be* evidence. Thus his account in *De Doctrina Christiana* seems to commit him to the view that all given signs are, or at least are meant as, evidence; and since, by (2) and (5), all words are given signs, he is committed to the view that all verbal signs are, or at least are meant as, evidence.

Sentences

We are now in a position to embark on an assessment of Augustine's theory. I shall start with the propositions numbered (1) and (2) above, that speaking is giving signs and that words are signs given in speech. I shall not yet hold Augustine to his strong claim (5) that *every* word is a sign, but shall first consider the more modest and more plausible view that words are signs at least when taken together in suitable groupings. We shall find that even the modest view is indefensible; and we shall then have to ask whether anything can be salvaged from this part of the theory.

The reason why it is more plausible to describe groups of words than individual words as signs is only partly that, as will later appear, some classes of individual words – for example prepositions – are recalcitrant. More importantly, we have seen that Augustine appears to be committed to the view that verbal signs are evidential; and what is signified by an evidential sign always can, and often must, be identified not as a thing (e.g. a passing animal) but as a purported fact (e.g. that an animal has passed). This is a perfectly general fact about evidence; and it has the consequence for a theory of speech that the best candidates for being evidential verbal signs are to be found among those groups of words – they are rarely single words – which constitute sentences: for example, a good candidate for being an evidential verbal sign of a recently passing animal would be the English sentence 'An animal has recently passed.' In this section, therefore, we are to test Augustine's theory as it applies to sentences.

It will be convenient to work with a single illustrative sentence, label-ling it 'S':

S Your grandmother was in Brussels.

Augustine's theory does not demand any particular answer to the ques-tions 'What is S a sign of?' and 'What does S signify?' In fact, there is no reason why he should not allow S to be a sign of anything whatever, because words are of arbitrary imposition; and even if we assume – as he invariably does – that our sentence is used in conversation between people who know and observe the conventions of the language to which it belongs, the answers to the questions may depend on who is addressing whom, which of the addressee's two grandmothers is referred to, and what time-period is referred to. (Actually I suspect that Augustine would give multiple answers to the second question, 'What does S signify?', but a single answer to the first question, 'What is S a sign of?': viz. 'S is a sign of *all* the things it ever signifies, or all the things it can signify'; for at *De Magistro* 4.10 he implies about the noun 'signum' that it is a sign of *all* signs. If so, signifying, for a word, is not the same thing as being a sign, despite proposition (6) above; rather, they are related as gardening is related to being a gardener, or drilling, for a drill, is related to being a drill: S's being a sign of X will be a disposition or capacity activated when S signifies X, just as being a drill is a disposition or capacity activated when the drill is drilling.) Let us further assume, then, that what S signifies does vary from one utterance of it to another, and let us reduce – with luck eliminate – the variability by specifying a context C in which speaker, grandmother, and date have all been identified – let us say: me, the Queen, and VE Day.

What, then, does Augustine's theory entail about an utterance of S in context C? We are confining indications to evidence; but because of the clash between the ordinary philosophical notion of a sign ('indication') and Augustine's special definition of given signs in *De Doctrina Chris-tiana* ('something intended as an indication'), and because of the doubt recorded in proposition (8) above about signifying things outside the mind, there are two uncertainties generating four basic interpretations of how the sign theory applies to S:

(9) In C, S is intended by me as evidence that I believe that the Queen was in Brussels on VE Day;

(10) In C, S is intended by me as evidence that the Queen was in Brussels on VE Day;

(11) In C, S is evidence that I believe that the Queen was in Brussels on VE Day;

(12) In C, S is evidence that the Queen was in Brussels on VE Day.

For each of (9)–(12) it is possible to think of circumstances (consistent with C) which show it, and so the interpretation of the theory it applies, to be false. For example, against (9): I will not intend S as evidence that I believe that the Queen was in Brussels on VE Day if I utter it to the empty air, or expecting to be taken as romancing. Against (10): I will not intend S as evidence that she was there then if I know that my hearer already knows whether she was and is testing me. Against (11): S will not be evidence that I believe she was there then if I utter it on the stage or in my sleep. Against (12): S will not be evidence that she was there then if I am known to be a liar, or known to be misinformed about the period. And against all four there is this vital fact: S may occur 'embedded' in some longer linguistic unit which is not an assertion, or at any rate not an assertion of S; for example it may be followed by a further sentence, 'So says my guidebook, but it is unreliable', or appended to a prefix, 'It is not true that'. On the other hand if Augustine's theory proposed that in such cases S has a different signification from any of (9)–(12), it is hard to see what that would be. S with its context C was an example, meant as a basis for generalization. These objections show that there is no way in which generalization from S to all similar sentences can yield a true theory, on any of the four interpretations (9)–(12). We do not need, therefore, to consider whether the sign theory would work for dissimilar sentences, such as interrogatives.

What, if anything, can be salvaged? Discussing lying in the *Enchiridion* Augustine wrote:

> And undoubtedly, words were instituted among men not so that men should deceive one another by means of them but so that anyone might bring his thoughts [cogitationes] to another's notice by means of them. Therefore to use words for deceit, not for the purpose for which they were instituted, is a sin. (*Ench.* 22.7)

The claim made here is different from, and importantly narrower than, the claim made by the sign theory under any of interpretations (9)–(12). For in the *Enchiridion* passage Augustine does not assert that a speaker's words *are* evidence of his thoughts, let alone of purported facts, or even are intended by him as evidence of either of those things; rather, giving evidence of thoughts (bringing to notice) is what speech is *for*. The claim is still bold, surely too bold, since like most activities speech has multifarious purposes, some of which, such as promising, need not go through exposure of the speaker's mind (promising is also a counter-example to the weaker claim made at *De Magistro* 1.1 that 'in speech we aim at nothing but to teach', i.e. inform, or, he later adds, remind). Nevertheless, given a suitably wide sense of 'thought' the *Enchiridion* claim will cover a great part of the human activity of speech: think how often one could append to a sentence 'That's what I think/feel/want/ want to know'. Now, the question may be raised about this central purpose, How does speech manage to achieve it? And that question is so abstruse and difficult that it will not be surprising if examination of it obscures, and enquirers into it wrongly deny, the fact that not all speech even aims to achieve such a purpose. What the new question really asks is this: given that speakers often do have the central purpose, of 'demonstrating an impulse of their mind', 'giving forth a sign of their will' and the like, and given that the purpose is often achieved, by what means is it achieved? Perhaps the use of language begins to look like magic, but it cannot really be magic. What is the secret? Well, one requirement of successful mind-exposure by speech will be that the hearer of the speech should trust the speaker to have the mind-exposing intention which (in the kind of case we are considering) he does have; but that is not difficult to grasp – trust is natural. The other requirement is that the hearer should *understand* the speaker's utterance. What is needed, then, is an account of understanding speech.

This is not the place to attempt even a sketch of such an account, but a few remarks may help to relate it to Augustine's unsuccessful theory. Understanding an utterance – for example S in C – is indeed a case of recognizing the utterance as a sign, but not as a sign of the speaker's belief – for example of my belief that the Queen was in Brussels on VE Day – let alone of the purported fact purportedly believed – that she was there then. Rather, the hearer understands S (i.e. the speaker's utterance of S) in C when he recognizes S as a sign of a certain *intention* which the speaker must have had if there is anything to be understood; and the intention is what the speaker *meant* by S in C (in the case of S, what the speaker meant by it in C was that the Queen was in Brussels on VE Day). So the final stage in accounting for the hearer's understanding of S in C will be to analyse what it is in general for a speaker u to mean by a sentence s that p. But by this point we have evidently moved a long way from Augustine.

Words

So far we have examined the application of Augustine's sign theory only to sentences. Although in Latin it is comparatively easy to construct single-word sentences ('ambulavi' – 'I went for a walk', 'precabantur' – 'they used to pray', 'i' – 'go') nevertheless most Latin words, of course, cannot function as sentences on their own, and even those that can usually do not. Consequently proposition (5), that every word is a sign, needs different arguments in its defence from any we have yet considered.

To be sure, one might attempt to extend Augustine's theory about sentences by stages into a theory about single words. Suppose, for example, that Augustine accepts interpretation (10) of the significance of sentence S in context C, and suppose he is then asked what the predicate-component of S, 'was in Brussels', signifies in C. One way of answering would be to indicate the contribution made by 'was in Brussels' to the significance of S as a whole, as might be done like this: in C, *any* sentence 'A was in Brussels' is evidence that the speaker believes that *anything* B was in Brussels on VE Day, if and only if 'A' names B. By further stages the contributions made by the elements within 'was in Brussels' could then be isolated similarly. This kind of explanation (characteristic of modern truth-theories of meaning) takes sentences as the minimum units of significance: parts of sentences do not signify anything but only contribute, in a rule-governed way, to the significance of the sentence in which they are parts (some parts of sentences must, however, *name*).

There is a hint of this procedure in the first answer which Adeodatus gives in *De Magistro* to Augustine's question about the line he has quoted from Virgil, 'If it please the gods that nothing should be left from this great city'. The question is, 'What does each word in the line signify?', and about the first word 'if' ('si') Adeodatus says: 'It seems to me that 'if' signifies doubt; and where is doubt if not in the mind?' (*Mag.* 2.3). Perhaps the suggestion is: the line as a whole is evidence of its speaker's doubt whether a certain purported fact obtains; and the contribution of 'if' is to make the line evidence of *doubt* whether it obtains rather than, say, belief that it does. However, the suggestion is not pursued, and Adeodatus' next answer, though reverting eventually to something similar, at first proceeds differently.

The second word in Virgil's line is 'nihil' – 'nothing'. Adeodatus says: 'What can 'nothing' signify except what is not' (ibid.). At once he and Augustine find themselves in trouble: signifying what is not is signifying nothing; but if 'nothing' signifies nothing, according to propositions (5) and (6) it is not a word.

Adeodatus seems to have been attracted to this troublesome second answer by some such principle as the following: when a word is put for the two occurrences of 'A' in the formula ' "A" signifies A', the result will always come out true provided that it is capable of truth. The proviso is important, and doubtless explains why Adeodatus did not apply the principle to 'if'; for ' "If" signifies if' is not capable of truth – it is not a complete sentence. The cases for which the proviso *is* fulfilled are, roughly speaking, the cases in which 'A' is replaced by a name. So the principle can be reformulated as ' "A" *signifies A' is the right formula for the significance of names.*

It is clear that in return for now assessing Augustine on his full statement that every word is a sign we shall have to abate the charge that by signs he means evidence. And it is only reasonable to do so, despite the fact that a word such as 'Brussels' in sentence S could be supposed to offer evidence for a mental state, viz. that the speaker is thinking of

Brussels, has Brussels in mind. Adeodatus' formula would exclude this reading, because it requires the word to be evidence not of a mental state at all, but of Brussels; and what could that mean – evidence that Brussels exists, evidence that it is present? The suggestions are absurd. On the other hand reminding, which is also a feasible way of being an indicative sign, is precisely the relation needed for constructing a legitimate application of Adeodatus' formula to words like 'Brussels'. Among the many descriptions that come to mind of the relation between 'Brussels' and Brussels some are unhelpful ('means', 'names', 'denotes', 'designates'), some wrong ('stands for' in the sense 'takes the place of', 'represents' in the sense 'depicts'); one that is both right and helpful is 'refers to', where what it means to say that 'Brussels' refers to Brussels (e.g. in sentence S in context C) is

'Brussels' is intended to bring to mind Brussels.

It is not possible, as Augustine saw, to bring to a person's mind by naming it something which was never in his mind before ('perception of the signification [of words] . . . occurs not by hearing the vocal sounds [vocum] uttered, but by recognition [cognitione] of the things signified', *Mag.* 11.36). The bringing to mind that is intended by utterance of a word such as 'Brussels' is therefore bringing back to mind, reminding, and the truth that 'Brussels' refers to Brussels can readily be understood as identical with the corresponding application of Adeodatus' Principle, that is, as identical with the proposition that 'Brussels' signifies Brussels.

In *De Dialectica* and *De Magistro* Augustine argues that this application can be extended to all single words. The argument is from two premises:

(13) Adeodatus' Principle can be extended to all names;
(14) all words are names;
therefore Adeodatus' Principle can be extended to all words.

But we shall have to conclude that (13) is false and (14), though true in a way, would not support the argument.

Names

What is a name? Augustine seems to have accepted a criterion which, owing its origin (so far as we know) to Plato's *Sophist* (262a), had been developed over the succeeding 700 years in the hazy tradition of ancient grammar (from which little survives complete before the Latin grammar of Priscian, early sixth century AD). In this classification names, nomina, comprised all that we call nouns, including adjectives, and often also pronouns. Among the examples of names cited by Augustine are (put into English) 'Romulus', 'Rome', 'virtue', 'silver', 'river', and 'great'. I

have already mentioned the first three; they and also 'silver' fit Adeodatus' Principle neatly, since each is (in correct usage) a referring
expression and each refers (in a context of correct usage) to one of the
things so named, 'Romulus' to Romulus and so on. Difficulties begin
with the common noun 'river' ('fluvius', *Mag.* 4.8). Augustine never
suggests that 'river' and its like are signs of the *class* of rivers and their
like (the 'extension' of the name): as we have seen, the word is a sign of
rivers, all of them. Thus the application of Adeodatus' Principle to 'river'
will presumably yield: in any context of correct usage, 'river' signifies
some (one) river. Given our understanding of 'signifies' as 'refers', this
application is always wrong for English, which requires combination
with some other word, minimally 'the', if a common noun is to refer to
some member of its extension; Latin however, lacking articles, could use
'fluvius' thus on its own. Nevertheless even in Latin a common noun
can also appear in combinations where it does not refer to a member of
its extension: for example, in the phrases 'nullus fluvius' – 'no river' or
'omnis fluvius' – 'every river' there is no river which the word 'fluvius'
– or indeed the phrase as a whole – serves to bring to mind (which river
would it be – the Danube?). The same is true of predicative combinations,
as in 'the Danube is a river'. These cases call for a distinction among
names which grammar may be able to do without but a theory of signs
cannot: perhaps the distinction between singular terms and universal
terms that underlies Aristotle's syllogistic logic, or the distinction
between subjects and predicates that underlies Frege's quantificational
logic. By building on such a distinction we may then also be able to
explain names like 'nihil' – 'nothing' and 'nemo' – 'nobody', the initial
troublemakers for Adeodatus' Principle in *De Magistro* and a source of
philosophical teasing ever since Homer's story of Cyclops (*Odyssey*
9.366, 408).

Augustine fails, then – and in the case of 'nihil' hardly tries – to
show that Adeodatus' Principle is satisfied by all names in his generous
acceptation of the word 'name'. In the 1940s Gilbert Ryle detected and
castigated in Carnap what he called the 'Fido'–Fido principle, that
'signify' in its modern sense of 'mean' states a relation which holds from
every expression to 'some extra-linguistic correlate to the expression,
like the dog that answers to the name "Fido" ' (Ryle 1971:226). So far
as that principle applies to names its recorded history begins, I fear, with
Augustine.

A passage from *De Dialectica* on the vices of obscuritas and ambiguitas
will serve both to confirm the failure of proposition (13) and to introduce
our examination of proposition (14):

Let us suppose that ‹a teacher in class› has said 'Great' ['magnus']
and then stopped. Notice what uncertainties result from hearing that

name. Perhaps he is going on to say, 'What part of speech is it?', or perhaps, 'What [metrical] foot?', or perhaps he is going on to ask a question in history, 'Great Pompey fought how many wars?', or to make a remark in literary criticism, 'Great, almost unique, is Virgil's contribution to poetry', or to deliver a rebuke to a lazy pupil with, 'Great idler that you are'. You can see, I expect, that when the fog of obscurity has been dispelled, the word said above stands out like a junction of many roads. For that single thing that was said, Great, is both a name and also a trochaic foot and also Pompey and also Virgil and also an idler; and numberless other things not mentioned, that are capable of being understood through utterance of the word. (*Dial.* 8.15)

'Great', being an adjective, already counts as a name by Augustine's relaxed criterion, and therefore is supposed by him to be a sign of all great things just as, I remarked earlier, 'sign' is supposed to be a sign of all signs (and 'river' of all rivers). The new point that needs to be noticed is that also among the things 'capable of being understood through utterance of the word' is, according to Augustine, the word itself, which is 'a name and a trochaic foot'. If a modern pupil wrote 'Great is a name', giving the Augustinian answer to Augustine's first question, 'What part of speech is it?', he would be taught to enclose 'Great' in its own further quotation marks in order to indicate that the word was being mentioned (a convention I have myself scrupulously observed in this chapter; there was no comparable device in ancient writing). Some twentieth-century philosophers hold that *mention* of a word excludes *use* of it. But Augustine's reasonable view is that what we would call quotation-mark utterances mention a word *by* using it. Thus the word occurs in such utterances; and what it signifies in them is itself.

This doctrine conflicts with the requirement in Augustine's definitions of 'sign' that signs 'show something *beyond* themselves' (*Dial.* 5.7, p. 35 above, cf. *Doct. Christ.* 2.1.1, p. 36 above). Nevertheless he labours the doctrine in both *De Dialectica* and *De Magistro*. It is not quite clear why so much effort is spent on it. There is some evidence that Stoics had used it as a basis on which to defend the paradox that all words are ambiguous (attributed by Augustine to 'the dialecticians', and endorsed by him, *Dial.* 9.15, cf. *Mag.* 8.22). In the early chapters of *De Magistro* we find it playing a part in a series of curious arguments in defence of proposition (14).

Augustine has begun by denying (14): in the lines from Virgil ' "If" ["si"] . . . and "from" ["ex"] . . . are words yet not names; and many such are found' (*Mag.* 4.9). But later he undertakes to show otherwise:

AUGUSTINE: Utter a few conjunctions for me, any you like.

ADEODATUS: 'And', 'too', 'but', 'also' [the Latin is 'et que at atque'].

AUG: Don't you think that all these you have said are names?

AD: Not at all.

AUG: But at least you think that I spoke correctly to you in saying 'All these you have said'.

AD: Quite correctly; and now I understand to my surprise that you have shown that I did utter names; for otherwise one could not rightly say of these, 'All these'. (*Mag.* 5.13)

'These' ('haec') is a pronoun referring to 'and', 'too', etc.; and in the preceding lines pronouns (pronomina) have been classified among names (nomina). At first sight, therefore, Augustine's case appears to be the preposterous one that 'and', 'too', etc. must be names because it is possible to refer to them by name. The real case is deeper, and emerges from details of the preceding passage:

AUG: I believe you have accepted and will agree that a so called pronoun, which does the work of the name itself [pro ipso nomine valeat], nevertheless denotes [notet] a thing with less full signification than the name does. This is how your grammar teacher defined it, I think: a pronoun is a part of speech which, put in place of the name itself [pro ipso posita nomine], signifies the same as it, although less fully. (*Mag.* 5.13)

So the reasoning is:

(15) what pronouns are put in place of are names;
(16) in the exchange quoted, 'these' was put in place of 'and', 'too', etc.;

therefore 'and', 'too' etc. are names.

Such conjunctions, he is arguing, are names because it is possible to use *themselves* to refer to them.

There follows a sound demonstration that at 2 Cor. 1:19 Paul must be understood as using 'is' ('est', Greek '*nai*' meaning 'yes') as a name – one *not* referring to itself – when he says of Christ that 'Is was in him [est in illo erat]' (*Mag.* 5.14). In case it is thought that Paul lacked linguistic finesse, another argument can be drawn from translatability: anyone who says that the Latin 'qui' ('who') means the same as the Greek '*tis*' is using 'qui' and '*tis*' as names; but he is correct to say so; therefore they are names (*Mag.* 5.15). The most eminent professors of logic (disputationum) teach that every complete sentence contains a name and a verb. Suppose then that I say of a dimly perceived object, 'Because it is a man it is an animal', while you prefer the more cautious, 'If it is a man it is an animal': where are the names in your comment to me, ' "If" is satisfactory, "because" is not'? (*Mag.* 5.16).

Every word, we are thus invited to conclude, can be used to refer to itself, and when so used it is a name. Here Augustine is surely right; and what is more, the kind of name in question is a referring expression, the kind for which Adeodatus' Principle holds good. We modern pedants would write such applications of the Principle with nested quotation-marks: ' "the word 'because' " signifies the word "because" ' or, more briefly but confusingly, ' " 'because' " signifies "because" '. But no notational purism will refute Augustine's intuition that the word 'because' is *used* to refer in these claims; and in that use it is a name satisfying the Principle (but see Geach 1972 for caveats).

Every word, therefore, *is* a sign, in the sense that every word is capable of being used with the intention of bringing something – itself – to mind. Unfortunately, as is obvious, this result is less than Augustine's sign-theory needs. *De Doctrina Christiana* asserts that 'no one uses words except for the purpose of signifying something' (1.2.2, proposition (4)); but words like 'because' the arguments in *De Magistro* show at best that they are exceptionally so used. Wittgenstein wrote:

> Augustine, in describing his learning of language, says that he was taught to speak by learning the names of things. It is clear that whoever says this has in mind the way in which a child learns such words as 'man', 'sugar', 'table' etc. He does not primarily think of such words as 'today', 'not', 'but', 'perhaps'. (*Brown Book* 1)

In his later *Philosophical Investigations* Wittgenstein quoted the relevant passage (*Conf*. 1.8.13), repeated the same criticism, asked us to 'imagine a language for which the description given by Augustine is right', and concluded that 'Augustine, we might say, does describe a system of communication [Verständigung]; only not everything that we call language is this system' (*Philosophical Investigations* 1.3). The criticism is essentially right: for although *De Dialectica* and *De Magistro* do show Augustine 'thinking of such words as "not" ', nevertheless when he thinks hard about them he comes out with the judgement that they are names. Not everything that we call language is like that.

Learning to speak

Wittgenstein also wrote:

> Augustine describes the learning of human language as if the child came into a strange country and did not understand the language of the country; that is, as if it already had a language, only not this one. Or again: as if the child could already *think*, only not yet speak. And 'think' would here mean something like 'talk to itself'. (*Philosophical Investigations* 1.32)

As Baker and Hacker note (1983:60), the evidence for this attribution seems to come not from the few sentences of Augustine's *Confessions* (1.8.13) quoted at the beginning of the *Investigations* but from slightly earlier passages in which Augustine, using his own observations of babies, imagines himself in infancy frustrated by inability to express (edere), and not merely to satisfy, his desires (*Conf.* 1.6.8, 1.8.13). Wittgenstein connects possession of an earlier language – which in the infant would have to be a wordless language of thought – with the effectiveness of ostensive definition in teaching a new language: only if the learner is already a talker, at least a talker-to-himself, will he be able to gain understanding when a teacher says to him such things as, ' "Purple" is the name of *that*'; for only then will he be equipped to know or guess the nature of his teacher's intention (Does he mean colours?) when the teacher points and says 'that'. Hence a false picture of the infant mind could tempt philosophers into too crude an account of language-acquisition.

Augustine's picture of the infant mind is certainly false, since it contains the inconsistent claims that adults 'have no means by any of their senses of entering into' a speechless baby's soul, and yet that he himself learnt about babies' frustrations by his own observation of them (*Conf.* 1.6.8). Certainly, too, his attitude is that of someone who models infant mentality on the mentality of a speechless stroke-victim; but how far that is a false model only empirical psychologists are in a position to tell us. Whatever the psychologists' verdict may be, however, we can at least exculpate Augustine from the philosophical error imputed to him by Wittgenstein, of inferring from this model to an excessively crude account of language-acquisition. Passages in *De Magistro* furnish, ironically, the best anticipation known to me of Wittgenstein's insights about ostensive definition. Augustine stresses how hard it is to explain signs except by means of other (given) signs; even explanation by gesture, as in pointing, is a use of such signs (*Mag.* 3.6, 10.34). If one seeks to explain a sign by manifesting what it is a sign of, e.g. 'walking' by walking, there will always be the possibility of misunderstanding:

> ADEODATUS: If someone . . . were to ask me what walking is, and I were to attempt to teach him what he asked without a sign, by promptly walking, how am I to guard against his thinking that it is just the *amount* of walking I have done? If he thinks that, he will be mistaken; for he will judge that anyone who walks farther than I have, or less far, has not walked. And what I have said about this one word can be transferred to every word which I had agreed could be exhibited [monstrari] without a sign, apart from the two we have excepted. (*Mag.* 10.29)

The exceptions were 'speak' and 'teach'; but Augustine later includes them too.

Writing

A brief passage of Aristotle which Kretzmann (1971:3) has called the most influential text in the history of semantics contains this claim: 'Spoken sounds are symbols of affections in the soul, and written marks of spoken sounds' (*De Interpretatione* 1.16a 3–4). Aristotle goes on to describe spoken sounds as also signs, *sēmeia*, of such affections, but he does not say that written marks are signs of spoken sounds. In each of our three main texts we find Augustine in partial agreement with this. Without acknowledging any distinction between sign and symbol – in his ecclesiastical Latin 'Symbolum' designated the Creed – he nevertheless denies that there is a direct relation between written marks and mental states (or between written marks and external things); according to Augustine, what writing signifies is *speech*:

> Every word makes a sound. For when it is in writing, it is not a word but the sign of a word, the reason being that when letters are seen by a reader, what [quid] would be issued vocally is suggested to his mind. For written letters show to the eye something beyond themselves, and show to the mind vocal sounds [voces] beyond themselves. (*Dial*. 5.7)

> AUGUSTINE: What happens when we find words written? Are they words? Are they not more truly understood as signs of words, a word being what is uttered in an articulate vocal sound with some signification? . . . Thus it is that when a word is written, a sign is made to the eyes by which something comes into the mind which pertains to the ears. (*Mag*. 4.8)

> But because words strike the air and pass, lasting no longer than their sound, signs of words have been devised through their letters [i.e. phonetically]. In this way vocal sounds are shown to the eyes, not through themselves but through what are signs of them. (*Doct. Christ*. 2.4.5)

The things called written words are not properly words at all, Augustine insists; nor are written letters properly letters – a 'letter', in Augustine's Latin usage, being something vocal, 'the smallest part of articulate vocal sound' (*Dial*. 5.7), i.e. a vowel or consonant.

It is not clear whether Augustine would have espoused this doctrine had Latin script not been, like its ancestors and descendants, phonetic. At any rate, it is correct to describe phonetic writing as *modelling* spoken words, whose internal sound structure gets represented by letters (in our sense of 'letter'); and accordingly written Latin words are signs, signa, of spoken Latin words in the accredited sense 'representations'. Whether or not encouraged by this – irrelevant – fact, Augustine makes written words signs of spoken words in his own official sense of 'sign': they indicate them – writing 'suggests to the reader's mind what would be issued vocally'.

The doctrine fits some kinds of writing well enough, for example the text of a play or the libretto of a song. The latter in particular can sensibly be regarded as giving an indication of vocal sounds, an indication not exactly in the sense of evidence, nor yet reminder, but in the sense of instructions for making sounds. Musical notation is similar, the prime function of a score being to give instructions for the production of – usually non-vocal – sounds. And a sacred text, e.g. a scroll of the Jewish *Torah*, could well be thought of in the same way, as intended to guide the performance of liturgical readers.

And if not vocal performance, then sub-vocal: for the kind of inner vocalization we shall find Augustine examining in the next section – what Evelyn Waugh called 'pronouncing ‹words› in the mind' (1962:107) – is often the effect of silent reading, when one reads *to* oneself. Perhaps Augustine would be content with the view that writing is a sign of vocal *or* sub-vocal pronouncing.

Yet even musical scores *can* be used differently, by those with the skill to 'read' them. Such people are able to learn how the music goes simply by following the notes with their eyes; they may or may not hear the music with the mind's ear, but they do not need to play or sing it, even sub-vocally, in order for their understanding to be activated. With written words this same non-vocalizing skill, now common, may also once have been rare, its exercise secondary to the use of texts for reading aloud or at best reading *to* oneself; and in such conditions there would be some justification for defining writing as an 'indication' of what to say (the sole reference to writing in Homer describes a missive as 'sinister signs', *Iliad* 6.168–9). Yet long before Augustine people must often have read without pronouncing; and even if in provincial Africa the custom was to speak or mouth the words (the young Augustine in Milan was startled to find that Ambrose read silently, *Conf.* 6.3.3), it cannot still have been reasonable in his time to conceive the writer's normal purpose as provision of a 'score' for vocal or sub-vocal performance. I think we have to rate Augustine's doctrine of written signs superannuated.

Inner words

According to Christian orthodoxy God's word is his deed; that is, God effects his will by speaking it (*Gen. Lit.* 1.3.8), as in 'Let there be light' (Gen. 1:3). Since God has no body, divine speech is not vocal: it is what Augustine called an inner word (verbum quod intus lucet, *Trin.* 15.11.20). God speaks in the same way to human beings, who hear his word internally (*Serm.* 180.7.7). He uses no 'tongue', i.e. language, neither Hebrew nor Greek nor Latin. The word of God that a man may hear is like the word of a man who has not yet uttered it:

Observe your own heart. When you conceive a word ‹that you wish› to speak – I shall describe, if I can, what we observe in ourselves, not how we come to grasp it – when you conceive a word ‹that you wish› to produce, there is some thing which you wish to say and the very conception of that in your heart is a word: not yet uttered, but already born in your heart and waiting to be uttered. You take note who it is to be uttered to, who you are talking to: if he is Latin, you search for a Latin vocal sound [vocem]; if he is Greek you think of Greek words; if Punic, you see whether you know any Punic. Matching the differences in your audience you employ different languages in order to produce the word you have conceived; but what you had conceived in your heart was confined to no language. (*Ev. Joh.* 3.14.7)

Similarly:

A thought that is formed from a thing that we know is a word that we say in the heart. It is neither Greek nor Latin nor any other language, but when we need to bring it to the notice [notitia] of those to whom we speak, a sign is picked with which to signify it. (*Trin.* 15.10.19)

Inner words occur not only when we are preparing to speak; for any kind of notion (notitia) is a word:

In one way we call a word what occupies a stretch of time by its syllables, whether it is pronounced or thought, in another everything of which we have a notion [omne notum] is called a word impressed on the mind, so long as it can be produced from the memory and defined, even if the thing itself displeases us; in another when what is conceived in the mind pleases us. (*Trin.* 9.10.15)

The purpose of the passage surrounding this quotation is to distinguish loved from hated notions, but that purpose is here overlaid by the more important distinction between thoughts (or perhaps knowledge or concepts) that are verbalizable and those that have been verbalized. The latter appear again in *De Quantitate Animae*:

AUGUSTINE: Now before the word ‹sun› itself is uttered from your mouth suppose that, wishing to pronounce it, you hold yourself in silence for a time. Does not something stay in your thought which someone else is about to hear vocally expressed? . . . Does it not seem to you that the name itself as it were received from you the signification it was to convey to me through my ears? . . .

The sound is a body, but the signification is, so to speak, the soul of the sound. (*Qu. An.* 32.65–6)

The complex details of these passages, since they come from different works and dates, need not be assumed to be all consistent with one another. A general picture emerges, however, according to which at least two kinds of thoughts *are* words: the thoughts which a thinker has already formulated in words, saying the words to himself perhaps in rehearsal before speaking or writing; and the thoughts in no language which, allegedly, he is able to draw on in these processes of silent and vocal formulation.

Augustine's construction of this doctrine is typical of his philosophical method. He starts from a familiar phenomenon that 'we observe in ourselves', the rehearsal of phrases and sentences in advance of speech or writing. He uses the phenomenon to elucidate a theological obscurity, the notion of the word of God. In doing so he moves beyond the evidence into a theory, that all thought is inner speech; and the theory is one which he can support both from the Bible (e.g. 'The fool hath said in his heart, There is no God', Ps 13 [Heb. Bib. 14]:1) and from Platonism (e.g. Plato, *Sophist* 263e). Finally, he leaves his own stamp on the theory, again for theological reasons, when he insists that the words in which thoughts are 'formed from a thing that we know' are not in any language.

Without commenting generally on this theory I shall end the chapter by looking at its relation to an earlier episode in the history of philosophy of language, the Stoic doctrine of *lekta*, sayables.

Cicero's and Seneca's allusions to the doctrine of *lekta* had refrained from the neologism 'dicibile' which would have been the most direct Latinization of the Stoics' Greek. 'Dicibile' got invented at some time between Seneca and Augustine, to be used by Augustine in a single passage of *De Dialectica*:

Whatever is perceived [sentit] from a word by the mind, not the ears, and is kept shut up in the mind itself, is called a sayable [dicibile]. When a word is uttered [procedit] not for its own sake but for the sake of signifying something else, it is called a saying [dictio]. The thing [res] itself, which is not a word nor the conception of a word in the mind, whether or not it has a word by which it can be signified, is called merely a thing in the proper sense of that name. So these four must be kept distinct: word, sayable, saying, thing. 'Word' [literally, What I have said: word] both is a word and signifies a word. 'Sayable' is a word; however it signifies not a word but what is understood in a word and retained [continetur] in the mind. 'Saying' is a word but signifies both together of the things signified by the first two, that is, both a word itself and what occurs in the mind by means of a word. 'Thing' is a word which signifies whatever remains beyond the three that have been mentioned [literally, said]. . . . But when they [sc. some words said by a teacher] are perceived in advance of vocal sound [ante vocem] they will be sayables; when for the purpose I have mentioned they are expressed in vocal sound, they become sayings, (*Dial.* 5.8)

According to this passage a dicibile is:

(a) perceived from a word by the mind not the ears, and kept shut up in the mind;
(b) a conception of a word in the mind;
(c) not a word but what is understood in a word and retained in the mind;
(d) what occurs in the mind by means of a word;
(e) a word perceived in advance of vocal sound.

It is hard to fit all these into a coherent account. (e) describes inner words in the sense Augustine was later to use for explaining how God speaks to men, while (b) suggests inner words in Augustine's extended sense, i.e. thoughts in general. (a) and (d) refer us to items that are given a place in a hearer's mind as a result of his exposure to speech: these also, in view of the sign-theory of speech, might be identified as thoughts, in particular the speaker's thoughts which he intends to convey. Alternatively, (a) and (d) could be interpreted so as to conform with (c), which appears to identify the dicibile with the meaning of a speaker – his intention to convey thoughts (or facts), rather than the thoughts conveyed.

Such uncertainty would not be surprising if Augustine were inheriting, doubtless in a changed and enfeebled state, the tradition of Stoic doctrine about *lekta*. According to the Stoics words are corporeal but *lekta* are incorporeal things 'signified' by them (Sextus, *Adversus Mathematicos* 8.11–12). Thoughts too are corporeal, they believed; and *lekta* 'accord with' a certain kind of thought, the 'rational *phantasia*' (ibid. 8.70). A central function of *lekta* is to be true or false, 'complete' ones being those whose 'utterance is finished, e.g. "Socrates writes" ' (Diogenes Laertius, *Lives of the Philosophers* 7.63), which therefore correspond to sentences rather than individual words; while the incomplete ones, we also learn, correspond to predicates. It appears therefore that the Stoics, or some of them, felt they had identified a need for incorporeal entities corresponding to sentences and predicates which was *not* matched by any need for incorporeal entities corresponding to names. Here is an emphasis on difference of function among words and word-groups which we have found Augustine playing down in his doctrine that all single words are names, and which he seems to ignore altogether in what he says about dicibilia. Like Locke in the passage quoted on p. 39 above but unlike the Stoics, Augustine was tempted to assume that whatever corresponds to a sentence, in the mind or in the world, must be formed of parts – be they 'inner words' or ideas – which correspond to the parts – words – forming the sentence. This beguiling error is the picture theory of language which I have already mentioned in connection with the non-Greek meaning of 'signum', 'representation'. It was to impede the philosophy of language for many centuries after Augustine.

Further reading

Against the sign theory see Price (1953). For alternative theories see e.g. Grice (1957) and Searle (1983: ch. 6). Blackburn (1984) is a good recent survey of philosophy of language. On Augustine's theory see Markus and Jackson, both in Markus *Augustine* (1972). Burnyeat (1987) is a penetrating examination of the *De Magistro*.

IV

God and bad

Dualism

Near the beginning of the dialogue *De Libero Arbitrio* Augustine makes
Evodius ask, 'How does it come to be that people misbehave?' ('Unde
male faciamus?' *Lib. Arb.* 1.2.4). Augustine replies: 'You raise a question
which exercised me a great deal when I was still quite young; worry
about it made me take up with heretics and brought me into a wretched
state' (ibid.). These heretics were the Manichees, who had been active
in Africa since the beginning of the fourth century.

Mani (or Manes or Manichaeus) was a Persian prophet of whom we
know that he was born about 216, had skill as a painter, travelled
extensively eastwards from Persia, and was crucified or met some other
revolting death about 278, apparently at the instigation of the official
Persian priesthood. He taught a fanciful cosmology, doubtless elaborated
out of earlier Persian good/bad dualisms. The cosmos is divided into a
realm of light and a realm of darkness. The princes of darkness fell in
love with light and attacked its realm to capture it. God, the prince of
light, sent primordial men to repulse them, but the men were defeated
by darkness and their finer elements became mixed with elements of
darkness. From the mixture God made the visible world, so that the
finer elements might be liberated upwards into the sun, as is gradually
happening. Mortal man – the men we are – was then formed by Satan
as a trap for these elements, to impede their rising. God sent prophets
including Jesus (a docetic phantom) to warn men against aiding Satan's
purpose by sinful living. In order to assist the liberation of the trapped
elements it is necessary for men to abstain from meat, wine, and sex.

It is disturbing to be told by Augustine that the sect which adhered
to this farrago of myth and taboo had attracted him by its appeal to
'the plain and simple way of reason' (*Util. Cred.* 1.2); perhaps a more
intellectually respectable version was purveyed to him at Carthage – by,

he reports, 'exceedingly witty and cultivated' missionaries (*Util. Cred.*
1.3). However that may be, one must admit that there is a certain
satisfaction, both intellectual and emotional, in the dualism underlying
Mani's fables, which accounts for the existence of good and evil by
postulating a struggle for dominion over the world between two primal
powers, in whose warfare we are all caught up. Augustine, however,
was not beguiled permanently, but came in the course of time to feel
uneasy about his co-religionists for a number of reasons, including their
cavalier attitude to astronomical calculation; so that by 382, when he
was a 28-year-old professor at Carthage, he was glad at last to have the
opportunity of laying his doubts before a visiting bishop and savant of the
sect, one Faustus. Faustus at first charmed Augustine by his unexpected
condescension; but the pleasure turned to anger as Augustine's impor-
tunity was continually rebuffed (Faustus would not accept questions
from his lecture audience). He had pinned his hopes on this man; and
as he came to think Faustus a charlatan, so his respect for Manicheism
began to dissipate. Yet without that doctrine, how could the existence
of evil be accounted for? 'By this stage you, my helper', he wrote to
God in the *Confessions*:

> had released me from those fetters ‹of Manicheism›, and I was trying
> to find out where evil comes from, and there was no way out
> [quaerebam unde malum, et non erat exitus]. . . . ‹I› was in a fever
> to discover where evil comes from. (*Conf.* 7.7.11)

In the following years, during which his conversion took place, it was
Augustine's main intellectual preoccupation to forge a 'Catholic' – i.e.
Christian – doctrine of evil.

As a Christian Augustine came to think that the dualist explanation
of evil suffered from two major defects. First, it derogated from the
supremacy of God by circumscribing his activities as creator:

> The consideration we wish to urge [he wrote in one of his anti-
> Manichean tracts] is the truth of the Catholic doctrine . . . that
> God is the author of all natures [omnium naturarum esse auctorem
> Deum]. (*C. Ep. Man. Fund.* 33.36)

Secondly, Augustine argued that in postulating the existence of powers
which are purely evil Manicheism was inconsistent both with its own
account of those powers and with the Neoplatonist thesis deriving from
Plotinus that 'the bad is nothing but a privation of the good' (*Conf.*
3.7.12).

This thesis is elusive. Some have understood it as stating that badness
is a species of non-existence, but so understood it is false since badness
admits of degrees while non-existence does not. Plotinus' own definition
employs a distinction drawn from Plato which shows that he at least

could not have been thinking of non-existence: 'Bad is . . . a form of what is not . . . ‹where› what is not is not what utterly is not but only what is other than what is' (*Enneads* 1.8.3.4). But if badness consists in being other that what is, we need to ask 'Other than what is *what*?'; and the answer seems to be the unsurprising one, 'Good' – so that the bad is a privation of the good in the sense merely of being a lack of it (not necessarily a *loss*, as Augustine sometimes assumes, e.g. *C. Ep. Man. Fund.* 35.4). But now there is a difficulty in seeing how this thesis can rise above the banal, and how it can have strength as a weapon against dualism or indeed any other ethical stance. Augustine takes us an important step further when he describes the bad, not indeed as a species of non-existence, but as a tendency towards that:

> For a thing to be bad is for it to fall away from being and tend to a state in which it is not [idipsum ergo malum est . . . deficere ab essentia et ad id tendere ut non sit]. (*Mor. Man.* 2.2, cf. *C. Ep. Man. Fund.* 40.46)

In another expression to similar effect he often says that badness is 'corruption', which makes it a stage on the way, rather than a movement, towards non-existence: to be bad on this conception is to be at least partly decayed. Because total decay is destruction, Augustine is now in a position to draw the inference he wants against the Manichees: what is wholly bad has been destroyed, so that no being can be purely evil. He compares a putrid limb:

> If the corruption has destroyed it completely, no good, and therefore no nature, will remain, because there will be nothing for the corruption to corrupt. (*Nat. Bon.* 20, cf. *City* 19.13)

Thus the logicians' rule that nothing contains contraries has a counter-example here, and everything evil is, also, good (*Ench.* 14.4).

But is the privation thesis true, so understood? It conceives the goodness of each kind of thing as what conduces to the thing's being good of that kind – a good specimen – and it construes goodness as that in virtue of which the specimen thrives or flourishes; then it reasons that if you deprive anything of all that contributes to its thriving you will have deprived it of the very means of existence. As a general account of goodness this oversimplifies in three different ways. First, although living things cannot exist in the absence of all that contributes to their thriving (since that includes what is needful to them, i.e. needful for life), other things can: a social club, for example, might through total inactivity have no good in it, yet continue to exist. Secondly, to be a good specimen is not the same as to be a thriving one; indeed the very idea of that kind of goodness is hard to understand in the case of a mountain, say, or a bed or a journey or a victory. Thirdly, even things which can be good by thriving can often also be good in quite other ways, and therefore can be bad without corruption of their natures. In particular what in English we call evil is generally badness of a more external sort, the word connoting especially hurtfulness and malice towards other people; and there is no inference from Augustine's privation thesis to the conclusion that nothing is purely hurtful or malicious.

Augustine does, however, support this last conclusion by a supplementary argument. Lacking a separate word for 'evil' (he always employs the generic 'malus' and its cognate noun 'malum') he nevertheless notices that 'hurtful', 'id quod nocet' (*Mor. Man.* 3.5), could be offered as a definition of 'malus', and that a hurt is a loss of goodness. Against Manichees who use this definition he then argues that the kingdom of darkness cannot be hurtful either to itself, since on the Manichean view it contains no good to lose, or to the kingdom of light, whose pure goodness must include immunity to losing itself. Yet even this supplementary argument is not strong enough to dispose of the princes of darkness, because there would appear to be no barrier to the existence of pure *malice*, which can become effective as hurt just so soon as there are beings like ourselves, both possessed of some goodness and vulnerable to its loss.

The problem of evil

Whatever the merits of Augustine's arguments against dualism, his Christianity obliged him to abandon it and so left him with a problem, the theist's Problem of Evil. Here is a statement of it by Pierre Bayle (1647–1706), from his article on Manicheism:

> Either God is willing to remove evils, and not able, or able and not willing, or neither able nor willing, or both able and willing. If he be willing and not able, he is impotent, which cannot be applied to the Deity. If he be able and not willing, he is envious, which is generally inconsistent with the nature of God. If he be neither willing nor able, he is both envious and impotent, and consequently no God. If he be both willing and able, which is the only thing that answers to the notion of a God, from whence come evils? Or why does he not remove them? (Bayle 1697)

Suppose that Bayle's concluding questions are unanswerable. Then a theist will have to concede that if God were both willing and able to remove evils, there would be none. From which it follows, since there are evils, that God does not exist. This generates out of Bayle's problem an argument for atheism, which could be stated as follows:

(1) It is necessary that if there is a God, he is neither envious nor in any way impotent;

> (2) It is necessary that any being who is neither envious nor in any way impotent will prevent at least some of the evils that occur;
> (3) No being does prevent any of the evils that occur;
> Therefore there is no God.

Such arguments as this have been described as presenting 'the most formidable objection to theistic belief' (Plantinga 1974:164). We must now examine how Augustine responded to the objection.

It is worth noticing at the outset that he followed in a long line of responses. Not all of them had been philosophical: the cries of pain in *Prometheus Bound*, or God's answer to Job out of the whirlwind, are intended to produce pity and awe rather than intellectual illumination. But philosophers too, and especially Epicureans and Stoics, had been at work before Augustine's day and had explored all the main ways of escaping the inference from evil to atheism (see e.g. Lucretius 5.198, Chrysippus, in von Arnim 1903–5:2.1125, 1170). It seems that Augustine was unfamiliar with all this previous work except that of Plotinus, whose solution he follows quite closely.

The argument from evil presses us to concede that if God exists he must either lack power or be deficient in qualities that are widely regarded as virtues when found in a human being. Augustine is not temperamentally averse to either concession. A passage in his long treatise against the deplorable Faustus shows him well aware of the pitfalls into which belief in the 'father almighty', 'patrem omnipotentem', can lead an incautious believer; and he specifies three things which the Catholic Christian ought not to think God capable of:

> Anyone who says, 'If God is omnipotent, let him make what has been done not to have been done,' fails to see that he is saying, 'If God is omnipotent, let him make what is true to be false in the very way it is true.' . . . God is not the adversary [contrarius] of truth. (*C. Faust*. 26.5)

> Now we do not say that God is omnipotent as if to believe that he is even able to die; or as if he should not be called omnipotent because he is unable to do that. (ibid.)

> God by his nature is unable to sin. (*City* 22.30)

On the other hand God's supremacy as creator, his freedom to choose whether there should exist such things as mosquitoes and droughts and potential torturers (or 'fire, frost and wild animals', *City* 11.22) must be upheld against the Manichees, as we have seen. As for moral defect, Augustine is oddly unconcerned to defend Plato's claim about the Demiurge that 'in someone good there is no malice [*phthonos*] ever about anything' (*Timaeus* 29e1), let alone to vindicate God's positive benevolence towards his creation. Rather than malice – Bayle's 'envy' – what Augustine most fears from the argument about evil is the imputation to God of *injustice* – so that his solution to the Problem of Evil is more aptly called a theodicy than many. Corruption, he seeks to show, takes nothing good from a nature

> except where God permits; and he permits it where he judges it to be required by good order and justice, in accordance with the gradations of inanimate things and the deserts of the animate [ubi ordinatissimum et justissimum judicat, pro rerum gradibus et pro meritis animarum]. (*C. Ep. Man. Fund.* 41.47)

We shall of course find Augustine defending the proposition that God is good, and without sin – indeed incapable of sinning. Mercy is also among the divine virtues (*C. Adim.* 7.3). But God's mercy does not extend to all men; his justice does.

All this shows that Augustine's aims are more limited than those of many Christian apologists. Nevertheless the atheist can, of course, mount a challenge against the limited project too, by changing his first two premises in some such way as this:

(1a) It is necessary that, if there is a God, he is maker of heaven and earth, and just, and sinless;

(2a) It is necessary that any being who is maker of heaven and earth and just and sinless will prevent at least some of the evils that occur.

Against the revised argument Augustine will not respond by denying (1a). Instead, then, he must deny (2a); that is, he must assert that

> It is possible for there to exist a being who is maker of heaven and earth and just and sinless but who does not prevent any of the evils that actually occur.

which involves asserting that the existence of such a God is compatible with the existence of such evils.

Behold, it was very good

That, then, is Augustine's project: to display the evils of the world as consistent with the existence of a just and sinless God who is 'author of all natures and substances' (*Mor. Man.* 2.3). His first step in carrying out the project is to argue that evils are, so to speak, no more than blemishes on an essentially healthy and beautiful creation. This is an invitation, not to cheer up and look on the bright side (something Augustine was constitutionally little disposed to do), but rather to see the world from the creator's point of view – to imagine God's problem, as it were. When you do that, Augustine thinks, you will understand that created things, while 'neither supremely nor equally nor unchangeably good, are yet each one of them good; and taken all together they are very good, because out of all of them is made an admirable beauty of the whole' (*Ench.* 9.3). He is not claiming that evil is an illusion; indeed he notices an argument to the contrary, that if we fear evils groundlessly, the fear itself is an evil (*Conf.* 7.5.7). Each creature is good in the sense merely that each has some good in it, as it must according to the corruption theory if it is not to go out of existence (see *Ench.* 12–14.4). Thus for example, if we look closely we shall find use (*City* 11.22), or at least no harm (*Gen. Lit.* 3.15.24), in poisonous animals; one man's solecism is another man's trope (*Ord.* 2.4.13); the defeated cock in a cockfight which Augustine witnessed was 'somehow consonant with the laws of nature and beautiful' (*Ord.* 1.8.25); and even eternal fire is not a bad nature, although it is bad for them who suffer it (*Nat. Bon.* 38). More important for theodicy is Augustine's conviction that the whole together is admirable: he agrees with God who on the sixth day of creation, we are told, 'saw every thing that he had made, and, behold, it was very good' (Gen. 1:31).

If someone were impiously to begrudge God's complacency on the sixth day, I think Augustine would not claim that reason can shift him from such an attitude. Admittedly he devotes some effort, like Plato and Plotinus before him, to convincing us that bad parts are compatible with a good whole (they may be 'absorbed', as Mackie (1982:154) has put it). Plotinus had pointed out, at length, how unreasonable it would be to expect all the characters in a play to be heroes (*Enneads* 3.2.11.17); Augustine's references (e.g. *City* 12.4) to beauty and fittingness – the joint subject, incidentally, of his earliest composition *De Pulchro et Apto*, now lost – echo Plato's opinion that a beautiful statue will not necessarily have beautifully coloured eyes (*Republic* 420c). God puts the wicked to good uses,

> embellishing the course of the ages, as if it were an extremely beautiful poem set off, so to speak, with antitheses; (*City* 11.18)

> the world is beautiful even with its sinners, although considered by themselves their ugliness befouls it [sua deformitas turpet]. (*City* 11.23)

It is a requirement of order that bad things should exist, and God loves their existence (*Ord.* 1.6.18). Yet the impious might concede these points without ceasing to doubt the goodness – even the overall beauty – of God's creation; and in reply to them Augustine does no more than protest that such doubts are induced by the obscurity of the divine purpose (*Ord.* 2.5.15).

Against two more particular objections, however, he offers a counter-argument. One objection is that even if the creation is good as a whole, it would have been better still without evil in it. No, says Augustine, because that would have been impossible. This response derives from Neoplatonism: the 'true' universe of mind, said Plotinus, was entirely good; yet 'it was not the sort of thing that could be last of the things there are' (*Enneads* 3.2.2.9); it had to create, and what it created was bound to be worse than itself (ibid. 38). In the same vein Augustine, addressing the pagans, says:

> In the range from the earthly to the heavenly and from the visible to the invisible some good things are better than others; they are unequal in order that all of them should exist [ad hoc inaequalia, ut essent omnia] (*City* 11.22; cf. 12.4, 12.27 (26), Plotinus, *Enneads* 4.8.6, Plato, *Timaeus* 41bc).

Although all natures are good, some, such as rational souls, are so much better than others such as bodies that their superiority persists even when they and not the others have been corrupted (*Nat. Bon.* 5). As Plotinus insisted, badness is the price of variety (*Enneads* 3.2.11.7).

At this point the doubter may retreat to an even less pregnable position: why, he may ask, is there *so much* evil as there is? Granted for argument's sake that the creation is good, and that it must contain evil, why must it contain all the terrible evils which it does contain, especially suffering and malice (the things we most properly call evils in English)? Augustine's reply to this final challenge is a curiously muted one. To be sure he will argue that all human suffering is just – we shall return to this later in the present chapter and in chapter 7. He is willing to assert that hangmen, and prostitutes, are necessary (*Ord.* 2.4.12); sometimes he hints that everything is for the best (*Nat. Bon.* 16, *Sol.* 1.1.2, *Lib. Arb.* 3.9.26). But there is in Augustine no systematic defence (so far as I know) of the thesis that God *could not have worked things better*, that as Leibniz (1646–1716) was much later to put it,

> if he had wished to do more, he would have had to make either other ‹more perfect› natures or other miracles to change ‹our› natures, things which the best plan could not admit. (Abridgement of the *Theodicy*, p. 518; compare the Stoic thought that nature has made the perfect product, Cicero, *De Natura Deorum* 2.34.)

In Augustine's Bible, as in the Vulgate, the Latin for 'very good' at Gen. 1:31 is 'bona valde', not 'optima'.

God's justice

The evidence we have considered so far reveals Augustine as asserting that God's creation, taken as a whole, is good and indeed very good. This is then argued to be consistent with the reality of all the manifold evils of the world; for a creation could not be wholly without deficient parts and relative inferiorities, while many of the evils which actually occur turn out on close inspection to be useful. So ends the first and, as we might call it, Platonic stage of Augustine's theodicy; and in his earlier years, beset by the Manichees, he may have been content to leave the matter there. But when later other pressures arose, and especially the controversy with the Pelagians, he came to feel that the Platonic consider-ations, while still potent, were not enough on their own to vindicate the justice and goodness of God.

One difficulty is this: however heavily the evils of the world are outweighed by countervailing goods, and however necessary is the exist-ence of evil to the goodness of the whole, God might still be blame-worthy if it turns out that the distribution of actual evils is unfair to some individuals. The objection here is familiar to us in the context of political and economic decisions: what secures, or even maximizes, benefit to a group may infringe the rights or disappoint the legitimate expectations of some members of the group. What if, similarly, God's dispensation permits the innocent to suffer? Augustine was especially perturbed – as his Pelagian critic Julian would be in the 420s – by God's treatment of babies. Here is part of a long letter he wrote to Jerome in 415 about the origin of the soul:

> But when we come to the sufferings [poenae] of small children, believe me I am stuck with no way to turn and I really cannot find an answer. I do not mean only the sufferings of damnation after this life, which have to fall on those who leave the body without the sacrament of Christian grace, but the ones which to our grief occur in this life before our very eyes, which if I were to list, time would run out before the list was ended. They are worn down by illnesses, agonised by pain, tormented by hunger and thirst, disabled, demented, pestered by unclean spirits. Unquestionably it needs to be shown how they can suffer all this justly when there is no cause in their own wrongdoing [sine ulla sua mala causa]. It is wrong to say either that these things happen without God's knowledge, or that he cannot put a stop to their causes, or that he causes or permits them unjustly. We do say rightly that irrational animals are available for the use of superior beings, even wicked beings, as we see clearly in the gospel that the swine were made over to demons to use for their own purposes [e.g. Mt. 8:31]; but can it really be right to say this about man too? He is an animal, but a rational one, even if mortal.

68

The soul in these bodies which is penalised with so much misery is rational, and God is good, he is just, he is almighty – only a madman doubts that. So we must be able to refer to some just cause for all these evils that happen to small children. Of course when older people are afflicted in such ways we are content to say that either their merits are being tested, as with Job, or their sins punished, as with Herod; and from the particular cases which God has wished to make plain it is allowable to infer to others that are obscure. But these are older people. Tell me how we should answer about small children, if there are no sins in them to be punished by all these sufferings, since there is obviously no justice to be tested at their age. (*Ep.* 166.16)

Jerome begged off responding (*Ep.* 172); but Augustine, as we shall see in a moment, was disingenuous in claiming to have been stuck for an answer.

Even this is not the whole of it; for, secondly, even if God were shown to be guiltless of discriminating unfairly in the distribution of suffering, it would also remain to exonerate him from complicity in human wrongdoing, or sin. Here is Augustine's statement of the second charge:

We believe that everything which is comes from one God, and yet God is not the author of sins. The disturbing thought is this: if sins come from the souls which God created, and the souls come from God, will it not be quite a short step from the sins to God [quomodo non parvo intervallo peccata referantur in Deum]? (*Lib. Arb.* 1.2.4)

Sins in men cannot be excused or justified by serving a good end; neither then can God be exonerated from his shared responsibility for human sins by the plea that all is for the best; therefore God is a sinner.

Augustine's justification of God against this double charge rests on two bold theses: all human *suffering* is just punishment, and God is not the author of human *sin*. At the very beginning of *De Libero Arbitrio*, from which the previous quotation was taken, he makes himself say:

If you know or believe that God is good (and it is out of the question to think otherwise), he does no evil. Again, if we grant that God is just (and denying that is blasphemy), he allots both rewards to the good and punishments [supplicia] to the bad, which, of course, are bad to those who suffer them. Hence if no one is penalised unjustly (which we must believe, since we believe that this universe is ruled by divine providence), God is in no way author of this first kind of evil [which men do], though he is the author of the second kind [which men suffer]. (*Lib. Arb.* 1.1.1, cf. *Conf.* 7.3.5)

Before I examine these theses there is a preliminary point to be made. It is an odd fact that Augustine, in addition to holding that human suffering and sin are the only evils which seriously challenge God's goodness, also often writes as if they are the only evils which exist: indeed at one place he presents it as an article of Catholic faith that every evil is either a sin or the penalty of sin ('aut peccatum aut poenam peccati', *Gen. Lit. Imperf.* 1.3, cf. *Ver. Rel.* 12.23, 20.39, *C. Fort.* 15, *City* 22.1). He himself has more than one reason to repudiate this restrictive view. For example, he does not regard the sufferings of irrational animals as punishment, because he believes that only rational animals are capable of incurring just punishment. More generally, we have found him acknowledging various corruptions and deficiencies in the world which, though neither sins nor sufferings, are evil in the sense of falling under his concept of malum. In other places he concedes that mere lack of excellence is not a penalty, asking ironically, 'How did the moon offend so as to be made so much inferior ‹to the sun›?' (*Simp.* 1.2.8), or speaks of faults (vitia) in earthly things which are 'neither voluntary nor penal' (*City* 12.4). The explanation of this apparent inconsistency may be that in the article of Catholic faith Augustine uses 'malum' narrowly, to cover only the evil doings and sufferings of men.

As for non-human animals, they suffer for our instruction:

> What is pain [dolor] but a certain kind of feeling that will not put up with division and corruption? . . . Only the pain of beasts makes apparent how great is the yearning [appetitus] for unity in the lower living creatures. If that were not apparent, we should be reminded less than is needful that all such things are framed by the supreme, sublime, ineffable unity of the creator. (*Lib. Arb.* 3.23.69)

This is part of the conviction that beasts are for human use, as Genesis was taken to imply (1:26,28) and as the Stoics also thought (Cicero, *De Natura Deorum* 2.63.158–64.161). Misuse is a sin, no doubt, so that if a wanton higher being tortures a monkey in a laboratory, the higher being will roast in eternal fire (and see *Conf.* 10.35.57 against cruel sports). But there will be no redress for the monkey.

For the thesis that all human suffering is punishment Augustine found plentiful support in the Bible. The tendency, widespread in the human race, to blame misfortunes on oneself – to look for offences of which one is guilty, and see the misfortune as punishment for the offence – is surely nowhere more marked in literature than among the prophets and priests who composed the major part of the Old Testament. When the men of God warn and threaten, and are not heeded, the threats come to pass:

> And the Lord spake unto Moses, Go unto Pharaoh, and say unto

him, Thus saith the Lord, Let my people go, that they may serve
me. And if thou refuse to let them go, behold, I will smite all thy
borders with frogs. . . . And the frogs came up, and covered the
land of Egypt. (Ex. 8:1–6 AV, alluded to at *City* 12.4)

More often it is Israel herself, or her rulers, who do 'evil in the sight of
the Lord' and are punished, as when Nathan tells David that his child
by Bathsheba will die because David has commanded the execution of
her husband Uriah so that he may marry her himself (2 Sam. 11:2–12:23).
'Fire and hail, famine and deadly disease, all these were created for
retribution' (Ecclus 39:29). And so on and on: the list is long and
Augustine, like Paul before him, embraced its message (by contrast, it
hardly appears in the gospels, Lk. 13:1–5 and Jn 9:1–5 having even been
cited as dominical resistance to it: Hick 1966:173).

Part of the message, a necessary part for the vindication of God's
justice, is that all sufferings are merited, each several instance a just
punishment. Here Augustine realizes that he is defending a paradox, in
that he faces the task of refuting the common opinion, held by everyone
not in the grip of a theory, that sometimes the *innocent* suffer.
Augustine's response rests on a single premise of breathtaking audacity:
no one is innocent. He will maintain that each and every human being
carries the burden of at least as much guilt as will justify God in causing
or permitting the sufferings he endures. Since, as we have seen Augustine
urging to Jerome, suffering often begins in the cradle, guilt begins there
too: it is original guilt, originalis reatus (e.g. *Simp.* 1.2.20). A Christian
must believe in this guilt, if God is to be justified (*C. Sec. Jul.* 1.27).

The question whether we *should* believe in original guilt I postpone
to chapter 7, confining myself at this point to a comment on Augustine's
conviction that those who refuse to do so are heretics because no alternative escape from the argument from evil to atheism is available to the
Catholic Christian. Needless to say alternatives have often been
proposed; a partial one even seems, quite often, to be adopted by
Augustine himself, when he says that the suffering of the virtuous is not
punishment but probation. For example: 'It is not unjust that objection-
able people should get power to do harm, both for testing the patience
of the good and for punishing the misdeeds of the bad' (*Nat. Bon.* 32;
but see the comment to Jerome cited above). Yet another solution
discards the distinction between sin and its penalty and attributes all
human suffering to the work of sinners: human sinners when it is proper
to blame them, otherwise unseen powers who are supposed to be loose
in the world, fallible (so as to avoid Manichean dualism) but sufficiently
potent and malicious to account for so-called misfortunes and so-called
natural calamities: Satan and the other fallen angels are often cast in this
role (see, for example, Plantinga 1974:192). This type of explanation

appears to be favoured by the gospel stories with their emphasis on unclean spirits (though the appearance has been argued to be deceptive, N. P. Williams 1927:108–10, 118–21; Augustine himself believed in demons, but generally regarded their work as deception rather than injury). However fanciful these alternatives may be, they surely demonstrate that Augustine is not entitled to his claim that a theory of universal guilt is necessary if God is to be justified.

God's sinlessness

With that comment I leave the punishment theory till chapter 7, and turn to Augustine's rebuttal of the charge which might be made against an almighty God of complicity in human (and angelic) sin. Augustine's counter-argument has two premises, the first of which is unexceptionable: sin is voluntary.

> Sins [he says] are not committed except by will [non igitur nisi voluntate peccatur]. (*Du. An.* 10.14)

> I say it is not a sin, if it is not committed by one's very own will. (*C. Fort.* 21)

> God is not the parent of evils. . . . Evils exist by the voluntary sin of the soul to which God gave free choice. If one does not sin by will, one does not sin. (*C. Fort.* 20)

> If I am not mistaken, the reasoning we have gone through demonstrates that we do it [evil] by the free decision of the will. (*Lib. Arb.* 1.16.35)

The reasoning for this, in the first book of *De Libero Arbitrio*, has been: to sin is to make bad use of things which can be used well, to attach and subject oneself to the 'temporal law [lex temporalis]'; but what a man elects to pursue and attach himself to lies with his will ('quid autem quisque sectandum et amplectendum eligat, in voluntate esse positum constitit', *Lib. Arb.* 1.16.34).

The identity of the second premise is not so clear. In one place Augustine seems to contend that voluntary actions have no other causal antecedents than the agent's will, which is itself uncaused:

> But what cause of the will will be possible, in the end, that is prior to the will? Either it is itself a will, in which case we have not got behind the root of will; or it is not a will, in which case there is no sin in it. Either, therefore, will itself is the first cause of sinning, or the first cause of sinning is not a sin. . . . Besides, whatever causes the will is either in fact just, or unjust. If it is just, anyone who obeys

it will not be sinning; if it is unjust, anyone who does not obey it will not be sinning either. (*Lib. Arb.* 3.17.49)

It is hard to make much of the two arguments in this passage, but enough will have been done if we test them against the strategy which Augustine's opponent would use. He would say that, when men sin, their bad wills are in turn caused by the will of God; and if God's will causes a bad will, God's will is unjust. It is irrelevant that *dis*obedience to an unjust will would be without sin, since the opponent presents sinners as obedient to God's will; and the fact that the opponent treats will as the first cause is not enough to show that every will is uncaused – at most it would show that everything uncaused is a will. Furthermore, Augustine cannot afford to assert that wills are uncaused, which is inconsistent, as we shall see in chapter 6, with his doctrine of prevenient grace.

On the other hand it would not be inconsistent with the doctrine of grace to hold that *bad* wills are uncaused, and we find that narrower thesis defended in book 12 of the *City of God* – or more exactly the thesis that bad wills have no 'efficient' but only a 'deficient' cause (cf. *City* 11.20–3). Augustine's subject in this twelfth book is the fallen angels, whose misery, he says, was caused by their voluntarily forsaking God. Nothing can have caused the first act of willing to forsake God, for nothing was then in existence that was not wholly good, and what is wholly good can cause nothing bad (*City* 12.6). He next argues that not even subsequent bad wills can have an efficient cause. Of two men watching someone with a beautiful body one may be stirred to lust while the other 'maintains a modest restraint of the will'; and this may happen, Augustine claims, without any antecedent difference in the viewers' constitutions or circumstances: 'those who wish to know what made [fecerit] the particular will of one of them bad, will find nothing, however carefully they look' (*City* 12.6). In order to explain the difference in the two viewers' responses Augustine now introduces the notion of a deficient cause (causa deficiens, *City* 12.7–8). The thought lying behind this unilluminating name is, I suggest, quasi-mechanical: goodness is like potential energy, and an efficient cause is like a motor which increases the energy by lifting; but a movement to badness is a movement down-hill, needing no motor; so that whereas the good man must be lifted by God, the bad man freewheels into sin. Unfortunately the mechanical ideas with which this suggestion plays are too naive, for they ignore the fact that gravity is as truly a force as any exerted by a lifting motor.

But the thesis that wills, or at least bad wills, are uncaused is not the only way of extricating God from complicity in human sin. An alternative is to maintain that, whether or not the causal antecedents of a sinful act run back beyond the agent's will, and whether or not, running back, they terminate in God's will, in any case *culpability* for a sinful act always rests wholly with its agent and not with any antecedent will. This doctrine appears in Plato's story of Er (*Republic* book 10) and passes through Plotinus (*Enneads* 3.2.7.19) to emerge as Augustine's denial that the links from God to evil form a chain:

> Here someone may perhaps say, Where do sins themselves come from, and where does evil in general come from? If from men, where do men come from? If from angels, where do angels come from? The answer that these latter come from God, though perfectly true, will give the impression to anyone who is inexpert and not very competent at investigating abstruse questions, that evils and sins are connected by some sort of chain to God. (*Du. An.* 8.10)

The inexpert's mistake is to assume that causal ancestry always transmits blame. Augustine ventures no proof that this is a mistake, although later in life he was to remind the Pelagians that a Christian could not afford to make it:

> In this way it can even be said that a bad will too should be attributed to God as its author; because not even that could exist in a man unless the man existed for it to exist in; but God is the author of the man's existence, and thus also of his bad will, which without having a man as its place of existence could not exist at all. However, to say this is out of the question [nefas]. (*Pecc. Mer.* 2.18.29)

Thus God's causal agency is not of such a kind as to lay on him any share of the responsibility for voluntary human acts; Augustine agrees with Plato's dictum that 'the blame (*aitia*) is the chooser's; God is blameless' (*Republic* 617e4–5).

The vindication will work provided that God himself is not one of the choosers but merely causes the sins of others without himself co-operating in them. Unfortunately there are two beliefs of Augustine which, taken together, do seem to commit him to the proposition that God co-operates in human sin. One, which is a part of Augustine's doctrine of grace, states that no *good* deed can ever be brought to execution without divine aid. A man wills, that is, chooses; but even if what he chooses is so simple a good thing as opening his front door, it is only by the grace of God that the door responds to the will. This doctrine is propounded as a counterweight to human pride, especially the pride of the Pelagians who held that God has given men all they need in order to achieve perfection and secure salvation. Yet although Augustine draws no inference for bad deeds, I think we must force him to generalize. For it is an obvious fact that some bad deeds are just as difficult to perform as some good ones, and just as likely to be botched; indeed often the mechanism by which a bad result is attained will be exactly the same as for a good one. Suppose that two men scatter leaflets from a balloon; one man's leaflets bring useful warning of a power cut, but the other's contain a maliciously false report that the water supply has been poisoned. If the good messages cannot be got successfully to their recipients without divine aid, it is wholly unreasonable to think that the bad ones can be. In general, at least some bad deeds must need outside help to pass from project to reality, if all good deeds are in need of such help. Augustine seems therefore committed to the view that at least some bad deeds are the co-operative work of God and man, so that God and man seem each liable to blame for them.

But it does not yet follow that God is implicated in human sin, because it might be that God's part in the co-operative work is blameless. If Augustine believed that the only sinful aspect in a bad deed is the intention to do it, then he could still hold God blameless on the ground that a man's intention to do a deed is his alone; whereas if there is also sin in the execution of bad deeds, it seems that God will share the imputation of that sin. On this issue Augustine vacillates. In *De Duabus Animabus* 11.15 he defines sin as 'the will to keep or pursue what justice forbids', and later he was to explain that 'here the sin defined is merely sin, not what is also sin's penalty' (*C. Sec. Jul.* 1.44, cf. *Retract.* 1.15.4 and see pp. 134–5 below). However, a wider definition is adopted in his interesting discussion of the Sermon on the Mount. He is examining the passage where Jesus says:

> You have learned that they were told, 'Do not commit adultery.'
> But what I tell you is this: If a man looks on a woman with a
> lustful eye, he has already committed adultery with her in his heart.
> (Mt. 5:27–8 NEB)

Augustine comments that there are three 'steps' to sin, or 'things which go to implement a sin [quibus impletur peccatum]' (*Serm. Dom. Mont.* 1.12.34), which are: suggestion (suggestio) of a bad act arising from memory or perception, attraction to it (delectatio), and finally consent (consensio).

> If consent has taken place [he holds], there will be a full sin, known
> to God in our heart even if it does not become known to man by
> deed. (*Serm. Dom. Mont.* 1.12.34)

He somewhat implausibly maintains (ibid. 1.12.33) that Jesus referred to this last step when he spoke of looking on a woman with a lustful eye ('viderit . . . ad concupiscendum'): a man who does that, Augustine asserts, not only desires adultery but consents to his desire and so – I think we may take it – intends adultery if he thinks it feasible; and this is a full sin, a 'sin in the heart'.

It would of course be possible to hold, as perhaps Jesus was implying, that the (conditional) intention is a full sin in the stronger sense that no further sinful component would be added by carrying it into action, which would make what Augustine calls 'a sin in deed' (ibid. 1.12.35). But (here I differ from Matthews 1981:50) Augustine takes a more lenient and realistic view, according to which in this part of the Sermon, where Jesus is extending the prohibitions of the *Torah* known to us as the Ten Commandments, Jesus's meaning is that the extensions set higher standards than the Commandments themselves. He comments;

> The smaller justice, therefore, is not to commit adultery by bodily copulation, but the greater justice of the kingdom of God is not to commit adultery in the heart. (ibid. 1.12.33)

Thus the deed is worse than the intention, and must have an extra sinful component (see also *Serm.* 352.3.8). By the corollary we have extracted from Augustine's doctrine of co-operative grace, this extra component will in many cases be at least partly the work of God. I conclude that it is not possible for Augustine to avoid the embarrassment of charging God with a share in the responsibility for some human sins, namely many of the graver ones which pass beyond sinful intention.

God's love

We are now in a position to make a preliminary assessment of Augustine's success in meeting the challenge to his faith that is posed by the existence of evil. We have seen that the challenge can be stated as an argument to an atheist conclusion whose second premise Augustine will repudiate; and his repudiation of it is the same as asserting that

> it is possible for there to exist a being who is maker of heaven and earth and just and sinless but who does not prevent any of the evils that actually occur.

In order to defend this assertion Augustine has tried to show, first, that the created world is very good, and, secondly, that the evils in it neither impute injustice to God nor implicate him in human sinfulness. In the first stage we have found that Augustine proceeds for the most part somewhat reticently, content to assert that God's actual creation is very good without claiming that it could not have been better. In the second stage he repels the charge that God lays suffering unjustly on the innocent with the astonishing thesis that no human being is innocent, and he exonerates God from complicity in human sin by insisting that guilt for sin originates with the sinners alone, presumed to exclude God. The former thesis, vindicating God's justice, rests on a still unexamined theory of natal or original guilt, while we have seen that the vindication of God's sinlessness cannot easily be combined with Augustine's ideas about co-operative grace. This summary shows, I submit, that even if we accept Augustine's rather limited aim, his theodicy has to be judged unsuccessful.

Finally, however, the question ought also to be faced whether Augustine's aim is not *more* limited than Christianity demands.

The God presented in Augustine's account of evil seems to fall short of being wholly admirable. The manifold miseries of human life display him, according to that account, as notably keen on punishment and, even if guiltless of sin himself, ready to permit a shocking amount of it in others. Yet according to Christian teaching God is love, and more kindly virtues are generally claimed for him than merely those of dealing justly and avoiding sin. Can we really concur in Augustine's sunny Neoplatonist view that the world which harbours all these evils is still (as perhaps it was on the sixth day) 'very good'? In spite of what I have said so far, Augustine is not deaf to such complaints, and he has two pleas to offer on God's behalf, to the effect that in imposing punishments and permitting sins God actually adds to the goodness of the world.

Suppose that all human suffering *is* just punishment; and suppose, what Augustine also believes, that God in his mercy remits a great deal of the punishment, so that many men suffer less than they deserve. Still, one might ask, would not a really good God remit more of it – or all of it? Does not the exaction of so great penalties reveal God as 'author of evil' even if not as author of injustice? Now one kind of response to this charge would be utilitarian: just punishment, it might be said, though 'in itself an evil' and a 'mischief' (Bentham, *Principles* 13.1.2), is a justified evil because of its useful consequences – deterrence, education, and the like. I think it would be peculiarly difficult to apply such a response convincingly to the Augustinian story of punishments, which (on earth) are largely by means of human outrages and natural calamity, and are partly for offences that have been committed before the culprit's birth. Save in a few passages (e.g. *Ep.* 210.1, suffering as a warning) Augustine does not make the attempt to do so, because, unlike the utilitarians, he is one of those thinkers (compare Plato, *Gorgias* 472e) who regard just punishment – punishment commensurate with an offence – as a positively good thing: not better than if there had been no offence, but good in itself given that there has been an offence. He states this view in various places (e.g. *City* 12.3, *Nat. Bon.* 9, 20), of which I quote two:

> If sins have been committed and there is no unhappiness [miseria], the order of things is marred by unfairness [iniquitas]. . . . The state of the will when a sin is committed is a foul [turpis] one, which is why a penal state is applied to it, to bring it into a setting [ordinet] where it is not foul that such a thing should be, and to force it into

77

congruence with the grace [decus] of the universe so that sin's disgrace shall be remedied [emendet] by sin's penalty. (*Lib. Arb.* 3.9.26)

If a soul does not repay [reddit] by acting as it ought, it will repay by suffering as it ought. No time interval divides the two, making the time of its not acting other than the time of its suffering; and this is in order to ensure that the beauty of the whole shall not be befouled even for a moment [ne vel puncto temporis universalis pulchritudo turpetur] by containing the disgrace of sin without the grace [decus] of its being avenged. (*Lib. Arb.* 3.15.44)

The subject of the present chapter does not include punishment after death, that being something which even some Christians have not felt bound to accept as among the 'evils that occur' – it is open to Christian theodicy to deal with hell by denying its existence. Nevertheless we have to remember, in judging Augustine's theory of the 'decus' of just punishment, that the punishments *he* is talking about include eternal fire.

The free will defence

When we turn to Augustine's defence of the divine toleration of sin, we naturally find him taking a different tack. For even those who can share his attitude of welcoming just punishment as redressing a balance rather than acquiescing in it as a last (if common) resort, even such people will agree that the sin which calls forth the punishment has no such positive value; and if the existence of sin too is ultimately to be seen as a good thing, that cannot be because the circumstances of the world are such as to make sins beneficial or healing or restorative. Rather it must be that their existence is a price worth paying for other goods that cannot be had more cheaply. The second part of Augustine's response to the complaint of God's deficient virtue is that there exists such a compensating good: free will.

In the *Enchiridion* (*Handbook on Faith, Hope, and Charity*) Augustine says of Adam's fall: 'God judged it better to bring good out of evil than not to allow evil to exist' (*Ench.* 27.8). The good that came out of Adam's sin is redemption by the Christ: 'for as in Adam all die, even so in Christ shall all be made alive' (1 Cor. 15:22; or rather some shall be made alive, as we shall see in chapter 7). The fault of Adam is thus a blessing, felix culpa, because in the later words of the Exultet, 'it has earned us so great and good a redeemer [talem ac tantum meruit habere redemptorem]' (Duchesne 1903:254). Augustine's doctrine, then, is that God at the creation of mankind saw himself confronted by the following choice: either he might make men in the likeness of other animals, innocent and incapable of moral fault (*Cont.* 16), or he might endow the species with freedom to sin, in which case (as he foreknew) they would use the freedom, some of them to be rescued and raised again by the redemptive death of the divine son. Faced with this choice God judged that the latter course was better. But why? Even if *all* were to be saved by Christ, it is not immediately obvious that it is better for them, or better in any other way, that they should sin, suffer, and be rescued than that they should never have been free to sin at all. And given that many are *not* to be rescued, but instead to be punished forever, it has seemed to many critics of Christianity, and to many Christians too, quite unintelligible why God should not have preferred to create man in perpetual innocence. Augustine's reply to this criticism is a version of what has come to be called the Free Will Defence.

Although the Free Will Defence is nowadays much elaborated and refined, we must not expect Augustine's exposition of it to anticipate modern subtleties. The version he gives may be taken as a conjunction of three propositions:

(4) Men have free will;
(5) To have free will is a good thing; and
(6) Sin is the price of having it.

Proposition (4) was destined to harass him during much of his activity as a controversialist, and especially in the anti-Pelagian campaign when he was tempted into pronouncements which the Pelagians branded as inconsistent with it. As we shall see in the next two chapters he clung nevertheless to the conviction that free will exists, motivated not only by the Free Will Defence itself but also by the thought that without free will there is difficulty in imputing guilt (which requires a will of some sort) and so in justifying divine punishment. He defends proposition (5) on the ground that the possibility of right living depends on the existence of free will:

> Now explain to me [asks Evodius], if it can be done, why God has given man free decision of the will [liberum voluntatis arbitrium]; for surely if he had not received it, he would not have been able to sin. . . . The problem you have posed [answers Augustine] is solved. For if man is a good thing, and if he could not act rightly except when he wills to, he ought to have free will, without which he would not be able to act rightly. (*Lib. Arb.* 2.1.1,3)

The argument seems to go like this:

(7) Men ought to be given the requisites for right action;
(8) Right action has to be voluntary action;
(9) Free decision of the will is a requisite for voluntary action;

Therefore men ought to be given free decision of the will.

The contentious premise in this argument for proposition (5) is (9), which will be examined in chapter 5.

That leaves proposition (6), that sin is the price of having free will. It too rests on an assumption about the nature of free will which I shall defer examining until chapter 5, but this time a highly plausible one: namely that one of the conditions necessary for the exercise of free will is the absence of compulsion. Given that assumption, Augustine's argument for proposition (6) goes as follows: if God's decision to grant men the exalted status of moral beings requires that they enjoy the gift of free will, it requires also that they suffer the peril of not being compelled, even by God, to refrain from lapsing into wrongdoing; hence if right or wrong choices of action are to be free, men cannot consistently be compelled to refrain from the wrong ones; and so (we are invited to infer) sin is the price of this freedom.

The Free Will Defence thus stated – and Augustine takes it no further – is not at all convincing as a justification of God's tolerance of sin. Admittedly it does succeed, given the plausible assumption about compulsion, in explaining why God should have decided not – or at least not always – to compel his human creatures into refraining from additions to the woes of their fellows; and also, a fortiori, why he should have given them powers of rational choice, unlike other animals. These decisions would follow from God's judgement that such powers, and freedom to use them, are a blessing and a dignity too valuable to be sacrificed for the sake of alleviating misery, even though God foresees the misery (similarly for the fallen angels, *City* 22.1). Yet Augustine's version of the Defence entirely fails to explain why God should not have created men with such a nature that they never choose – and would never even when tempted by the serpent have chosen – to lapse from godlike standards of behaviour. We get no answer if we ask Augustine why God should not have *caused* blameless conduct without *compelling* it or, as one might frame the question, why he should not have so arranged men's affections as to prevent the commission of sins without any need to *prevent the men* from committing them (see e.g. Bayle 1697: article on the Marcionites).

I agree with those recent philosophers who believe that the Free Will Defence can be fortified against this objection. Two extra propositions will be needed: that an exercise of free will requires not only absence of compulsion but also, more generally, the ability to do otherwise than as one actually does; and that a deed caused by God (even if not all deeds caused in all other ways) could not have been done otherwise than as it is actually done. It follows from these two extra propositions that a deed caused by God is not an exercise of free will, and so by premise (9) – if that can be accepted – is not voluntary and by (8) not commendable as right action; hence God's decision to bestow on men the status of moral beings will require him to abstain from causing blameless conduct whether by compulsion or by any other kind of cause. Thus if (9) and the two extra propositions are true, the Free Will Defence looks safe.

It will be argued in the next chapter that (9) is not true; but perhaps it could be circumvented. It will also be argued that the first of the two extra propositions *is* true. However, chapter 6 will then seek to show that Augustine himself cannot afford to accept these two extra propositions as true together, for reasons again connected with his doctrine of grace: for the grace doctrine, besides maintaining as we have seen that God co-operates in bringing men's good choices to fruition, will maintain also that God is operative in causing the good choices themselves. If my interpretation in chapter 6 is right, it will follow that Augustine is bound to regard God as the author of such virtuous conduct as men manage to achieve, so that we shall still lack an explanation why he should not have seen to it, without compulsion, that all men's conduct is virtuous; and we shall be forced to conclude that Augustine's version of the Free Will Defence is broken-backed.

Further reading

Hick (1966) criticizes the Augustinian approach and commends Irenaeus (*c*.130–*c*.200) as a better foundation for Christian explanation of evil. For the atheist stance see e.g. Mackie 1982: ch. 9, or McCloskey 1960. For the Free Will Defence see Plantinga 1974: ch. 9.

V

Defending free will

Degrees of freedom

Augustine says somewhere: 'Only let no one so dare to destroy the decision of the will as to wish to excuse sin.' We have already in the previous chapter observed his vivid sense of sin. And we have also uncovered his intellectual motive for imputing it universally: all men suffer; all suffering is God's punishment; all God's acts are just; all punishment not for sins committed is unjust; so all men commit sins. Moreover sin requires freedom. Augustine says of the double souls imagined by the Manichees:

> Whatever these souls do, if they do it by nature not will, that is, if they lack a movement of the mind free both for doing and for not doing; if in fact they are not granted the power of refraining from operating, we cannot maintain that a sin is theirs. (*Du. An.* 12.17; cf. *Lib. Arb.* 3.18.20)

Thus human freedom has to be defended in order to vindicate God as a just punisher. It has to be defended also, as we have seen in discussing the Free Will Defence in the previous chapter, in order to vindicate him as a caring creator. From the defence of it, begun in the *De Libero Arbitrio*, Augustine never finally retreated in his long life. Belief in 'free decision of the will' is the main philosophical difference between him and the Protestant reformers. Luther and Calvin were deeply influenced by him; it was indeed from his own later writings that they drew the materials from which they, unlike him, concluded to what Luther called the bondage of the will.

What is this freedom which Augustine must defend? Its *range* is quite determinate: men must be free to sin, that is, to do wrong. Its *degree* is much more problematical, and we shall have to examine in some detail not only what is needed for Augustine's two purposes but also what he thought was needed and how much of it he thought the facts attested. I shall distinguish three degrees of freedom, and I shall argue that Augustine requires the first two but not the third.

The first degree of freedom is present in anyone whose will is operative or, what I take to be the same thing, whenever what happens to someone is properly described as an action of his rather than something that happens *to* him. You lack this first degree if, for example, you are pushed into the path of a bicycle race, perhaps by a gust of wind (cf. Aristotle, *Nicomachean Ethics* III 1.1110a 3), perhaps by the act of some other person. But you are possessed of it if you are like the dog in the story of Zeno and Chrysippus, two Stoics who, according to the third-century antipope Hippolytus (*c.* 230),

> Also insisted that everything is in accordance with fate; and they employed examples like this: a dog tied to a cart which it wants to chase will chase it *and* be dragged [*helketai*] by it, doing its own will but with necessity, viz. fate; and if it does not want to chase the cart, it will simply be forced to. The same is true of men; if they do not want to acquiesce, they will simply be forced to accept their destiny. (*Philosophoumena* 21, von Arnim 1903–5:2.975)

The dog is unfree, in this first degree, only if it chooses not to acquiesce and is dragged none the less.

The compatibility of will with fate urged by these stories may be an illusion (it depends what 'fate' is). Likewise divine omnipotence exposes those who believe in it to the risk of having to regard *all* human wills as inoperative, rendered so by God's activity if God is conceived as the only genuine agent, so that men become merely instruments of his will; and reduction to this status is one kind of force or compulsion, 'coactio'. Although compulsion and coactio can also, as we shall see, be understood in a looser sense, when taken in this strict sense they will destroy even the first degree of freedom in their victim, by acting not through the victim's *will* but in such a way as renders his will inoperative. This degree is the freedom in John Wesley's dictum, 'He that is not free is not an *agent*, but a *patient*' (1829: Sermon 67, p. 80); it is commonly called freedom of spontaneity (e.g. Kenny 1973:90).

One might protest that the first degree is not really freedom at all. Although in Christian philosophical controversy it was sometimes distinguished as 'libertas a coactione', 'freedom from compulsion' (see for example the bull of Innocent X *Cum Occasione* which condemned the Flemish Catholic theologian Cornelius Jansen (1585–1638) for maintaining that the first degree suffices for ascribing merit and demerit, Denz. no. 2003), that designation no more exhibits it as a genuine kind of freedom than does, say, the description of a picnic as free from wasps. Calvin (1509–64), who also held that the first degree is all that is needed by a Christian apologist, preferred not to dignify it with the name of freedom. 'What difference does it make', he asked, 'whether we sin by free or enslaved decision, provided it is by voluntary desire?' (*Christianae Religionis Institutio* 2.5.2.); if you call voluntary action free, you use a proud name for a slight thing (ibid. 2.2.7). Many other thinkers have joined this linguistic protest, for example the Aristotelian commentator Alexander of Aphrodisias (fl. *c*.200), probably referring to Stoics:

> They say that what is up to [*epi*] us is in impulse and assent . . . which ‹however› constitute and indicate the voluntary. (*De Fato* 14, 183.22–7)

And Locke:

> Again, suppose a Man be carried, while fast asleep, into a Room, where is a Person he longs to see and speak with; and be there locked fast in, beyond his Power to get out: he awakes, and is glad to find himself in so desirable Company, which he stays willingly in, *i.e.* preferrs his stay to going away. I ask, Is not this stay voluntary? I think, no Body will doubt it: and yet being locked fast in, 'tis evident he is not at liberty not to stay, he has not freedom to be gone. (*Essay* 2.21.10; cf. Moore 1912:126)

Both the Protestant Calvin and the Roman Catholic Jansen claimed Augustine's authority for their view that the first degree – however you call it – suffices for his apologetic purposes. A passage apparently in this sense (and even agreeing with Calvin's nomenclature) occurs in the *Enchiridion*, where Augustine writes:

> In using free decision badly, man destroyed both himself and it. Just as someone who kills himself, unquestionably kills himself by living [sc. by exercising the powers of a living thing] but does not live by killing himself and will not be able to resuscitate himself when killed; so, though he has sinned by free decision, with the victory of sin free decision is lost [amissum est liberum arbitrium]. (*Ench*. 30.9)

Yet in spite of the scattered occurrence of passages like this one, there can be no doubt that Augustine generally demanded for sinners more freedom than the first, 'slight' degree.

The second degree of freedom which I shall distinguish is that defined by Hume (1711–76) in his *First Enquiry*:

> By liberty, then, we can only mean *a power of acting or not acting, according to the determinations of the will.* (*Enquiry Concerning Human Understanding* 8.73)

(Many earlier philosophers and theologians had offered definitions of the same kind, for example Erasmus, *De Libero Arbitrio*, LCC, p. 47;

Calvin, referring to 'the philosophers', *Christianae Religionis Institutio* 2.2.3; Molina, *Concordia* 14.13 d2 n3 apud Kenny 1979:61; Descartes, *4th Meditation*, in Adam and Tannery (eds) 1897: VII. 57; Locke, *Essay* 2.21.8; and the label 'freedom of indifference' is sometimes used to describe this kind of freedom, although, confusingly, Hume regarded himself as rejecting indifference in favour of spontaneity, *Treatise* 2.3.2.) The word 'or' in Hume's definition must be understood with care. It does not, as might appear, ascribe the single power which would be exercised in acting (even if there were no power of not acting) and would be exercised in not acting (even if there were no power of acting); but a double or two-way power, what the scholastics called potentia ad utrumque, one part of which is exercised in acting, the other in not acting. Both halves of the power must be possessed together by anything enjoying Hume's liberty, although of course it is not possible that both halves should be exercised together; for example, the power of frowning or not frowning is possessed by normal men, but not by a frowning statue. (This way of reading 'or' within the scope of 'possible' is common: for example it would be false to say 'I can get you tickets for Tuesday or Wednesday' if I can get them only for Tuesday.) If 'power' were taken widely, as possibility or potentiality, two-way powers would belong to anything which has a property contingently: for example, the sun when shining has the potentiality of not shining, which it is not exercising, together with the potentiality of shining, which it is exercising. Yet when the sun is shining we do not think that it is in the *sun's* power not to be shining: as the Greeks put it, shining is not 'up to', '*epi*', it (e.g. Aristotle *Eudemian Ethics* 2.10.1226a 17–28). This Greek expression never got carried over into the Latin tradition; instead, the kind of power intended by assertions of the second degree of freedom came to be characterized by reference to the will, voluntas (I usually stick to the old fashioned English noun 'will', and shall often use the even more stilted verb 'will to', because no alternatives have the range of Augustine's 'voluntas' and 'velle', which cover 'choose', 'want', 'wish', and 'be willing'). Among the various ways of using the will in the role of distinguishing freedom from mere contingency, one is to take it as specifying the conditions under which each half of a two-way power is exercised. That is Hume's way: the power is 'according to the determinations of the will'; that is: which half of it the free man exercises depends on the determinations of his will.

Augustine in many places connects freedom with power, for which his word is 'potestas', as when he says at *De Libero Arbitrio* 3.3.8, 'Besides, since ‹the will› is in our power, it is free for us'; and at least one of his discussions allows us to infer that the power is two-way. This occurs in a chapter of the *De Spiritu et Littera*, a late anti-Pelagian work, where, after remarking that the will to do a thing and the power to do it are logically independent, he concludes, inconsistently with that remark, as follows:

> We say there is power [potestas], when to the will is joined the possibility [facultas] of doing. Hence someone is said to have in his power what he does if he wills, and does not do if he wills not to [non vult]. (*Sp. Lit.* 31.53)

The second sentence here is reminiscent of G. E. Moore's

> suggestion . . . that we often use the phrase '*I could*' simply and solely as a short way of saying '*I should* if I had chosen'. (1912:131)

Moore's suggestion is now generally and rightly rejected, on the ground that conditionals such as 'he will do it if he chooses' could be true of someone who lacked the power to do *or* choose. I doubt, however, whether Augustine is vulnerable to this objection. If we take his two sentences together, it seems not excessively charitable to read him as laying down not two but four conditions for 'potestas', viz. X has it in his power to φ if and only if

> it is possible for X to φ
> X φs if X wills to φ
> it is possible for X not to φ
> X does not φ if X wills not to φ.

Applied to freedom, as the passage from *De Libero Arbitrio* invites, this definition is the same as Hume's, with 'facultas' doing duty for Hume's 'power'.

It is surprisingly rare for Augustine to describe men's wills as *being* free; his regular formula (which goes back at least to Ambrose) is 'free decision of the will', 'liberum voluntatis arbitrium'. Aquinas was to connect the contrast between arbitrium and voluntas with Aristotle's contrast between choice (*prohairesis*), which is of things in our control and doable at will, like coughing, and wish (*boulēsis*), which is of outcomes not achievable at will, like sneezing (*Summa Theologiae* 1a 83.4). But Augustine's distinction seems to be different. When he does say that the human will is free (e.g. *Du. An.* 12.15), he usually means, I think, that men are free *whether* or not to exercise their wills – to engage in the activity of willing. For example, the sentence already quoted from *De Libero Arbitrio* is introduced as follows:

> ‹Suppose someone says that› because it is necessary that he should will, he does not have the will itself in his own power, ‹we will reply:› Our will would not be a will, if it were not in our own power. Besides, since it is in our power, it is free for us. (*Lib. Arb.* 3.3.8)

The meaning comes out in the preceding discussion, where he has supported the claim that 'Nothing is so much in our power as the will itself' by means of a contrast between growing old, which we do not do by will (voluntate), and willing, which we do by will (*Lib. Arb.* 3.3.7; cf. *Retract.* 2.12, *C. Sec. Jul.* 1.101, we cannot be compelled to will anything, sc. in the strict sense of compulsion). The same claim that it is in our power *whether* we will should be understood in a passage (to be examined on pp. 91ff.) in the *City of God* where he says, 'When we say that it is necessary that, when we will, we will by a free decision, that is undoubtedly true' (*City* 5.10). By contrast, a man's will has 'free decision' only when it is in his power *what* he wills (for the contrast, compare Locke, *Essay* 4.13.2). Augustine believes that this is true of some but not all acts of willing. He would agree with Aquinas that

> We have free decision with respect to those things that we will not of necessity or by natural instinct. For the fact that we will to be happy [felices] does not pertain to free decision but to natural instinct. (*Summa Theologiae* 1a 19.10)

Augustine:

> It is thoroughly absurd to say that the fact that we will to be happy [beati] does not pertain to our will, on the ground that we are quite unable, owing to some unknown but beneficial limitation in our nature, to will not to; nor would we dream of saying that God has the necessity and not the will to be just, on the ground that he is not able to will to sin. (*Nat. Gr.* 46.54)

Thus Augustine's settled opinion is that free decision of the will is more than mere will, an opinion which will come out correct if we assume that he is speaking of the second degree of freedom. His use in the Free Will Defence of the proposition which in the last chapter I numbered (9) ('Free will is a requisite for voluntary action') ought to be seen as a lapse from this correct conclusion, a lapse which was perhaps aided by his slide in the text of *De Libero Arbitrio* 2.1.1–3 (quoted there) from liberum arbitrium, which is what he seeks to prove the goodness of, to libera voluntas, which would justify (9) if taken in the sense I have just examined, but at the cost of being irrelevant.

Although someone exercising the second degree of freedom cannot be compelled in the sense, or to the extent, of being used as an instrument (for his will must be operative, as it must even in the first degree), he may be compelled in a different way. For he may be under pressure or duress, as when one says 'The weather compelled me to turn back', or 'The vote forced the government to resign.' These cases are not in conflict with the second degree of freedom provided that, first, the force operates through the will ('Nero forced Seneca to the decision of choosing death', 'ad eligendae mortis coegit arbitrium', Boethius, *Consolatio Philosophiae*

3.5.28) and, secondly – as may well be the case – it does not remove all possibility, 'facultas', of doing otherwise. The expressions used of people under threat, or pressure of circumstances, that they have 'no option' or 'no choice' are, after all, usually mere bluff, since alternative courses of action usually do remain open, even though not eligible ones. So here is still freedom, of Hume's kind. On the other hand, it is a poor sort of freedom to be offered the choice between, say, penury and death, or resigning and being sacked; and 'You are free to defy me' would be a cruel joke from someone threatening one's friends or children with torture. Such freedom being, in circumstances of duress, of little or no value, there is therefore a motive for inventing a third and higher degree of it – the kind you really want – which you have only when acting and not acting are not only alike possible but also alike eligible.

The connection between blame and this third degree of freedom is a tricky topic for moral philosophy, and for jurisprudence; but Augustine ignores it. His attitude to culpability, at any rate to culpability before God, is the stern one that if an apparently sinful act is not *justified* by circumstances (something which it is important to notice that he does make room for – see for example his treatment of consent to rape, p. 138 below), then it merits punishment if it could have been avoided, however high the cost of avoiding it would have been. So the third degree is irrelevant to his theodicy, and does not need to be defended. Nevertheless he occasionally notices its existence, as when he says:

> If we consider the matter exactly, even what someone is compelled against his will to do, if he does it, he does by will . . . admittedly, not a full and free will, but he does not do it without will. (*Sp. Lit.* 31.53)

This person's will, Augustine goes on, is forced from him, extorta.

The culpability of sin

The second degree of freedom, Hume's liberty, is therefore what matters for Augustine, and is what he refers to as free decision of the will. Although not necessarily present whenever the will is operative, this freedom does exist, Augustine believes; that is, all men have two-way power, and exercise it in some of their voluntary actions. In particular they exercise it whenever they sin; for all sin is culpable, and culpability requires the two-way power ('a mind free both for doing and for not doing', *Du. An.* 12.17 quoted above). That at any rate is the simple way in which Augustine presented the connection between sin and freedom in his early campaign against the Manichees, when he was explaining suffering as God's just punishment. The 'cause of grace' against the Pelagians, however, was eventually to force him into greater complexity.

We can usefully approach the more complex doctrine by resuming the previous chapter's discussion of Augustine's treatise on the Sermon on the Mount. In the course of his comments there on Jesus' remarks about adultery, he says:

> So just as sin is reached by three steps, suggestion, attraction and consent, so there are three varieties [differentiae] of sin itself; in the heart, in deed, and in habit. Three deaths, one might say: one, as it were, in the privacy of the home [in domo], when there is consent to physical attraction [libido]; one out of doors in public, when assent proceeds to action; the third, rotting in the tomb, when force of habit weighs down on the mind like a mound of earth. (*Serm. Dom. Mont.* 1.12.35)

Augustine's apologetic purposes do not require him to hold that *all* sins are culpable: God's activity as a punisher will have been justified if only some are, provided that those ones are grave enough to merit the penalties actually inflicted. So the question arises whether he is equally ready to attach blame to sins of all the three kinds distinguished in the above passage. I think the answer is as follows: he sees good reason for excusing sins in habit, if these are understood as habits of sinning; he becomes willing to eliminate responsibility for sins in deed, as the imagined price of avoiding Pelagius' heretical view that human powers suffice for achieving the 'perfection of justice'; but sins in the heart *must* remain culpable, as the last bastion against Manichean derogation from God's omnipotence. I confine myself here to defending the first part of this answer; the other two parts belong to the discussion of grace in chapter 6.

Bernard of Clairvaux wrote:

> Thus the soul in some strange and evil way, under a certain voluntary and wrongly free necessity, is held both in servitude [ancilla] and free: in servitude because of necessity, free because of will. (*Sermons on the Song of Songs*, 81.7.9, quoted by Calvin, *Christianae Religionis Institutio* 2.3.5)

The pull of this paradox was felt by Augustine too. It may be at work, softening his apparent agreement with Calvinism, in the *Enchiridion* passage quoted above which confesses that by sin's victory free decision is lost. For Augustine goes on:

> What kind of freedom has the indentured slave, I ask, except when he enjoys his sin? For he *does* serve freely if he does his master's will gladly, becoming thereby free for sinning, who is a slave of sin. (*Ench.* 30.9)

Augustine toys with various ways of solving the paradox of the free slave (or free servant: it is important to remember that in the ancient world most personal servants were slaves, so that words for slave often lacked their modern connotation of a harsh subjection). The least appealing is his confused suggestion – quite often repeated, I am sorry to say – that the unregenerate are free to commit sins ('free for sinning') though not free to avoid them (and in similar vein he says the opposite about God, e.g. *C. Sec. Jul.* 1.100). Better is Paul's idea that a man may be slave to two 'laws' that fight one another, and so able in one way to do right in accordance with the good law, but disabled in another way by the 'law of sin' (Rom. 7:21 ff.). But the famous verse 21, 'I discover this principle, then: that when I want to do the right, only the wrong is within my reach [*parakeitai*, adjacet]' (Rom. 7:21 NEB), will not have suggested disablement to Augustine as it has to some modern philosophers, because his Bible (like the Vulgate) translated the Greek quite differently as 'I discover a law which is good for me when I want (to obey it), since the wrong (which I desire) lies in me (not in it)' (see *Nupt. Concup.* 30.33). Thirdly, a number of Augustinian passages gesture towards a use of the distinction between act and habit, according to which the sinner remains able, and so free, to do good deeds, but not able until sanctified to have the habit of doing them (nor therefore, perhaps, able to be a good man). This may be the thought in:

> The decision . . . of the will is truly free at the moment when it is not slave to faults [vitia] and sins. That is the gift of God, which when lost by one's own fault cannot be restored except by him who was able to give it. (*City* 14.11)

The same interpretation seems better than Calvin's imputation of irony in the passage where Augustine says that sinners have an arbitrium that is free but not freed ('liberum sed non liberatum', *Corr. Gr.* 13.42), despite Augustine's continuing with the feeble pun 'free from justice but the slave of sin'. Discounting the reappearance of this pun, I suggest the same understanding of 'slave' in:

> It must therefore be confessed that we have free decision both for bad and for good [et ad malum et ad bonum]; but in doing bad everyone is free from justice and the slave of sin, whereas in good no one can be free unless he has been freed by him who said, 'If the son has freed you, then you will be truly free'. (*Corr. Gr.* 1.2, quoting Jn 8:36; cf. *C. Du. Lit. Pel.* 3.7.20)

And compare:

> The human will . . . cannot be said to be free, so long as it is trammelled in the bonds and bondage of desires [vincentibus et vincientibus cupiditatibus subdita]. (*Ep.* 145.2)

Freedom and necessity

Luther (1483–1546), applauding an article of Wyclif (c.1330–84) that had been condemned at the Council of Constance in 1415, wrote:

> I was wrong to say that free decision before grace is a thing [res] only in name. I ought to have said simply, free decision is a fictitious thing, or a name without a thing. For no one has it in his own power [manu] to think a good or bad thought, but all things . . . happen by absolute necessity [de necessitate absoluta]. (*Assertio*, article 36)

Augustine rejected the sentiment, but not the antithesis: for him too, I shall argue, freedom is incompatible with absolute necessity.

The qualifier 'absolute', like its contrasting 'conditional', seems to go back no further than Boethius (*Consolatio Philosophiae* 5.6, p. 98 below), but the same distinction had been used by others before him, back to Aristotle. Augustine himself might have been helped by a version of it in the *City of God* book 5, chapter 10, a puzzling passage which must now be examined. The preceding chapter 9 of this book has propounded a refutation of Cicero's view that, if God foreknows the future, 'there is nothing in our power and no decision of the will' (see pp. 98–102 below). Next Augustine turns to the question 'Whether any kind of necessity overmasters men's wills', 'an voluntatibus hominum aliqua dominetur necessitas'. In answer he distinguishes two kinds of necessity, and argues that neither kind overmasters the will. But the nature of the kinds, and their relation to freedom, are so obscure that the passage needs to be quoted at length (in my translation I try to reproduce Augustine's word-play on the cognates of 'posse' and 'potestas'):

> If we are to speak of that necessity of ours which is not in our power [non in nostra potestate] but brings about what it is empowered to [potest] even if we will that it should not – for example, the necessity of death – then it is clear that our wills, by which life is well or ill conducted, are not under necessity of that kind. For we do many things which we should certainly not do if we willed not to. Among these is primarily willing itself: for if we will ‹that willing should be›, it is, and if we will it not ‹to be›, it is not – we should not will if we willed not ‹to›.
>
> But if necessity is defined according to the way in which we say that it is necessary that something should be so or happen so, I fail to see why we should be frightened that it will take away freedom of will from us. For equally we do not place God's life and foreknowledge under necessity if we say it is necessary for God to live for ever and to foreknow everything; in the same way, neither is his power diminished when he is said not to be empowered to die or be deceived. So far from his being thus empowered, a more

powerful view [potius] is that, if he were thus empowered, he would really have less power. It is right, of course, to call him all powerful [omnipotens], even though he is not empowered to die or be deceived. . . . His being all powerful is the reason why in some things he is not empowered. Similarly when we say it is necessary that when we will we will by a free decision, undoubtedly we say this truly, and we do not thereby subject free decision itself to necessity, which eliminates freedom. (*City* 5.10)

Let us start with the second paragraph and its comparison with God's necessities. On the one hand, Augustine asserts, it is necessary for God to live for ever and have foreknowledge; but on the other hand these facts do not place him 'under' necessity, or diminish his powers. One way of understanding this would be through a distinction between active powers and passive liabilities: in lacking some of the latter, such as liability to death or deceit, God is not brought 'under' necessity, because his active powers are not diminished; yet absence of liability has to be counted as a *kind* of necessity since, without constricting the manner in which things can act, it does constrict the manner in which they can 'be or happen'. The case of human will seems on the face of it quite different. For there the point in Augustine's second paragraph appears to be that while willing itself is not, willing-by-free-decision-if-you-will is, subject to necessity; and this tells us, not that a single object is bound by only one out of two related kinds of necessity, but that a single kind of necessity binds only one out of two related objects. At any rate there is no need to distinguish different 'definitions' of necessity in order to explain how the necessity that an exercise of the will should occur by free decision, if it occurs, is consistent with the non-necessity of its occurring. What *that* requires is the distinction alluded to by Luther, between the conditional necessity of 'q' if 'p' and the absolute necessity of 'q'.

The other clue to Augustine's meaning is his description of the first kind of necessity, in his first paragraph, as 'what is not in our power, but effects what it is empowered to [potest] even if we will it not to'. The kind so identified is, presumably, the contradictory of Augustine's freedom, freedom in the second degree; so it might be that Augustine means to contrast this first necessity with a kind which *is* compatible with freedom. Yet if so, his examples do not suffice for the purpose, because the necessities he specifies under the second kind are not the sort of thing to which the concept of freedom can be applied at all. God's omniscience and immortality are states, which might be freely acquired or lost but cannot be freely retained: as the Dutch Protestant theologian Arminius (1560–1609) was to say in reference to a similar suggestion about divine goodness: 'No man is said to be freely learned although he has obtained erudition for himself by study which proceeded from free will' (*Apology* p. 167a, Nichols: vol 2, p. 34). As for the idea that Augustine means to attribute freedom to the necessity that willing-is-by-free-decision-if-it-occurs, that suffers from the disadvantage of imposing on him a doctrine which it is surely impossible to make any sense of.

Cornelius Jansen has an argument designed to show that Augustine is committed in this passage to the view that freedom is compatible with the second kind of necessity, which accordingly Jansen calls 'simple or voluntary' (simplex seu voluntaria, *De Gratia Christi Salvatoris* 6.6; cf. 'What occurs voluntarily, even if it occurs necessarily, still occurs freely . . . only violence [violentia] is opposed to natural human liberty', condemned as errors in the bull of Pius V *Ex Omnibus Afflictionibus*, 1567, Denz. nos. 1939, 1966). If I understand Jansen rightly the argument is (*De Gratia* 6.6, 633c–634c):

(1) In the case of simple necessity, 'x necessarily ϕs' is compatible with 'x necessarily wills to ϕ';
(2) the latter entails 'x wills to ϕ';
(3) 'x wills to ϕ' in turn entails 'x is free to ϕ or not';
therefore simple necessity is compatible with freedom.

Jansen interprets Augustine's 'undoubted truth' – that when we will we will by free decision – as expressing (3). But we have seen that the interpretation is implausible, as is the thesis it enunciates, without which Jansen's argument for compatibility collapses. I conclude that Augustine does not suppose that either of his two kinds of necessity is compatible with freedom, as indeed he conveys in his final reference to 'necessity, which eliminates freedom' (Jansen has to take this as referring only to the first kind). But this result leaves the distinction between the two kinds still obscure. We shall not need to adopt Jansen's view that the first kind is (strong) compulsion, i.e. what renders the will inoperative: it can extend also – as 'not in our power' naturally suggests – over cases where the will is operative but not free. This permits interpretation of the first kind as necessity which limits active powers, and attributes to Augustine the view that the power of willing is never so limited, since anyone who wills retains the power of not exercising his will at all (but instead, presumably, being carried along by circumstances). The second kind is evidently wider – at any rate Augustine says that it applies in cases, such as God's immortality, where the first kind does not. But I see no way for Augustine to escape the charge that what he puts under this second kind is actually an amalgam of two quite unrelated things: necessity as limitation on passive liabilities, and conditional necessity. If that is right, then Augustine's conclusion will be that although there is a way in which necessity applies to the will – namely that willing has

93

the *necessary consequence* of being exercised freely – nevertheless that way is not such as to put the will 'under' necessity, because, so far from making exercises of the will necessary, it requires them not to be.

Arguments for freedom

It is in general open to a theist to use his belief in God as support for the contention that men are free. We must be free, he could argue, or God would not permit us to suffer so; and we must be free, or God would have made us behave ourselves better. But these arguments were not available to Augustine, once he had been obliged to proceed in the contrary direction against the Manichees, reasoning that *because* we are free, there is no need to postulate malevolent divinities in explanation of our faults and our ills.

There are, however, other lines of argument for freedom from which Augustine is not debarred, among them the need to justify *human* punishment (*Ep.* 246.2). One which sometimes attracted his attention is the argument from exhortation. Erasmus (1469–1536), defending free will against the onslaught of Luther, wrote:

> The Lord said to Moses, 'I have set before your face the way of life and the way of death. Choose what is good and walk in it' [Deut. 30:19]. . . . It would be ridiculous to say 'Choose' to someone in whom the power was not present of applying himself one way and the other, as though one should say to a man standing at a road junction, 'You see these two roads; take which you like,' when only one was open to him. (*De Libero Arbitrio* II a 14, *LCC* p. 54)

The argument can be expanded like this: no sane being will command what he believes to be impossible; so no sane and omniscient being will command what is impossible; God is sane and omniscient; so what God commands is possible. We shall find Pelagius urging a similar point (p. 106), except that his plea is that for God to lay impossible commands on us would be uncaring: Erasmus thinks it would be absurd.

This argument was effectively challenged by the Protestant reformers, and in particular by Luther in his reply to Erasmus, *De Servo Arbitrio* (a title taken from Augustine, *C. Jul.* 2.8.23). Luther's first objection was that imperatives do not imply indicatives. But that objection misfires, since the argument from exhortation claims only that 'do A' implies 'you can do A', not that it implies 'you will do A'. Moreover the sense of 'imply' must be special: not that 'do A' cannot be *true* without 'you can do A' being true – for no imperatives can be true – but that utterance of 'do A' is somehow improper unless accompanied by belief in the truth of 'you can do A'. This evokes, however, a second objection from Luther: there is no reason for the possibility implied by an imperative to be contemporary with the utterance of the imperative. Exhortations might sometimes *cause* the impossible to become possible, and might thus be expected to cause it to become actual:

> It has pleased God to impart the Spirit not without the Word but through the Word. (Luther, *De Servo Arbitrio* p. 161, *LCC* p. 214)

Thirdly, and somewhat less plausibly, other acceptable motives might be ascribed for God's commanding what is impossible:

> Hence the words of the law are spoken not to affirm the force [vim] of the will, but to enlighten blind reason so that it sees that . . .
> the virtue of the will is nothing. (ibid. p. 126, *LCC* p. 190, citing Rom. 3:20, 'Law brings only the consciousness of sin')

Just so one might tell the traveller to choose his road in order to show him that only one road was open, 'To teach us', as Luther perversely puts it, 'what we ought to do and what by the same token we cannot' (ibid. p. 160, *LCC* p. 213).

Poor Augustine! Both these antagonists drew their arguments from his works, indeed from works of similar, late, date. Here is the Erasmian side:

> Surely wherever it is said 'Don't do this' and 'Don't do that', and wherever divine warnings direct the operation of the will towards doing something or not doing something, free decision is adequately proved. (*Gr. Lib. Arb.* 2.4; cf. *Lib. Arb.* 3.1.3)

And here is the Lutheran riposte, against Celestius, a follower of Pelagius whom we shall meet again:

> 'Besides,' he [Celestius] says, 'we have to enquire whether there is a command [praeceptum] on man to be without sin; for either he cannot, in which case there is no command; or else, because there is a command, he can. For why should anything be commanded which cannot be done at all?' The answer is that there is every reason to command a man to walk with right steps so that, when he has realized that he cannot, he may seek the remedy for the inward man to cure the lameness of sin, which is the grace of God, through our Lord Jesus Christ. (*Perf. Just.* 3.6)

Foreknowledge: De Libero Arbitrio

Yet in Augustine's eyes, as in those of nearly every other philosopher, free will requires not so much a proof as a defence against refutation. We shall examine in the remainder of this chapter how he responds to the threat posed to it by divine foreknowledge; the next chapter will turn to the far greater threat, given Augustine's theological standpoint, from divine causality.

In two places Augustine discusses the question whether God's fore-knowledge (praescientia) of human acts is not inconsistent with the acts' being freely chosen: *De Libero Arbitrio* book 3, and *City of God* book 5 chapter 9. In the former he makes himself say to Evodius:

> I am sure that your problem – what puzzles you – is this: how can there fail to be a contradiction and an inconsistency between God's foreknowing all the future and our sinning by will, not necessity? For if, you say, God does foreknow that a man will sin, it is necessary that he sin; and if it is necessary, there is no decision of the will in his sinning, but rather unavoidable and fixed necessity. Your fear clearly is that this reasoning will lead to the result that either, disrespectfully, God must be denied foreknowledge of all the future or, if we cannot deny that, we shall have to agree that sins are committed by necessity, not will. (*Lib. Arb.* 3.3.6)

Although this argument, as befits the anti-Manichean theme of the dialogue in which it appears, concerns only sinful acts, Augustine begins his response by treating it, reasonably enough, as resting on more general premises concerning all acts, in effect:

(4) If God foreknows that a will ϕ at t, it is necessary that a ϕs at t;
(5) if it is necessary that a ϕs at t, a ϕs at t not by (decision of) will.

Having secured Evodius' agreement to the generalized premises, Augustine proceeds to show that there must be counter-examples to the conclusion they jointly entail:

> Who would be so mad as to venture to say that we will not by will? Accordingly, although God foreknows our future wills, it does not result from this that we will anything not by will. . . . Since he foreknows our will, what he foreknows will itself be. So it will be a will, since it is a will that he foreknows. And it will not be able to be a will, if it is not in our power. So he also foreknows the power. Power is not, therefore, taken away from us by his foreknowledge; it will be all the more certainly present, because he whose foreknowledge does not fall into error [non fallitur] has foreknown that it will be present to me. (*Lib. Arb.* 3.3.7–8)

Thus the counter-example is yielded by

(6) If a *wills* at t, a *wills* by will; and
(7) For some a and t, God foreknows that a will *will* at t.

(4)–(7) are jointly inconsistent, if willing falls within the range of 'ϕ'. From that outcome Augustine now intends us to infer that the conclusion generated by (4) and (5) is false, and hence that (4) or (5) must be false; and it is evident that he selects (5) as the culprit, because Evodius is allowed to conclude the discussion by saying:

I do not now deny either that whatever God has foreknown, necessarily comes to be, or that he foreknows our sins; and both of these in such a way that the will nevertheless remains free for us and set in our power. (*Lib. Arb.* 3.3.8)

How good is this response? Since Augustine's aim is to refute an alleged inconsistency, and that is equivalent to proving a possibility, it is reasonable that he should use the method of example, displaying a case in which the desired possibility is actualized. The possibility he seeks to prove is

It is possible, for some a, t and ϕ, that God foreknows that a will ϕ at t, and a ϕs at t by will;

and he argues that, because of (6), this possibility is actualized by *any* example of divine foreknowledge of an act of willing, that is, by the truth of (7). The strategy is ingenious, but there are some evident weaknesses in Augustine's execution of it. First (6), together with its supporting thesis that willing is in our power, remains challengeable. Secondly (7), the proposition that God foreknows at least some wills, has to be assumed, which is not satisfactory in an argument designed to show that his total foreknowledge is compatible with human freedom. Thirdly, the conclusion will reconcile foreknowledge with *freedom* only if all decisions of the will have to be free. As we have seen earlier in the chapter, Augustine is not entitled to this extra claim ((9) from p. 79), which needs to be distinguished from the thesis, used in the present passage in support of (6), that it is in our power *whether* we exercise our wills.

Finally, the modern reader will jib at (4), and will suspect that, in conceding it, Augustine is guilty of an elementary modal muddle. Luther was to say that granted foreknowledge and omnipotence it follows 'by an irrefutable logic [irrefragibili consequentia]' that nothing in a man is 'free to become now in this way now in that way other than what ⟨God⟩ has foreknown or is now bringing about' (*De Servo Arbitrio* part 4, LCC, p. 243). But the logic had long since been refuted, at any rate as regards foreknowledge, by the scholastic distinction between absolute and conditional necessity, a distinction which Luther dismisses in his coarse way as 'playing with words [ludibriis verborum]' (ibid. p. 120). What is irrefutable is the truth of (4) when it is read as asserting conditional necessity, instantiating the general fact about propositional knowledge that

Necessarily, if something is known, it is a truth.

However, in order for (4) to play its part with (5) in generating an inconsistency when (6) and (7) are added, we should have to deduce from it the corresponding instantiation of

If something is known, it is a necessary truth,

thereby asserting the absolute necessity of 'it is true'. The fallacy in this deduction was well explained by Boethius (c.480–c.524), writing a century after Augustine ('I.T.' 's translation of 1609):

> For there be two necessities: the one simple, as that it is necessary for all men to be mortal; the other conditional, as if thou knowest that any man walketh, he must needs walk. . . . But this conditional draweth not with it that simple or absolute necessity. . . . These things therefore [viz. future free acts] being referred to the divine sight are necessary by the condition of the divine knowledge, and, considered by themselves, they lose not absolute freedom of their own nature. (*Consolatio Philosophiae* 5.6; cf. Aquinas, *Summa Theologiae* 1a 14.13)

Augustine's complacent confidence in (4) invites the suspicion that he overlooked the whole distinction.

Foreknowledge: the City of God

Twenty-five or thirty years after writing *De Libero Arbitrio* Augustine made his second attempt on the problem of freedom and foreknowledge in a chapter of the *City of God* composed, with the appearance of haste that is characteristic of much of that work, against an argument of Cicero. Book 2 of Cicero's dialogue *De Divinatione* had denied foreknowledge on the ground of its incompatibility with human freedom, whereas Augustine will declare that 'the religious mind chooses both' (*City* 5.9). Here is his reconstruction of Cicero's line of argument:

> What is it, then, about foreknowledge of the future that frightened Cicero into the appalling argument in which he tries so hard to undermine it? Evidently that, if all future events [futura] are foreknown, they will occur in the order in which it is foreknown that they will occur; and if they occur in that order, the order of things is determined [certus] by the foreknowing God; and if the order of things is determined, the order of causes is determined, for nothing can happen that is not preceded by some efficient cause; but if the order of causes, which makes all that happens happen, is determined, then, he says, all that happens happens by fate; and if that is so, nothing is in our power, and there is no decision of will.

Therefore in order to escape these consequences, so intolerable,
absurd and dangerous to human affairs, he decides [vult] that there
is no foreknowledge of the future. (*City* 5.9)

The conclusion stated here, that there is *no* foreknowledge, is neither
Cicero's (whose target is divination, defined as 'presentiment of things
that happen by chance', 'praesensio fortuitarum rerum') nor justified by
the argument, which presents the absurdity that nothing is in our power
as a consequence of *total* foreknowledge, and thereby escapable provided
that foreknowledge is not total. What this means is that *some* things are
not foreknown to *anyone*, from which it follows that some things are
not foreknown even to God (who appears before his cue in Augustine's
reconstruction). Thus the Ciceronian argument, as seen through
Augustine's eyes, can be sanitized as follows:

  (8) If everything is foreknown to someone, everything occurs in
      foreknown order;
  (9) if everything occurs in foreknown order, everything's order is
      determined by its foreknower;
  (10) if everything's order is determined, the order of causes is
      determined;
  (11) if the order of causes is determined, everything happens by fate;
  (12) if everything happens by fate, nothing is in our power and there
      is no decision of will;
  (13) but there is decision of will;
  therefore some things are not foreknown to anyone, even God.

This is a valid argument, which refutes God's foreknowledge of all the
future (divine omniprescience, as I shall call it), provided that its premises
are true; and establishes that no rational mind can 'choose' both divine
omniprescience and human freedom, provided that the freedom in question requires decision of the will and the remaining premises, (8)–(12),
are true. Augustine sees all this, as the core of his response reveals:

But it does not follow that if the order of all causes is determined
by God there is therefore nothing in the decision of our will. In
fact, even our wills themselves are in the order of causes determined
by God and contained in his foreknowledge, since human wills too
are causes of human deeds [operum], and so he who foreknew all
the causes of things certainly could not have been ignorant even of
our wills among those causes, which he foreknew to be the causes
of our deeds. (*City* 5.9)

This fixes the blame on (11) or (12), between which Augustine hesitates
through uncertainty as to the appropriate meaning of 'fate', 'fatum', the
word which Cicero had used to translate the Stoic '*heimarmenē*'. Cicero

makes his brother Quintus, speaking as a Stoic, define *heimarmenē* as 'the eternal cause of things, ‹explaining› why the past has happened and the present is happening and the future will happen' (Cicero, *De Divinatione* 1.55.126), which suggests that to be fated is no more than to be part of a causal nexus; certainly, as Augustine records earlier in the chapter, many Stoics denied that *heimarmenē* entails necessity. But Augustine, like other critics of the Stoics before and since, failed to grasp this definition, and instead presented 'fatum' as ambiguous between our modern sense (he speaks nebulously of 'how [the word] is applied in common parlance, that is, to the configuration of the stars at the time of anyone's conception or birth', ibid.) and, secondly, 'spoken, or decreed' – which is in fact the correct etymology of the Latin word. Under the former meaning he then denies (11), believing that although causes are determined, nothing happens by fate; while under the latter meaning he denies (12), believing (as we shall see) that God's decrees can act through a human will.

Two other key words in the argument are at least as obscure as 'fate', although neither gets any comment from Augustine. One is 'certus', which I have translated 'determined' in an attempt to reproduce the obscurity. Like the English 'certain' this word can be applied to people, and then it bears the English sense; but when, as here, it applies to actions or events, its basic meanings are 'resolved, or decided' (of a would-be action) and 'assured, or dependable' (of any event). In the Ciceronian argument Augustine uses 'certus' both in a relative construction, certus *to* God ('determined by' in my translation) and absolutely. Since the former requires the meaning 'decided', premise (9) is not so innocent as would appear if the word were translated by 'certain': what it asserts is that universal knowledge of the future comes not by foreseeing how things will be, but only by deciding or ordaining how things shall be. If the argument is to work, this same sense must then be preserved in premise (10) (and presumably (11)), by understanding the absolute 'determined' as elliptical for 'determined by someone'.

The other difficult word is 'order', 'ordo', an Augustinian favourite which he shamelessly imports into the argument despite its appearing hardly if at all in Cicero's text. As a young man Augustine had written a dialogue *De Ordine* on the question 'Whether everything good and bad is confined [contineat] by the order of divine providence' (*Retract.* 1.3). Order, we learn in that work, would not exist if everything were wholly good, because it would not then be needed (*Ord.* 2.1.2); but as things are, God imposes it so as to keep evil in check. Thus order is limitation, restraint, control, and we must read 'foreknowledge of the order of things' not, or not merely, as foreknowledge of which things succeed which, but as including knowledge of the rules or laws that ensure these successions. Augustine's thought in premise (8) is presumably, therefore, the inductivist thought that only by learning such rules of working could anyone hope to tell how things will go on from the point at which, at any given moment, they have arrived. This then explains premise (10), for given the extra assumption, made explicit in the argument, that everything has a cause, limitation on the way things go will require limitation also on the way things are caused to go, so that a creator who imposes the former must proceed by imposing the latter.

Suppressing the dubious notion of fate, we can thus discern in Augustine's Ciceronian argument the following overall structure: God's foreknowledge of all the future requires knowledge of the laws by which things work; these laws are causal; no one can foreknow all causal laws without foreordaining them; nothing foreordained by God is in human power; so if anything is in human power, God does not foreknow all the future.

We have seen that Augustine's response is to reject the final premise: since human wills, he argues, are among the things foreordained by God, their existence cannot be inconsistent with his foreordaining them. How successful is that answer? In the first place, we must surely rate it *more* successful than its predecessor in the *De Libero Arbitrio*. There Augustine reconciled foreknowledge with freedom only by means of the assumption that God foreknows some human wills; here that very assumption is under challenge, and the case is strengthened by his not relying on it. On the other hand the assumption which he now substitutes, that God *foreordains* human wills (they are 'certae Deo'), is still open to challenge on the ground that what is foreordained cannot be a will. More seriously, Augustine remains vulnerable to the charge that, here as in the argument of the *De Libero Arbitrio*, he is altogether too cavalier about the distinction of will from free will. The inconsistency alleged by Cicero is between divine omniprescience and things being 'in our power' – the second degree of freedom. Augustine will not defeat that allegation by showing merely that a man's willing to φ may come within the scope of God's ordinances; he must also show that when it does so the man retains the power not to φ. Arminius, accused of maintaining the article that 'God has not by his eternal decree determined future contingencies to one side or the other', was to protest that if God determines in the sense of 'resolving that something shall be done [statuit ut aliquid fiat]' by a human agent, God does not thereby determine in the sense of bringing it about that the agent 'remains no longer free . . . so as to be able to suspend his own action' (Arminius, *Apology* p. 143b, Nichols: vol 1, 696). This is the position which Augustine needs, but fails, to substantiate.

Obversely to these doubts whether Augustine can get away with the challenge he makes to Cicero, we may also object that another of Cicero's assumptions ought to have been challenged by him, and was not: this is the implication I have derived from (9) that the laws of nature can be fully foreknown only to one who foreordains them. Many theologians have solved the foreknowledge problem by denying that connection, as when Milton makes God say:

> if I foreknew,
> Foreknowledge had no influence on their fault,
> Which had no less proved certain unforeknown.
>
> (Milton, *Paradise Lost* 3.117–19)

With respect to 'knowledge of creatures' Augustine thought otherwise:

> ⟨God⟩ is not acquainted [novit] with any of his creatures, whether spiritual or corporeal, because they are, but they are because he is acquainted with them. For he did not lack knowledge of the things he was to create; he created, therefore, because he knew [scivit], not knew because he created. (*Trin.* 15.13.22; cf. Kenny 1979:34)

Aquinas was to cite the first half of this passage in support of his contention that 'God's knowledge is cause of things', but gave a better argument (in effect, you cannot predict a poem without composing it, *Summa Theologiae* 1a 14.8). Augustine's argument, in the second sentence, seems to rely on the quite implausible claim that anyone's knowledge of his own future actions must be causative of them. We shall return in the next chapter to the question whether Augustine's and Milton's views on this matter are really in conflict.

Conclusion

These attempts by Augustine to reconcile divine omniprescience with human freedom leave us with two general difficulties, the first of which, not yet mentioned, is this. According to Augustine, God stands outside time; so nothing is future from his point of view; but foreknowledge, prescience, is knowledge of what is future from the knower's point of view; so God can have *no* foreknowledge. The two passages we have surveyed give every appearance of contradicting this conclusion when they assert that it would be 'crazily disrespectful' ('insanissima impietas', *Lib Arb.* 3.2.4) to deny foreknowledge to God, and that 'anyone who lacks foreknowledge of all the future is not God at all' (*City* 5.9). These vehement assertions will have to be qualified by Augustine, or reinterpreted, if they are to square with his mature doctrine about God's relation to time, which I shall examine in chapter 9.

Second – and this difficulty we have confronted at the end of the preceding section – there is a special problem about reconciling human freedom with *divine* foreknowledge arising from the status of God as creator. If that status makes him cause of everything, and if, as we have seen Augustine assuming in the *City of God* and apparently asserting in the *De Trinitate*, no one who is the cause of an event can predict it without causing it thereby, then the freedom of human acts is compatible with divine knowledge of them only if it is compatible with divine causation of them; and God's foreknowledge of human wills, being forewilling of those wills, must operate on them in such a manner as not to detract from their freedom. In this way the problem of reconciling human freedom with divine foreknowledge connects with the problem of reconciling it with divine causation, which is the subject of my next chapter.

Further reading

On free will consult e.g. Dennett (1985) or Lucas (1970). On the *De Libero Arbitrio* passage see Rowe (1972).

VI

Free will at bay

Pelagius

At a council attended by Augustine at Carthage in May 418, eight canons were issued against the followers of Pelagius, among them these three:

> Canon 3. Item: it was resolved that whoever says that the grace of God, by which man is justified through Jesus Christ our Lord, avails [valet] only for the remission of sins already committed, not also for aid in not committing them, is to be anathema.
>
> Canon 4. Item: whoever says that the same grace . . . aids us not to sin only because understanding of commands is revealed and disclosed by it so that we know what we ought to seek and what avoid, but that our also desiring and having strength to do what we know should be done is not produced in us through it, is to be anathema.
>
> Canon 5. Item: it was resolved that whoever says that the grace of justification is given us so that we should be able more easily to fulfil what we are bidden [jubemur] to do through free decision, although even if grace were not given we should be able to fulfil the divine commands without it, even if not easily, is to be anathema. (Denz. nos. 225–7)

Seven years before this council Pelagius had arrived in Palestine, after flight a year earlier from the impending sack of Rome. There he might have passed the rest of his days in peace, had not his younger companion Celestius, left behind at Carthage when Pelagius passed through, annoyed the Catholic authorities by indiscreet dissemination of his views on baptism – a touchy subject in Africa, as we shall see in chapter 11 – and been excommunicated. In Hippo Augustine was quickly informed of these proceedings and, fresh from his triumph over Donatism (chapter

11), at once decided that here was a 'new heresy' (*Retract.* 2.23, *Ep.* 178.1) needing to be smashed. It was he who dispatched Orosius, a young Spanish presbyter (and future historian), with letters to Jerome in Palestine (*Epp.* 166, 167) asking advice about two matters bearing on Pelagius' views: the origin of souls and the meaning of Jas. 2:10. Orosius arrived at Bethlehem to find Pelagius installed five miles away in Jerusalem under the patronage of its bishop, enjoying the admiration of high-minded Christian men and women in exile in the city (Kelly 1975: 309 ff.). Dispute about Origenism and the value of marriage was already raging between the irascible Jerome and his new neighbour, 'that fathead, bloated with Scotch porridge' (Jerome, *Commentaries on Jeremiah*, prologue); and one can only guess at the motives which led to the two of them being invited at this moment to address letters of advice – both surviving – to one Demetrias, daughter of a wealthy Roman family, who had come also into Augustine's ambit in Africa (*Ep.* 150, see p. 193 below) and had decided to take vows of chastity. In this climate it was not long before Orosius contrived a confrontation: in 415 Pelagius was summoned before a council of Greek-speaking bishops at Diospolis (Lod, near Tel Aviv) and accused of heresy. He was acquitted.

News of the acquittal caused consternation in Africa, and when Orosius returned with a first-hand account, councils were held which drew up petitions to pope Innocent I (*Epp.* 175, 176), seconded by a private letter (*Ep.* 177) from bishops Aurelius (of Carthage), Augustine, Alypius, Evodius, and Possidius. The bishop of Rome, flattered by deference to the pretensions of his see on such an important matter, replied with an assurance of support that was construed in Africa as amounting to excommunication of Pelagius, Celestius, and all their followers, till they should recant. Innocent then died, leaving his successor Zosimus to face the Roman Pelagians. Zosimus, summoning Pelagius and Celestius to appear before him, pronounced once more in their favour. But he had reckoned without the civil authority. Within a few months riots broke out at Rome which were blamed on the Pelagians; separately, the African bishops may have exerted influence at the imperial court in Ravenna. At the end of April 418 an edict of the emperor Honorius, soon echoed by the unhappy pope, banned the expression of support for Pelagians and exiled the leaders from Rome (for an account see Brown 1967:357–63). Next day the council of 418 met at Carthage.

Since most of Pelagius' writings have been lost, it is difficult to know how much of the Carthaginian anathema applies to him. But the main lines are clear. He gained from Augustine himself or from others of like mind the conviction that the justice of divine punishment requires human freedom; he saw a threat to that justice in the Pauline doctrine of the fall, and a threat to freedom in the Pauline doctrine of grace. Augustine was no less sensitive to the threats (*Pecc. Mer.* 2.18.28): on grace he urged the monks of Adrumetum (Sousse, in Tunisia) to read and reread two tracts he had sent in response to their request for guidance (*Corr. Gr.* 1.1); he acknowledged that the question is 'obscure' (*Gr. Lib. Arb.* 1.1), its true answer 'very difficult, and intelligible to few' (*Ep.* 214.6). These two Christians faced, then, a common problem, and the 60–year-old Augustine's outrage at the Pelagian solution to it spurred him to a decade of hectic literary activity. Having noted the cause of that activity I shall not, in what follows, attempt to unravel the true from the false accusations against Pelagius (on whom see Ferguson 1956 and Evans 1968). Grace will be discussed in this chapter, the fall and original sin in the next.

Two graces: enabling and co-operative

We can concentrate on canon 5 of the council of 418, picked out from the three I have quoted for reaffirmation eleven centuries later by the Council of Trent (Denz. no. 1552). Our evidence that Pelagius opposed it comes from his letter to the young virgin Demetrias, in which he scorned the suggestion that God

> forgetful of human frailty, whose author he is himself, should impose commands [mandata] that cannot be borne. . . . He, who is just, did not will to demand [imperare] anything impossible; he, who is caring [pius], did not propose to convict [non damnaturus] a man for what the man could not avoid. (*Letter to Demetrias*, section 16)

In this or like texts the bishops may have discerned a threat to Canon 5 as follows:

(1) No divine command is unfulfillable by men;
(2) There are divine commands;
Therefore men can fulfil the divine commands without the aid of God's grace.

To make the argument valid it is clear that (1) needs strengthening into 'Every divine command can be fulfilled by men unaided'. But this could be understood in either of two ways, according as 'unaided' qualifies 'can' or 'fulfilled'; for in general '*a* has the power to ϕ unaided' may mean either 'the power to ϕ is *a*'s without aid' or 'the power to ϕ without aid is *a*'s'. In the second sense a normal man will have the power, for example, to write a letter unaided, but not to push a lorry uphill unaided; whereas in the first sense he will lack even the power to write a letter unaided, since others must supply him with paper, pen, desk, food, and other such euphemistically named 'facilities'.

When we think in human terms, we commonly ignore the first of these qualifications on our power, and so freedom, of action – the fact that our powers are contingent and removable. But a theist may have occasion to glorify God by asserting the contingency, which he will trace back, perhaps through other human 'facilitators', to God the fountain of every power, *enabler* of all things. The same motive of glorifying God in comparison with his creatures may lead a theist also to emphasize men's need for aid in the execution of their projects; and this need may even come to be thought, like the first, quite general, so that nothing can be done by a man on his own, no project carried to fruition without divine *co-operation*.

The accusation against Pelagius of resisting these tendencies often failed to make clear how far his opposition to them was supposed to go. Yet it is obvious that the quotation from his letter opposes at most the second kind of qualification, i.e. asserts at most that if God has commanded *a* to φ, the power of φing without aid belongs to *a*. This will deny men's need for the co-operation of God in their execution of good deeds, without denying their need for God's grant of power to execute them; it will assimilate good deeds to letter-writing, which nearly anybody can do on his own who can do it at all, even though without outside aid he will lack the power of doing it at all. If we distinguish two graces, one a gift of power, enabling, the other an aid to execution, co-operative, we have no reason to suppose that Pelagius denied the need for the former, at least. What, then, was the position of his opponents?

The difference between enabling and co-operative grace, although not difficult to understand, is exceptionally easy to hide in ordinary language. Canon 5 itself is ambiguous between them (and therefore, I submit, is void for uncertainty as an anathema). Equally ambiguous is Jn 15:5, 'Without me you can do nothing', quoted in the same canon and often by Augustine; and so is Augustine's admonition in a letter of 426/7: 'Do not defend free decision in such a way as to attribute good deeds [opera] to it without God's grace' (*Ep*. 215.8; cf. *Simp*. 1.1.15). In other places however a judgement between the different meanings becomes, if not often certain, at least probable.

Two important biblical texts appear to favour the 'Pelagian' view that men have no general need of co-operative grace.

> He made man from the beginning, and left him in the hand of his own counsel. If you will, you shall keep his commands, and true fidelity [fidem bonam] is at your pleasure. . . . In man's purview are life and death, and whichever he pleases will be given to him.
> (Ecclus 15:14–17)

This text was discussed by Augustine in *De Gratia et Libero Arbitrio* (2.3) and, responding to Julian's citation of it, in his last, unfinished work (*C. Sec. Jul*. 1.45); the Reformation writers also argued over it (e.g. Erasmus, *De Libero Arbitrio*, p. 47, Luther, *De Servo Arbitrio*,

LCC pp. 182 ff., Calvin, *Christianae Religionis Institutio* 2.5.18). A similar stumbling block for the anti-Pelagians was:

> The command that I lay on you this day is not too difficult for you, it is not too remote. . . . It is a thing very near to you, upon your lips and in your heart ready to be kept. (Deut. 30:11, 14, NEB)

This also is discussed by Erasmus, Luther, and Calvin; Paul had quoted it at Rom. 10:8.

In a number of places Augustine himself gives the impression that enabling grace suffices for good deeds:

> By ‹grace› it also comes to be that the good will itself, which has now begun to be, is increased, and becomes so great that it is able to fulfil the divine commands which it wills to, when it wills firmly and completely. . . . 'If you will, you shall keep his commands'. (*Gr. Lib. Arb.* 15.31)

The same view is suggested in the *De Peccatorum Meritis* when Augustine likens God to the eye without whose help we cannot see (*Pecc. Mer.* 2.4.4), and in the unfinished work when he says that the power of living well 'is not given without the grace of God' (*C. Sec. Jul.* 1.94). Nor was he alone among Pelagius' opponents in being sometimes content with this mild doctrine: Jerome's remark to Demetrias that 'It is ours both to will ‹to do a thing› and to will not ‹to›; and this very thing that is ours is not ours without God's mercy' (Jerome, *Letter to Demetrias*, section 12), could equally well have been penned by her rival spiritual adviser.

Typically, however, Augustine thinks that there is also need for co-operative grace. The word 'co-operative' comes from Paul:

> And in everything, as we know, he co-operates [*sunergei*] for good with those who love God. (Rom. 8:28, NEB preferred interpretation, which is also Augustine's; the word occurs in pagan philosophy too, e.g. Sextus, *Adversus Mathematicos* 8.199)

This grace, according to Augustine's settled view, is needed in everything that men do well, because without it their good acts will not be crowned with success:

> When we will, and so will as to act, he co-operates with us. But without him, either operating so that we will or co-operating when we will, our caring achieves no good results [ad bona pietatis opera non valemus]. (*Gr. Lib. Arb.* 17.33)

I shall return later to the first part of this, 'operating so that we will'; here it is enough to note that, as the surrounding context makes clear, Augustine thinks both parts necessary, despite the 'either . . . or' (vel . . . vel).

The doctrine of co-operative grace puts together two thoughts: first, that succeeding in a project or enterprise, even when it occurs, is beyond what the succeeder can be said to *do* (compare Aristotle: 'It jars to say that we choose ‹to be healthy or happy›, for in general choice is thought to be concerned with what is up to us', *Nicomachean Ethics* 1111b 29–30); and, secondly, that the gap between endeavour and achievement is bridged by God. Sometimes Augustine cites biblical illustrations from farming:

Thus it is not the gardeners with their planting and watering who count, but God, who makes it grow. (1 Cor. 3:7, NEB)

‹Yahweh› will add prosperity, and our land shall yield its harvest. (Ps 84 [Heb. Bib. 85]:12, NEB)

The verse from John's gospel which I have already quoted follows after a viticultural simile telling in the same sense – or even suggesting, perhaps, that God's grace is both enabling and co-operative:

No branch can bear fruit by itself [*aph' heautou*], but only if it remains united with the vine. . . . Apart from me you can do nothing. (Jn 15:4–5, NEB)

Sometimes God's crowning of endeavour is identified with his strengthening of an already formed, but weak, will (e.g. *Corr. Gr.* 12.38), for Augustine accepts the cruel doctrine that faith can move mountains (Mt. 17:20, Mk 11:23). ' "If it says so in the Bible it is so, Philip," said Mrs Carey gently' (Somerset Maugham, *Of Human Bondage*, ch. 14). Philip Carey's failure to cure his club foot by prayer must 'just mean that you hadn't got faith' (ibid.), for, as Augustine puts it, mountain-moving 'would occur if the will exerted were great enough for so great a matter' (*Sp. Lit.* 35.63).

It was Pelagius' view, according to Augustine, that

Power [posse] ‹God› placed in ‹our› nature, but will and action [velle et agere] are ours by his will; accordingly he does not help us to will, he does not help us to act, he only helps us to be able [valeamus] to will and act. (*Gr. Christ.* 1.5.6)

By contrast, Augustine himself held that both posse and agere need God's help.

Freedom and co-operative grace

We are now in a position to broach the question whether either of these two kinds of grace, enabling and co-operative, conflicts with human freedom. Plainly the former kind does not. Enabling grace is, indeed, a condition of some freedoms, since if the power to 'achieve good works' is a gift of God, people to whom the gift is denied lack freedom to achieve them. Whether Augustine thinks that there are such people will be a question for chapter 7. However, when enabling grace *is* granted to a man, his freedom may be as extensive as anybody has ever imagined human freedom to be.

It is with his defence of co-operative grace that Augustine begins to risk having, in Erasmus' image, 'fought with an enemy in front so incautiously that he received a wound in the back' (*De Libero Arbitrio* IV 16, *LCC* p. 96). Suppose that I can shift a broken-down lorry, but only with someone else's help: am I free to shift it? Whether it is even *possible* for me to shift it depends, I think, on whether it would be right to say, when I had got it moving in co-operation with the rest of my team, that the lorry had been shifted by *me*. Yet even if this possibility exists, it is not enough for freedom unless it is the possibility of shifting the lorry by my own will or decision; and it seems reasonable to say that a man engaged in a co-operative undertaking actualizes the latter kind of possibility only if his helpers' wills are his to command. This is implicit in Calvin's remark that a man is free in the ordinary sense only if he is 'able by himself [a se ipso] to turn himself to either part', namely good or evil (*Christianae Religionis Institutio* 2.2.7). Since God's will is not at the command of any human will, the condition is not met if God has to be among our helpers.

If that is right, Augustine's position is far from the ordinary man's. Most of us would agree that it 'jars to say' that we are free to be healthy or happy, but would find nothing odd about saying that we are usually, for example, free to open our front doors. In both these kinds of case there is the same logical gap between trying or making an effort or taking steps towards a desired outcome, and achieving that outcome; but in the latter kind of case we do not pay attention to the gap, either because we do not believe, or at least because we do not acknowledge in our speech, that bridging it is dependent on the co-operation of another agency – or, alternatively, on any noticeable degree of luck. *My* opening my front door is something that usually happens or not according to the determinations of *my* will. Augustinian Christians think otherwise: for them all human actions are like lorry-shiftings. Luther's colleague Melanchthon (1497–1560) said: 'Although Christian doctrine on this topic differs altogether from philosophy and human reason, philosophy has gradually crept into Christianity' (*Loci Communes Theologici, LCC* 19, p. 23).

Melanchthon referred to the scholastics; no such 'philosophy' pollutes Augustine's anti-Pelagian writings. His conception of the relations of God to man demands God's assistance for even the most commonplace projects, if they are to be brought to fruition. In particular, then, men lack the power of avoiding bad outcomes unaided, and therefore are not free to avoid them. The steps by which an Augustinian must advance to this conclusion are:

(3) The power to secure any outcome without divine aid belongs to no man;

so (4) The power to secure any good or neutral outcome without divine aid belongs to no man;

so (5) The power to avoid any bad outcome without divine aid belongs to no man;

so (6) No man has the power of avoiding a bad outcome by the determination of his own will;

so (7) No man is free to avoid any bad outcome.

I said on p. 82 that the freedom which Augustine's theodicy requires him to preserve is freedom to sin. If we now invoke the distinction made in his treatise on the Sermon on the Mount between sins in the heart and sins in deed (*Serm. Dom. Mont.* 1.12.35, p. 89), it is tempting to go beyond (7) by inferring from it that, although freedom to avoid the former kind of sins (which are sinful intentions) is not yet ruled out, freedom to avoid the latter kind is; that is,

(8) No man is free to avoid sins in deed.

I think Augustine tended to assume that this extra step could be taken; but he should not have done so, because it is invalidated by his own doctrine that all sin requires will to sin (*Du. An.* 12.16.17, p. 82). That doctrine ensures that any serious effort to avoid a bad outcome, even if it is not crowned with success by God's co-operation, will acquit a man of the charge of committing a sin with respect to the outcome he sought to avoid, which, whether or not it is judged to be his *doing*, will not in Augustine's eyes be his *sin*, provided that he has not willed it. Therefore, in order to infer from (7) to (8) it would need to be shown in addition that men lack power to engage their wills in projects of avoiding bad outcomes.

Prevenient grace

From what we have considered so far the following doctrine of sin seems to emerge, where sin is taken to cover sins in the heart and in deed (but not in habit): *men are free to avoid sins, provided that they have power to will to avoid sins in deed.* Here is the argument: (i) freedom – in the second degree – to avoid sins consists in power to avoid or commit them, according to the determinations of the will; (ii) it seems reasonable to hold that power to *will* to avoid sin in deed brings with it power to avoid willing them, which on Augustine's view (p. 75) is the same thing as power to avoid sins in the *heart*; (iii) as we have seen at the end of the previous section, power to avoid sins in *deed* follows from power to will to avoid them; (iv) and finally the other half of freedom to avoid sins, namely power to *commit* them, is not yet in dispute.

In the light of this result a compromise position suggests itself, which would reconcile human freedom with human dependence on divine co-operation. The dependence theory states that, for any outcome that-*p*, men lack the power to bring it about that *p* (on their own); but the above freedom theory requires only, what is compatible with this, that for some outcomes that-*p*, men have the power to *will* to bring it about that *p*. Such a compromise had already been fashionable among Christians unaffected by the Pelagian controversy. Augustine's eastern contemporary John Chrysostom (*c*.347–407) was to be reproved by Calvin for maintaining that 'We must strive to bring what is ours, so as to make ourselves fit for what is the gift of God' (*Homilies on Genesis* 25.7, *PG* 53.228, see Calvin, *Christianae Religionis Institutio* 2.2.4); and the part that we bring, he and others believed, is a good or bad will. This idea was taken up by a western contemporary of Augustine's, John Cassian (*c*.360–435) of Massilia (Marseilles), who held that when Nathan accused David of adultery and murder (2 Sam. 12:1–14), 'It was ‹David's› own doing that he was humbled and acknowledged his guilt' (Cassian, *Collationes* 13.13). Two young men, an unknown Hilary and Prosper, later to be Augustine's doughty champion in controversy and canonized as St Prosper of Aquitaine, wrote to Augustine for support against Cassian's followers. According to Hilary, the Massilians were claiming that '‹Grace› avails to help someone who has begun to will, not to grant him to will' (*Ep.* 226.2), and Prosper reports that they found a reason for this view in their fear that otherwise

> However they behave it cannot fall out otherwise for them than God has determined [definivit]; . . . so all effort is abolished, all virtues destroyed, if God's arrangements [constitutio] precede [praeveniat] human wills, and under the name of predestination a kind of fatal necessity is introduced. (*Ep.* 225.3, also in *ACW* volume 32)

'Obedience', they infer, 'comes before grace' (ibid. 6; and compare Augustine's embarrassment in *Ep.* 2* to Firmus, see Chadwick (1983:427); and how Pelagius was scandalized by *Confessions* 10.31.45, 'Give what you command and command what you will', *Don. Persev.* 20.53). The compromise led its defenders to affirm, then, that at least in some actions God's grace towards the agent is conditional on the agent's antecedent good will, from which it would follow that his will is not conditional on antecedent, or as it was called, prevenient, grace (Cassian, *Collationes* 13.11,18; the word is from Ps 58 [Heb. Bib. 59]:10, 'The God of my mercy shall prevent me', AV).

This Semipelagianism, as the Counter-Reformation was to label it, received its condemnation a century after Augustine's death, at a council in Orange in 529. The acts of the council (lost in the Middle Ages and rediscovered during the Council of Trent) contain the following canon 6:

> If anyone says that the divinity has mercy on us when without God's grace we believe, will, desire, try, work, pray, watch, study, seek, ask, or knock, but does not admit that it is through the infusion and inspiration of the Holy Spirit in us that we believe, will, or have the strength to do all these things as we ought, and subordinates the aid of grace to human humility or obedience without agreeing that it is a gift of grace itself that we are obedient and humble, he contradicts ‹Paul's teaching in 1 Cor. 4:7 and 1 Cor. 15:10›. (Denz. no. 376; reaffirmed at Trent, ibid. no. 1553)

He also contradicts Augustine, who a year before his death had written:

> The wills of men are preceded [praeveniri] by God's grace, and no one can be adequate in himself either for beginning or for completing any good work. (*Praed. Sanct.* 1.2)

At Orange, Augustinianism triumphed over the Massilians.

The triumphant doctrine contains an ambiguity not unlike that between enabling and co-operative grace, according as it represents a man's good decisions as depending on God's causing him to have the power to make them or on God's causing him to make them. Several of Augustine's dicta suggest the former – that prevenient grace is merely enabling. Paul had written of there being gentiles who fulfil the law 'by nature' (Rom. 2:14); Augustine comments that what was at first natural to man by his creation in God's image (Gen. 1:27) must, since Adam's fall, be restored to him through grace: 'through grace nature is repaired' (*Sp. Lit.* 27:47). Hence

> Free decision is not made vacuous by grace, but given its grounding [statuitur], because grace heals the will by which justice is freely loved. (*Sp. Lit.* 30.52)

Similarly, quoting the Septuagint version of a verse of Proverbs (Prov. 8:35 LXX) which reappears around fifty times in his works (see Sage 1964):

> ‹It is› in the decision of the human will to believe or not believe, but in the elect 'The will is prepared [praeparatur] by the Lord.' (*Praed. Sanct.* 5.10)

In the late sixteenth-century Iberian controversy *de auxiliis* (on aid) the Jesuit, Molinist, party were understood by their opponents to ascribe no more than this 'sufficiency' (as they oddly called it) to prevenient grace. God, as it were, gives us the fare; when his gift is effective in securing a ticket, he foresees but does not make it to be so (see Suarez (1548–1617) *De Gratia* 5.24.12). In an appendix (ibid. app. 1.36) Suarez adduces an important early work of Augustine's, the *Ad Simplicianum*, in which we find

> Whoever God pities, he calls in a way he knows will fit him [ei congruere] not to reject the caller. (*Simp*. 1.2.13)

Nevertheless, according to Augustine healing, preparing, and calling are not the whole of God's contribution to the good decisions made by the elect. Free decision

> Is ascribable [pertinere] to the grace of God . . . not only for its being but also for its being good, that is, converted to doing the Lord's commands. (*Pecc. Mer*. 2.6.7)

It would be absurd to suppose that free will comes from God (obtineamus . . . a Deo) but good will, which is better, comes from ourselves (ibid. 2.18.30). Pelagius, who allowed that God helps us to be able to will, should have allowed also that he helps us to will (*Gr. Christ*. 1.5.6). Again, in the *Ad Simplicianum* (on Rom. 9:11):

> The merit of having faith follows a man's call rather than preceding it. . . . So unless God's mercy precedes by calling him, no one has the power to believe. (*Simp*. 1.2.7, cf. 1.2.10)

And again

> We must notice and realize that this will has to be attributed to God's gift not only because it comes from free decision, which was created with us in our natures, but also because God acts [agit] on us, by our being persuaded by what we see, to will and to believe. . . . God works in men to will and to believe and his mercy prevents us in everything. (*Sp. Lit*. 34.60)

As usual, Augustine leans on biblical authority in defence of this stronger doctrine which makes prevenient grace *operative* as well as enabling. When the Christians at Philippi were quarrelling about the government of their church, Paul adjured them to

> Work out your salvation in fear and trembling; for it is God works in you as to both willing and doing, for his own good pleasure. (Phil. 2:12–13, quoted e.g. at *Simp*. 1.2.12, *Corr. Gr*. 9.24; Augustine's Latin preserves the Greek infinitive construction '*kai to thelein kai to energein*')

No man can come to me unless the father who sent me draws him. (Jn 6:44, quoted e.g. at *Praed. Sanct.* 8.15)

You have not chosen me, but I have chosen you, and I have arranged (*ethēka*) that you should go out and bear fruit. (Jn 15:16, quoted e.g. at *Corr. Gr.* 12.34)

Thus it does not depend on man's will or effort, but on God's mercy. (Rom. 9:16, quoted e.g. at *Simp.* 1.2.12)

In two late treatises Augustine supplements these biblical texts with argument. The *De Gratia et Libero Arbitrio* quotes Paul's assertion (Rom. 4:4) that

To those who are repaid according to merit 'The wages are reckoned not as a grace [i.e. favour] but as a debt'. (*Gr. Lib. Arb.* 5.11)

Augustine agrees – and incidentally reports Pelagius as having been brought to agree (*Gest. Pel.* 14.30, 17.40) – that no grace can be 'given according to our merits' (non ex operibus, *C. Jul.* 6.19.59). If then, he argues, good will were not caused by prevenient grace, it would be meritorious, so that subsequent – i.e. co-operative – grace would be accorded to that merit, and 'grace would not be grace' (*Gr. Lib. Arb.* 5.11). The argument is:

(9) Subsequent grace is given in accordance with a man's good decisions (in order to fructify them);
(10) No grace is given in accordance with anything meritorious;
(11) If a man's good decisions are of his own making, they are meritorious;
Therefore, a man's good decisions are not of his own making (but of God's).

The argument fails through equivocation. Premise (10) is in fact doubly ambiguous, since 'in accordance with (secundum)' might mean either (A) 'conditionally on' – i.e. only in the presence of – or (B) 'in acknowledgement of', and 'meritorious' might mean either (a) 'for which reward is fitting' or (b) 'for which reward is due'. In senses (A) and (Ba) the premise is implausible (although in sense (Ba) it is apparently upheld by the thirteenth of the 39 Articles of the Church of England). In sense (Bb), surely intended by Augustine, (10) expresses the conceptual truth that what pays a debt is not a favour. But at least one of the other premises invokes a different sense. Some Christian theologians hold that (9) is true only in sense (A), on the ground that subsequent grace cannot be conceived as any sort of prize, even the sort awarded irrespective of merit, as in a beauty contest. However that may be, it is certain that premise (11) requires sense (a), ascribing what the scholastics were to call 'congruous' rather than 'condign' merit. A good decision, being acceptable to God, is a suitable object for God to reward, 'Just as someone is said to have merited a bishopric, i.e. he is worthy or suitable for a bishopric' (William of Auvergne (c. 1180–1249) De Meritis p. 298a). Yet the decider need have performed no 'service obliging recompense' (ibid. p. 297), and no injustice need be done if reward is withheld. Augustine is therefore wrong to infer, from the conceptual Pauline truth that condign merit cannot be acknowledged by grace, to the conclusion that the good will of which subsequent grace is, perhaps, an acknowledgement has no merit at all.

Three years later, in his De Praedestinatione Sanctorum, the same chapter 4 of Paul's letter to the Romans provided Augustine with a different, but no more successful, argument to a similar conclusion, that faith is the gift of God. Paul is commenting on God's promise to Abraham that he and his seed – both Jew and the gentile 'nations' – would inherit the world (Rom. 4:17), which Augustine understands as a promise of salvation and thereby of right living, 'good works' (Praed. Sanct. 10.20). There are no good works without faith, as Paul had made plain (Heb. 2:4, 11:6). Augustine concedes that, in general, it is allowable to make a promise when some of the conditions of fulfilment are not themselves promised but only foreknown (thus one may sign a will without promising to die). However, anyone making a promise whose conditions he does *not* promise, promises what he lacks power to effect. And Paul rightly commended Abraham (Rom. 4:21) for believing that 'what [God] promised he has power to effect too [potens est et facere]'. Therefore, Augustine concludes, God did not merely foreknow the faith of the nations, but promised it; and he can fulfil his promise only by granting that faith. Here is the argument in Augustine's words:

> Did God perhaps, so as to promise what *he* effects [facit], promise Abraham in his seed the good works of the nations, but not the faith of the nations which *men* effect for themselves, although, so as to promise what he effects, he foreknew that they would effect that faith? . . . That way it would be in the power of man, not God, that God should be able to fulfil his promises. . . . [But] we must believe with Abraham that what he promised he has power to effect too. . . . Therefore he gives faith too. (Praed. Sanct. 10.20)

This confuses use of aid with use of luck (see Tichy and Oddie 1983: section 5): although as we have seen (p. 110) it might be right to deny God the power of effecting good works if he were to require men's help in effecting them, that is different from denying him the power merely on the ground that in order to exercise it he would need to make use of advantageous circumstances lying outside his control (e.g. I may be able to push a lorry with a locked cab, but only because someone else has left the brake off). So even if God were not in a position to promise Abraham all the conditions for the good works of the nations, it would not follow that his promise was one which he lacked power to fulfil.

These arguments fail. Nevertheless Augustine held to the opinion that God's prevenient grace causes good decisions, as well as holding that it makes them possible. The next thing to ask is whether freedom can still be preserved under these new constraints.

Freedom and prevenient grace

We have now arrived at a version of the question whether *compatibilism* is true, that is, whether freedom of the will is compatible with determinism. When the question is put in that schematic way it is indefinite, because of the habit of different philosophers to use the name 'determinism' for two different theses, that everything *is necessary* and that everything *has a cause*. We are interested in the second of these two, and even that can be narrowed down for our purposes to something a good deal more specific. Nicene Christianity, with its belief in God 'the father almighty, maker of heaven and earth', tends to cast God in the role of universal cause, so that the Christian may find himself faced with the task of accommodating human freedom not only to 'everything has a cause' but to the stronger claim, entailing but not entailed by it, 'everything has a cause in common', and the still stronger 'everything is caused by God'. Assuming that the 'things' will be events or states, we could represent this Christian determinism as the view that

(12) every event and state of the world either is God's act or is brought about by God's act.

Augustine himself would be committed to (12) if he accepted two premises from which it follows:

(13) God knows everything; and
(14) Everything that God knows he causes.

(13) is, seemingly, Augustinian, although I have not been able to find a statement more comprehensive than those considered in chapter 5 which ascribe to God foreknowledge of all the future. But (14) he repudiates on the ground that God foreknows sins, of which he is not the cause (p. 73 above):

> But ‹God› has the power to foreknow even things that he does not do [facit] himself – any sin, for example. (*Praed. Sanct.* 10.19; cf. *An. Orig.* 1.7.7)

Thus, after all, Augustine agrees with Milton (p. 102 above) about the 'faults' of creatures, such as those of Adam and Satan; as with a craftsman, it is only of the things which God does cause that his knowledge is causative. Nor is it only sin which in Augustine's view supplies counter-examples to (14) and thereby to (12): he sought to show that God is not the cause of other evil either, despite Isaiah 45:7, 'I am God, making good and creating bad' (e.g. *C. Adv.* 23.48, *C. Sec. Jul.* 3.127–8):

> There is no way out of the religious argument about good and bad unless whatever is, in so far as it is, is from God; while in so far as it lapses from being [ab essentia deficit], it is not from God, albeit always ordered by divine providence as befits the whole [universitati]. (*Mor. Man.* 7.10)

This Neoplatonist treatment of bad as the privation of good leads Augustine (*pace* Calvin, citing e.g. *Contra Julianum* 5.3.13 on Ezekiel 14:9) to reject the Christian determinism of (12).

His counter-examples to (12) concern bad states and events; good or neutral ones will still have to be ascribed to God as creator. Among the good or neutral states are many human actions and their results, themselves caused by decisions of human wills. God's will might be conceived in such cases as operating *through* human wills, so that God causes the outcomes by causing the decisions. Acts of operative prevenient grace will then fall within this class – presumably a wider one – of divine acts which cause human decisions which cause good or neutral states and events.

The Pelagian controversy over grace now appears in a wider perspective. Grace did not itself create the problem of reconciling human freedom with divine activity: the problem was there already for any Christian, or other theist, who rated God's power and majesty high enough to wish to give him credit for the success of human arrangements – such as it is. One solution to the general problem would invoke the idea of a causal tree, branching backwards, so as to give credit to both God and man as joint, co-operative, causes of successes without having to suppose that the will of God works through the wills of men. This is the Semipelagian solution, that man proposes but God disposes. What was new for Augustine was rejection of that shared credit, as overgenerous to man and derogatory to God, whose benign activity, though still allowed to work jointly on outcomes as subsequent grace, must *also* in Augustine's view be routed as prevenient grace through human decisions. So we arrive at the particular form which the compatibilist question takes for Augustine: can God's activity do that, and yet leave human decisions free?

If the prevenient grace were merely enabling, there would be no more a problem here than with subsequent grace: furnished by God with the power of willing the good, I may still retain the power of not willing it; and since these are powers of willing, we can hardly deny that, given both of them, it will depend on my will which one I exercise. In this way 'free decision is not made vacuous by grace, but given its grounding' (*Sp. Lit.* 30.52).

But since prevenient grace is also operative, causing good decisions, the battle over compatibilism has now been joined: can a decision be at the same time free and caused by God? If it cannot, then prevenient grace will also destroy freedom *to avoid sin* in those to whom it is granted. For without freedom to decide in favour of the sin which grace causes them to decide against, they will lack power to decide in favour of it and so, since sin requires decision of the will, they will lack power to sin; but without the power to sin, they will possess only one half of the two-way power that is needed in order to be free to avoid sin.

Necessity and divine causation

In discussing whether decisions caused by God can be free, my strategy in the remainder of this chapter will be as follows. First, I shall assume that freedom excludes necessity; specifically, if it is ever a necessary fact that a man decides to do something, his decision to do it was not an exercise of freedom. Jansen, as we saw in chapter 5, thought that Augustine denies that assumption in the *City of God* 5.10; but I argued there that he does not deny it; and in any case it is true. Given the assumption, it follows that victory will go to the incompatibilist if causation implies necessity, and I shall consider four arguments, of increasing subtlety, purporting to show that causation does imply necessity. I believe that all these arguments are faulty, and that the compatibilist position they try to overthrow is the correct one. I shall also argue that Augustine is innocent of adherence to the first three of the arguments. About the fourth I am not sure what opinion he held.

The first argument goes like this. Suppose God causes me to decide to smile at a friend; then I cannot refrain from so deciding; for were I to refrain, God's will would be inefficacious:

(A) If God caused me to decide now to smile, it follows that I decide now to smile;
God caused me to decide now to smile;
Therefore it is necessary that I decide now to smile.

This is fallacious, confusing conditional with absolute necessity: a decision may be necessary conditionally on its being caused (by God or anyone) without being itself necessary. Some of Augustine's commentators have fallen into this confusion (e.g. Chadwick 1967:232), and we have already found reason to suspect that Augustine was blind to it in his discussion of foreknowledge in the *De Libero Arbitrio* (p. 97). On grace, however, various passages count for his acquittal, suggesting that he noticed that there is room for causes to act in two ways, either by taking away the possibility of their being inoperative, or just by being operative. The distinction is important to Aquinas:

> The effect of divine providence is not merely that a thing should result somehow, but that it should result either contingently or necessarily. Therefore what divine providence disposes to result infallibly and necessarily results infallibly and necessarily, and what divine providence has reason should result contingently results contingently. (*Summa Theologiae* 1a 22.4)

And in several places Augustine seems to be aiming at the same point. Like Aquinas, he contrasts the behaviour of a man and a stone:

> For God works our salvation in us not as in senseless stones, or as in things in whose nature he has not placed reason and will. (*Pecc. Mer.* 2.5.6)

Against Cicero's argument retailed in the *City of God* book 5 chapter 9 (p. 98) he responds with the claim that *all* efficient causes are 'voluntary', implying, I think, not just the Berkeleyan thesis that only a will can be an efficient cause, but also that what it causes is not thereby made necessary (compare *De Libero Arbitrio* 3.1.2, where 'voluntary' impulses are contrasted with those that impose necessity). In a sermon on chapter 6 of John's gospel preached at Carthage in 417, while pope Zosimus was trying the Pelagian cause in Rome, he says:

> 'No one comes to me unless the father who sent me has drawn him [traxerit]' [Jn 6:44]. 'Drawn,' he said, not 'dragged [duxerit]'. This force [violentia] is applied to the heart, not the flesh. Why are you looking puzzled [miraris] then? Believe, and you come; love, and you are drawn. Don't think this is a rough, irksome force. It is soft, it is delightful. You are drawn by delight itself. Isn't a sheep drawn when it is shown some tasty grass? I would say it is not pulled by the body but caught up [colligatur] by desire. (*Serm.* 131.2.2; cf. *Ev. Joh.* 26.4 quoting the poet, 'trahat sua quemque voluptas'.)

What presumably puzzled Augustine's congregation is his evident intention in this remark to interpret the evangelist's 'trahere' (*helkusei*) as the non-compelling word in contrast with 'ducere' as the compelling one, which goes against both Latin usage and a famous Stoic tag ('Ducunt volentem fata, nolentem trahunt', Seneca, *Epistulae Morales* 107.10). Erasmus put the point better:

> The word 'draws' [trahendi] sounds as though it implied necessity and excluded freedom of the will. But in fact this drawing is not violent [violentus], but makes you will ‹to do› what nevertheless you

are able to will not ‹to do›, just as if we show a boy an apple and he runs for it, or show a sheep a green willow twig and it follows it. (*De Libero Arbitrio* III c 3, *LCC* p. 80)

As Prosper had meanwhile said, by grace free decision is 'conversum, non eversum', changed not smashed (*Ad Rufinum* 17).

Perhaps the same message is carried in a passage of the *De Spiritu et Littera* in which Augustine seeks to combine two theses: that God 'acts upon us to will and to believe', and that 'to consent to God's call, or reject it, is ‹the act› of our own will'. The latter

Not only does not count against the saying 'For what do you have that you did not receive?' [1 Cor. 4:7] but actually counts in its favour. For the soul cannot receive and have the gifts here referred to, except by consenting. (*Sp. Lit.* 34.60)

The gifts of faith and good will can only be received by consent; therefore in causing their receipt God must be causing their receipt by consent.

So much for the first argument. The next two that I shall examine depend on the assumption that each divine grant of prevenient operative grace is prevenient in *time*, occurring before the human decision which it causes. Augustine often quotes the saying of Paul that God chose the elect 'before the foundation of the world' (Eph. 1:4) and the saying of Isaiah that the Holy One of Israel 'has made the things that are future' (Is. 45:11 LXX). The latter pronouncement (absent, incidentally, from Jerome's version, which had adopted a different punctuation and sense many years before some of Augustine's uses of this proof-text, e.g. *Corr. Gr.* 14.45) asserts either that every event has a divine cause before it happens or, more strongly, that whatever time you select every event has a divine cause already before that time. Even the weaker thesis yields a second argument for necessity which can be exemplified as follows:

(B) If God caused me to decide now to smile, it follows that I decide now to smile;
God's having (in the past) caused me to decide now to smile is now necessary;
Therefore it is now necessary that I decide now to smile.

The first premise is common to (A) and unexceptionable, being an instance of the general truth that a thing's being caused to happen entails its happening. The new second premise, stronger than in (A), appears to rest similarly on a very general principle, viz. that everything which happens is necessary thereafter – the Necessity of the (relative) Past. Before discussing it, let us consider whether by containing this strengthened second premise (B) avoids the fallacy in (A). The inference from the two premises of (B) appeals to a theorem of modal logic stating that

121

necessity (present in the new second premise) is transmitted by entailment (as asserted in the first premise), *from* any entailing proposition which possesses it, *to* what that proposition entails. This theorem has been known since the time of Aristotle, and was to receive the following formulation from Jonathan Edwards (1703–57) in his discussion of divine foreknowledge:

> 'Tis also very manifest, that those things that are indissolubly connected with other things that are necessary, are themselves necessary. (*Freedom of the Will* 2.12, p. 258)

The kind of necessity to which Edwards' theorem is applied in argument (B) is temporal – the kind which something has at a time if it is inevitable at that time, *then* unavoidable, unable then not to be (or have been, if the 'something' antedates the time of inevitability, as in (B)). In that application the theorem has been challenged (see e.g. Lamb 1977), but I shall be content to assume that the challenge can be met, as I believe it can.

So we return to the second premise of (B), and its sustaining principle, the Necessity of the Past. Like Edwards' theorem, this principle has a long history going back to Aristotle at least, and it too is championed by Edwards, who says:

> In things which are past, their past existence is now necessary: having already made sure of existence, 'tis too late for any possibility of alteration in that respect. (ibid. p. 257)

Is Edwards right? He argues here to the past's necessity from its unalterability, but in order to see whether the past really is unalterable in such a way as to be necessary, we need to examine quite carefully what the claim to have altered it amounts to. Consider what it means to say that the weather has altered. It has altered if and only if it was one way in the past and is not that way now, e.g. if rain was falling at dawn but is not now falling at noon. Correspondingly, the *past* weather will have altered if and only if *it* was one way in the past and is not that way now, e.g. if the *dawn* rain was falling at dawn but is not now falling at noon. Plainly there is no possibility of such a thing: whereas other dimensions, for instance place, can of course make a difference to what happened at a given time, time itself cannot make a difference; so nothing counts as its *coming to be* the case that something has already happened. In this sense, then, the past is indeed unalterable: it cannot be revoked – 'Nor all thy Tears wash out a Word of it' (cf. *Doct Christ.* 2.28.44). On the other hand the future is unalterable in exactly the same sense: if something so far won't happen, it cannot come to be the case that it will happen. This should make it clear that the sort of unalterability which belongs alike to past and future is not enough to make what is past at a time necessary at that time. We might still have *power* over the past; for such power no more consists in being able to change what did not happen into what did (or vice versa) than power over the future consists in being able to change what will not happen into what will (or vice versa).

What is intended, rather, by distinguishing the past as unalterable is that there is no possibility of a thing's being caused after it has happened: nothing counts as *bringing it about* that something has already happened. From this it would genuinely follow, as Edwards asserts, that what is past is necessary – necessary because no power remains of causing it to have been otherwise (for there is no power to do something if nothing would count as doing it). But is the past in fact unalterable in this further sense? Paradoxically the answer is no, for there might be cases of backwards causation: for example, a brigand might have caused Augustine *to have seen* Hippo for the last time by catching him on the road to Carthage and selling him into permanent exile. The example, it must be admitted, is phoney in a way, perhaps because there is 'a covert future reference' (Swinburne 1977:170, cf. Plantinga 1976) in the word 'last' which makes the caused event not purely past relative to its causing event. In any case, the second premise of (B) can be defeated only by finding a counter-example to the narrower principle that *everything God causes* is thereafter necessarily caused by him, and the narrower principle looks a good deal firmer than the principle that *everything that happens* is thereafter a necessary happening.

Yet even the narrower principle is vulnerable. A theist might propose, for example, a doctrine of prayer according to which my prayer could be effective in securing that there is a letter waiting for me from the friend I long to hear from. If such prayers are ever effective, what they do is either to cause God now to cause the letter *to have been* written and posted earlier, or cause God *to have caused* the letter to be written and posted. Thus either he who prays or God who answers the prayer will be causing the past. In either case the causing is not of the phoney variety, but makes a real difference to how the past was; and in the second case the prayer causes God to have caused something, so admitting the continuing possibility that he should have caused it even in cases in which he did not. Whether Augustine's doctrine of prayer encompasses this idea that prayers sometimes affect the past, I have not managed to elicit (he certainly thinks that the outcome of successful prayers is fore-known to God – *City* 5.10, *Gen. Lit.* 6.17.28 – but leaves it unclear whether he thinks such prayers efficacious in causing an earlier decision by God). That, however, is irrelevant to the case against the second premise of (B), which rests on its being *possible* – whether or not actual – that prayers should operate in such a way (for dispute on this see Geach 1969 ('Praying'): 90, and Dummett 1964: 338–42). It would be unsafe, then, for a theist to rely on argument (B); moreover, I know no evidence that Augustine does rely on it.

There are two ways of trying to patch (B) up: here is one.

(C) God's having in the past willed that I decide now to smile causes me to decide now to smile;
God's having in the past willed that I decide now to smile is now necessary;
Therefore my deciding now to smile is now necessary.

This changes the second premise into something safer than in (B); for now it says nothing against the project of bringing it about that a previous act of will *did not cause something* – such might still be possible, and so the causing not yet necessary – but only rejects the possibility of bringing it about that a previous act of will *did not occur*. However, the first premise also is changed, and this makes the validity of (C) correspondingly more disputable. For (C) must now rely for validity not on Edwards' theorem that entailment, or 'indissoluble connection', transmits necessity, but on the claim that *causation* transmits necessity, *from* a now inevitable cause *to* the effect of which it is the cause. If that claim were true, it would be a serious and notorious threat to freedom, not only for theological reasons. Very many atheists too would allow that decisions often have causes (or causal ancestors, which turns out to be almost equally worrying) which occurred before the lifetime of the decider, and over which therefore he had no control even at the time of their occurrence. If their inevitability relative to him is transmitted to the decisions they cause, then many if not all human decisions are inevitable. However, this new claim about the transmission of necessity should not be accepted; and was not accepted by Augustine, who admitted 'causes of the will' that can be resisted (*Lib. Arb.* 3.18.50).

Strict omnipotence

There remains however the possibility that divine causes are special, and special in such a way that they, at least, do transmit necessity. Perhaps God's will cannot be resisted, either by causing him not to have willed in the past, 'before the foundation of the world', or by causing his past will not now to be efficacious. If so, we can construct a theological challenge to freedom which combines the advantages of validity (according to Edwards' theorem), absent from argument (C), with a safe second premise, absent from argument (B). It goes as follows:

(D) If God in the past willed that I decide now to smile, it follows that I decide now to smile;
God's having in the past willed that I decide now to smile is now necessary;

Therefore my deciding now to smile is now necessary.

At this point the theist is really hard pressed, and must explore every route of escape with care. Let us start by considering whether Augustine can, after all, deny the 'safe' second premise (common to (C)). Wyclif (c.1330–84) would have said that he can, but at the expense of placing God outside time; for Wyclif formulates argument (D), but puts its statements of God's activity into the present tense with the purpose of expressing timelessness:

> For the following argument is valid: God ordains this; therefore this
> will necessarily come to pass at the appropriate time. The antecedent
> is outside any created power and is accordingly altogether
> unpreventable. Similarly, therefore, is everything which formally
> follows from it. (*De Universalibus* 342, quoted in Kenny 1985:36)

The objection to freedom in the argument so tailored 'is answered', Kenny tells us, 'in dramatic fashion. Wyclif simply denies the antecedent: God's ordaining is not altogether outside our power' (Kenny 1985:38). Thus Wyclif's suggestion is that a divine decision to cause a human decision can in turn be subject to that human decision, and so is not a necessary or inevitable circumstance of the human decider's situation. And this can happen because the human decider's power to thwart God's will is not a power over the past, but over a divine act which happens altogether outside time.

Augustine was well situated to anticipate these Wycliffian tactics against argument (D), since he also – despite the many contrary indications we have met in the two last chapters – places God outside time (see chapter 9); but the opportunity was not grasped by him. Perhaps this was wise, for it is not at all clear that the mutual dependence which Wyclif urges, of a human on a divine decision and the latter on the former, is easier to accept in the absence of any temporal relation between the two of them than it would be if one preceded the other in time, or they were simultaneous. In any case, Augustine gives us no indication of dissent from the second premise of (D), so that we can now turn back to the first premise.

An appealing way of understanding omnipotence is as efficacy of will: to say that God is omnipotent is to say that whatever he wills to be so is so. This efficacy will have to be regarded as *universal* and may, but need not, be regarded also as *necessary*: that is, we may either treat God's omnipotence as ensuring that if he wills something that thing always happens as a matter of fact, or we may treat it as ensuring more strongly that if he wills something that thing always happens as a logical consequence of his willing it – the divine will entails the occurrence. Let us call the latter *strict omnipotence*. (D)'s first premise then represents God

as strictly omnipotent; and accordingly argument (D) proffers a case –
a powerful one – for the view that strict divine omnipotence is incompatible with human freedom. On the other hand omnipotence that is not
strict (as in the first premise of argument (C)) has not been shown to
pose the same threat.

Bare theism would presumably be indifferent between these two
conceptions of God's omnipotence; so we need now to turn to the
particular dogmas of Christian orthodoxy. On the question whether
Christians must regard divine omnipotence as strict three things remain
to be said: theologians have differed, Augustine wavers, and my own
view is that they need not. I shall end this chapter by substantiating the
first two of these claims, leaving the third to take care of itself.

In favour of strict omnipotence is Calvin's opinion that:

‹God› moves the will not, as has been taught and believed by many
generations, in such a way that it is afterwards in our choice whether
to comply with the movement or thwart it, but by working on it
effectively [efficaciter afficiendo] (*Christianae Religionis Institutio*
2.3.10);

and a century after him the Roman Catholic Jansen was papally
condemned for denying that 'Prevenient . . . grace is such as the human
will can resist or comply with' (Bull, *Cum Occasione*, Denz. no. 2004).
We note here that by Jansen's time this philosophical dispute cut across
the division between Catholics and Protestants, and among the latter
also there were dissentients from the official Calvinist line, such as
Arminius who – chiming with the Vatican – could write:

The whole controversy reduces itself to the solution of this question,
'Is the grace of God a certain irresistible force [vis]?' That is, the
controversy does not relate to those actions or operations which may
be ascribed to grace (for I acknowledge and inculcate as many of
these actions or operations as any man ever did), but it relates solely
to the mode of operation – whether it be irresistible [irresistilis] or
not. (*Declaration* 4, p. 122b, Nichols vol 1, p. 600).

For their own affirmative answer to Arminius' crucial question both
Calvin and Jansen claimed Augustine's authority; and a celebrated foot-
note of Gibbon, concurring, opines that the real difference between
Calvin and Augustine 'is invisible even to a theological microscope'
(*Decline and Fall* chapter 33, note 33). My own conclusion will be that
it is just not clear whether Augustine was a Calvinist and a Jansenist on
this matter. (The scholarly dispute, incidentally, had earlier origins: in
the ninth century a monk called Gottschalk had been kept in prison
by archbishop Hincmar of Rheims for maintaining that Augustine disbelieved in free will; Armstrong 1967: 579.)

'Thy will be done.' Augustine certainly believed at least the plain omnipotence doctrine that God's will *is* done, always: it is unvanquished, 'semper invicta' (*Sp. Lit.* 33.58); infidels who 'act against God's will when they do not believe his gospel, do not thereby vanquish it' (ibid.); and God 'does what he wills when he wills even with the very wills of men' (*Corr. Gr.* 14.45). The last of these dicta is offered as a reason for concluding that

> It is therefore not to be doubted that the will of God, who 'has done everything in heaven and earth, whatever he willed' [Ps 134 [Heb. Bib. 135]:6] and who also 'has made the things that are future' [Is. 45:11 LXX], cannot be resisted [non posse resistere] by human wills so as to prevent him from doing what he wills (*Corr. Gr.* 14.45).

This on the face of it is an inference from plain to strict omnipotence, from 'God's will is never thwarted' to 'men have no power to thwart it', an inference so evidently fallacious that we may suspect Augustine of not intending it, but merely using 'cannot' as a rhetorical flourish. Earlier in the same book he has addressed the question of a correspondent whether Adam was granted the gift of perseverance. No, he answers, because Adam did not persevere; the gift to Adam and the angels was only free decision whether or not to sin, God's purpose in the gift being to demonstrate what free decision could do (posset, *Corr. Gr.* 10.27). Because that experiment failed, we later men need, and the elect among us get, a greater gift, 'such aid in perseverance . . . that not only can they not be persevering without that gift, but also they are not other than persevering by means of [per] it' (*Corr. Gr.* 12.34). Although this sentence might, on its own, be understood as displaying the difference between enabling and operative prevenient grace, the gift of ability not to sin and the gift of not sinning, Augustine's preceding explanation has ascended to a different difference, that between being able not to sin and being *unable* to sin:

> We must carefully and attentively consider the differences within the following pairs, being able [posse] not to sin and not being able to sin, being able not to die and not being able to die. . . . Initially freedom of the will was . . . the power of perseverance; ultimately it will be the happiness of perseverance, of not being able to lapse from good. (12.33; cf. *Pecc. Mer.* 2.8.10, *City* 22.30)

Are the living saints in this 'ultimate' state? Evidently not, for 'as long as they live here they are fighting the lust for sin, and some sins creep up on them [subrepant]' (12.35). On the other hand Augustine goes on to tell us that the weakness of human will is helped 'So as to be inflexibly and invincibly [indeclinabiliter et insuperabiliter] effected by divine grace'

(12.38). 'Some editions', according to a commentator, 'read "inseparabi-
liter", in a dogmatic interest.'

A passage from the *Enchiridion* leans quite far towards the doctrine
of strict omnipotence. In discussing the troublesome Pauline text, '‹God›
wills that all men should be saved' (1 Tim. 2:4) Augustine found himself
obliged to interpret the apostle as meaning that all who are saved are
saved by God's will (*Ench*. 103.27; this and other passages contain
alternative suggestions – *Corr. Gr.* 15.44,47; *City* 22.1,2; *C. Jul.* 4.8.44).
The reason why the straightforward interpretation will not serve is that
it permits inference to the falsehood that all men *are* saved; and the
inference would be unimpeachable, Augustine says, because 'God cannot
will in vain anything that he has willed' (*Ench*. 103.27; Aquinas, incidentally, was later to agree: 'God's willing a man to be saved and his actually
being damned are incompatible', *De Veritate* 23.5). Is the word 'cannot'
again a rhetorical exaggeration, or does Augustine, like Aquinas, mean
what both of them say? His *argument* does not need the word, since
the actual but non-necessary truth of 'God's will is always done' suffices
for raising his problem how to square Paul's text with the doctrine that
some of us are damned. On the other hand if he does regard the divine
will as *necessarily* efficacious in this one department, when God wills to
save a man, there seems no reason why he should deny it in other
departments, as when God wills that a man should make a good decision;
and if he accepts it in all departments, he believes in strict omnipotence.

Thus in his treatment of Arminius' crucial question Augustine's
expression is unclear. But the candid critic will conclude not just to that,
nor even just that his thought is confused. Commenting at the end of
his life on one of the questions addressed long before in the *Ad Simplicianum* he wrote, 'On the solution to this question I tried hard to maintain
the free decision of the human will, but the grace of God was victorious'
[vicit] (*Retract*. 2.1). Probably in the same year as composing the *Retractationes* in which this comment occurs he had assured a Carthaginian
named Vitalis that Catholic Christians know that 'Those who in their
very own heart believe in the Lord do so by their own will and by free
decision' (*Ep*. 217.8.16, cf. *Gr. Lib. Arb.* 2.2). I fear that on this difficult
matter Augustine was among those 'theologians ‹who› are insufficiently
reluctant to contradict themselves' (Lucas 1970:76).

Further reading

The fullest recent study is Burns (1980). Warfield's introduction to
NPNF 5 summarizes Augustine's writings on Pelagianism. Augustine is
defended point by point in Jauncey (1925). On the treatment of Jonathan
Edwards see Plantinga (1986).

VII

First and last things

The existence of original sin

Julian (*c*.386–454), bishop of the small town of Eclanum in southern Italy, landowner, son and son-in-law of bishops, well connected inheritor of the traditions of Roman culture and imperialism, was out of tune with the spirit of his age, a man doomed to be one of history's failures, a defender of causes that were lost. The Pelagians gained in him a clever and pertinacious disputant, but not the astute politician they needed. The tone of his controversy with Augustine shows both parties aware of these facts of power: Julian strident in his hatred of the new provincial barbarism which he discerned in western Christianity, with its Jewish sense of despondency before the crimes and inadequacies of men, its dark self-abasement; Augustine harsh and contemptuous, unwilling to offer the courtesies of sober debate which he had used even against pagans in the *City of God* and always against his antagonists nearer home, but demolishing Julian like a house in the path of road improvements. It is a sorry episode.

Julian comes to the notice of history as one of eighteen recusant Italian bishops who would not sign the letter issued by pope Zosimus in 418 as a test of anti-Pelagian orthodoxy (p. 105). Deprived of his see in his mid-30s he spent the remainder of his life in exile from Italy, at first in the east, later in Sicily. None of his writings survive for sure except quite extensive quotations in Augustine. He was the author of two public letters to which Augustine replied in *Contra Duas Epistolas Pelagianorum*, and of an attack on the first book of Augustine's *De Nuptiis et Concupiscentia* which was answered in the second book and, more fully, in *Contra Julianum*. Julian responded to the former answer, promptly and at length. Then there was a lull, while this 'Second Response' made its slow way westwards, eventually reaching Augustine via Alypius, who copied and forwarded it from Rome where he was staying. Augustine replied in the six scornful books of his unfinished work, *Contra Secundam Juliani Responsionem, Opus Imperfectum*.

The dispute between Augustine and Julian ranged over four main topics, marriage, grace, baptism, and original sin. The connection between these four is revealed in a long letter written by Augustine about 427 to a certain Carthaginian, Vitalis, containing an affirmation of twelve propositions against the Pelagians, of which the first encapsulates in his admirable Latin most of the twists of his teaching on original sin:

> Since by Christ's atonement we are Catholic Christians, we know that unborn children have done nothing in their own lives, good or bad, and have not come into this wretched life following [secundum] their deserts in some previous life, which none of them can have had as his very own [propriam]; and yet, being born carnally following Adam, by the first moment of their birth they contract the contagion of an ancient death, and are not freed from the penalty [supplicio] of eternal death – a penalty imposed by just conviction [damnatio] transmitted [transiens] from one man to all men – unless through grace they are reborn in Christ. (*Ep.* 217.5.16)

In commenting on Augustine's doctrine of original sin we shall not need to look far beyond the contents of this masterly summary.

Augustine's proof that original sin exists is perfunctory, for all the importance of the concept to him. The concept's role, as we saw in chapter 4, is the crucial contribution to his explanation of evil that is made by asserting that all men, even newborn babies, merit punishment; for once that premise is accepted, suffering can be represented as entirely within the plan of a just God, who is never outsmarted by the malevolent princes of darkness. It can be represented, for example, like this:

> This life itself, if you can call it a life, full of evils of every shape and size, is evidence that the whole race of mortals has been convicted [damnatam], in its first origin. What other conclusion can be drawn from the shocking abysses of ignorance to which are due all the errors that have gathered every son of Adam to their dark bosom and which men are unable to escape without labour and pain and fear? Or from our love of so much that is trashy and injurious, and the heartache that results, the worries and sorrows and panics, the sordid fascinations, the conflicts and struggles and wars and plots and animosities, the hatred, lies, flattery, fraud, theft, robbery, and betrayal; the insolence and self-seeking and envy; murder at large and in the family; cruelties and brutalities, depravity and dissipation, impudence, shamelessness, and indecency; the lechery, the adultery, the incest, and those unnatural and disgusting acts between members of the same sex which it is foul even to

mention; sacrilege, heresy, blasphemy, perjury, and victimization; slander, deception and duplicity; evidence false and verdicts unjust; violence, terrorism, and all the other evils which do not occur to the mind but occur sure enough to human lives? Of course, these are the doings of bad men; but they stem from that root of error and misdirected love with which every child of Adam is born. You can see ignorance of truth in an infant, and attraction to trash of all kinds begins to show in childhood. Surely everyone knows that men come with these things into this life and, if allowed to live as they will and do as they will, advance to many if not all of the crimes and misdeeds I have listed, and to the many I have not managed to list. (*City* 22.22, cf. *C. Sec. Jul.* 2.89, 3.76)

'Men come with these things into this life.' If we brush aside Augustine's rhetorical claim that everyone knows this, and ask for a proof of it, he offers nothing satisfactory. For 'other conclusions' *can* be drawn, as we have noticed already in chapter 4 (p. 71). Writing to Jerome in 415 Augustine had been willing to quote an earlier suggestion of his own that the value of infant suffering may be to teach parents a lesson; for the children quickly forget their experience, and in any case God can make it up to them later (*Ep.* 166.18, quoting *Lib. Arb.* 3.23.68). Why then persist in the fantastical view that there is original sin? According to N. P. Williams (to whose valuable study (1927) I am indebted greatly) he relies on five biblical texts:

For I was conceived in iniquity, and in sins my mother nourished me in the womb. (Ps 50 [Heb. Bib. 51]:7, quoted e.g. at *Enarr. Ps* 50.10; *Pecc. Mer.* 1.14.34, 3.7.13; *Conf.* 1.7.12)

Who is clean from sin? Not even a child whose life on earth is of one day. (Job 14:4–5, repunctuating the LXX which itself is wrong; NEB, following Vg, has 'Who can produce pure out of unclean? No one. The days of his life are determined. . .'; quoted e.g. at *Pecc. Mer.* 2.10.15)

Unless one is reborn out of water and spirit, one is not able to enter the kingdom of God. (Jn 3:5)

Through one man sin entered into this world, and through sin death, and thus death was transmitted to all men, in whom [sc. the one man] all have sinned. (Rom. 5:12, misinterpreting 'in quo omnes peccaverunt', the Greek original of which must mean 'in that all have sinned', see pp. 138–9 below.)

For we too were once in our natures children of wrath. (Eph. 2:3, 'fuimus enim et nos aliquando naturaliter filii irae'; the right sense is more probably 'We were once ourselves too objects of wrath.')

Williams comments, 'The slenderness of the Biblical foundation upon which Augustine's terrific dogma is reared will be realized when it is pointed out that of his five proof-texts three are mistranslations' (1927:379); and one might add that of the other two the psalmist at that juncture in his lament appears to be ascribing sin to the pregnant woman, not her foetus (cf. Clement, *Stromateis* 3.17.100, apud Williams 1927:207), while the saying of Jesus to Nicodemus in John's gospel is not explicitly about sin at all.

I conclude that this philosophical inquiry need take no further notice of that part of Augustine's doctrine which asserts that there *is* original sin. On the face of it the assertion is preposterous; and although something might be done to raise its plausibility by sensitive interpretation of the name 'peccatum originale' – which I have so far left in its considerable obscurity – Augustine's arguments give us no sufficient motive for understanding the task.

The nature of original sin

However, a connected question remains which is of philosophical interest: if there *were* original sin, how could it merit punishment? It is on this further question that most of Julian's strictures bear, and I shall argue that Augustine cannot evade them. Of course, much turns on what the expression 'original sin' means, so we must now turn to the question what Augustine meant by it.

If babies are sinners one might infer that they have sinned in a previous life; but in the *De Peccatorum Meritis* (1.22.31) Augustine argues against the (Platonist) idea of reincarnation, quoting Paul's description of Jacob and Esau as 'not yet born, and not having done anything, good or bad' (Rom. 9:12). We have seen the same conclusion, and the Pauline phrase supporting it, worked into Augustine's letter to Vitalis; and it is reinforced elsewhere by his insistence that a baby's original sin is not voluntary (voluntate, *Pecc. Mer.* 1.9.10; propria voluntate, ibid. 15.20; voluntarium, ibid. 17.22; 'actual', the theologians' later word, seems not to have been used by Augustine). On the other hand the assertion that there is original sin means more in his general usage than to say that Adam, our origin, was a sinner (albeit that is the sense of 'originale peccatum' at its first occurrence in his works, *Ad Simplicianum* 1.1.10). Usually the sin of Adam is imputed to each of his descendants also, as Donne was to impute it to himself – 'Which is my sin, though it were done before' ('To Christ', *Poems*, p. 338; another version has 'was' for 'is') – while in the next breath Augustine is willing to say, as in the Vitalis letter, that it is not their 'own' (proprium): 'Babies . . . are born sinners by origin, not personally [parvuli . . . nascuntur non proprie sed originaliter peccatores]' (*City* 16.27, cf. 16.35).

All this threatens incoherency within the concept of original sin, and the threat is a double one. In the first place, Augustine is obliged to explain how someone can *be* a sinner through a sin which is not his *own*. He attempts to discharge the obligation by means of a horticultural metaphor, traduction, literally 'bringing across'. A tradux is a layer, that is, a plant-shoot which has bent back to the earth and struck root, eventually to be detached from the parent plant; hence traductio is propagation by layers. Augustine's theory states that 'We have brought across from Adam [ab Adam . . . traduximus], in whom we all sinned, not all our sins but only the original one' (*Pecc. Mer.* 1.13.16). Sometimes alternatively he uses the legal metaphor of inheritance, as when he speaks of our being 'Born in the inherited nappies of a flawed origin' (*C. Jul.* 2.6.15).

The metaphors fit with a theory of infirmity or disease – 'contagion' in the letter to Vitalis – such as that which makes the erect habit in Lombardy poplars, all propagated asexually (Julian in one of his crasser objections pointed out that human beings, by contrast, need two parents, *C. Sec. Jul.* 2.56–9). The sources of this theory have been traced, for example by Williams (1927), to Jewish literature of the last three centuries BC, including the pseudepigraphic 1 Enoch which builds its account on the Adam-story in Genesis 2–3 and on the even more primitive Watchers-story in Genesis 6:1–8 (Williams 1927: lectures 1,2). Its attraction springs from the fact that it reduces the problem why sin exists in most of God's human creatures (or in all, Job 15:14–15, Ps 129 [Heb. Bib. 130]:3) to the apparently more manageable problem why it came to exist in one of them. And it performs the reduction by postulating a taint or corruption introduced into the stock as a result of the first transgression by Adam (or in some accounts Eve). Augustine was among the Christians to whom this theory had descended. He speaks of the human race having a 'corrupted origin, like a diseased root' (*City* 13.14). He ruminates on his own case as a 15-year-old, when with a gang of other boys he had stolen pears out of pure mischief (*Conf.* 2.6.12–9.17). He is particularly struck by the waywardness and incompetence of infants: they struggle during baptism (*Pecc. Mer.* 1.36.67), lose their tempers if thwarted (*Conf.* 1.6.8), and won't be told what is good for them (*Conf.* 1.7.11). Admittedly the womb is small, but God could have made children 'grow up at once' (*Pecc. Mer.* 1.37.68). Human babies cannot even find the nipple (ibid. 38.69).

The trouble with the taint theory is that it imputes not sin but at worst sinfulness, a tendency or liability to sin; and such a tendency, when not yet actualized in sinful deeds, seems not to be blameworthy, let alone good cause for eternal damnation. Despite Augustine's insistence that 'This great infirmity of flesh points to something, I do not know what, but great enough in my judgement to be penal' (*Pecc. Mer.* 1.37.68), the uncommitted reader is more likely to sympathize with Julian's outburst:

> Babies, you say, carry the burden of another's [aliena] sin, not any of their own. . . . Explain to me, then, who this person [iste] is who sends innocents ‹to punishment›? You answer, God. . . . God, you say, the very one who commends his love to us [Rom. 5:8], who has loved us and not spared his son but handed him over to us [Rom. 8:32], *he* judges in this way; *he* persecutes new-born children; *he* hands over babies to eternal flames because of their bad wills, when he knows they have not so much as formed a will, good or bad. . . . It would show a just and reasonable sense of propriety to treat you as beneath argument: you have come so far from religious feeling, from civilised standards, so far indeed from common sense, that you think your Lord capable of committing kinds of crime which are hardly found among barbarian tribes. (*C. Sec. Jul.* 1.48, after Brown 1967:391)

This passage also exposes the second of Augustine's conceptual difficulties with original sin: all sin is voluntary, but original sin is not voluntary, not 'propria voluntate'. Rubbing at an old wound Julian had earlier written: 'The greatest difference between Manichees and Christians has always been this . . . that we attribute all sin to a bad will, they to a bad nature' (*C. Sec. Jul.* 1.24). He pointed out that many years earlier Augustine had contended against the Manichees in his *De Duabus Animabus* that 'Sin is the will to bar or admit what is forbidden by justice and is free to be avoided' (*C. Sec. Jul.* 1.47, quoting *Du. An.* 11.15). The *Retractationes* contain a lengthy comment on the treatise in which this earlier definition had appeared. In the course of it Augustine makes the surprising remark that the definition on which Julian was to fasten applies only to sin, not sin's penalty. The point is elaborated against Julian:

> That definition of mine which you approve of has reference to Adam. . . . To be sure Adam, when he sinned, had absolutely no bad in him to urge him unwillingly to doing bad [ad operandum malum] and make him say, 'The good that I will I do not do, but the bad that I will not, that I do' [Rom. 7:19]; and that is why in his sin he did what was forbidden by justice and had been free for him to avoid. For when someone says, 'The bad that I will not, that I do', it is not free for him to avoid. And *that* is why, if you keep in mind . . . that sin is one thing, the penalty of sin another, and the combination of them a third (that is, a sin which is itself also a penalty of sin), you will understand which of these three the definition applies to [viz. the first]. . . . An example of the second

kind is the bad which someone in no way does, but only suffers, as when someone who has sinned is put to death for his own offence. . . . The third kind . . . can be understood ‹as exemplified› in him who says, 'The bad that I will not, that I do'. (*C. Sec. Jul.* 1.47)

This is terribly confused. 'Sin' cannot *mean* 'penalty of sin', nor can anyone be said to have sinned (erred, offended, transgressed) *in* suffering the penalty for a sin – let alone be said to incur liability to (further) penalty in so suffering! Augustine's point about his third kind is that some post-Adamic sins (he does not think all) fail the test for freedom (in the second degree, see chapter 5) by failing to be such that the sinner 'does not do' them 'if he wills not to' (*Sp. Lit.* 31.53, see p. 86 above): they are committed unwillingly (nolens). But here the problem is spurious and the remedy misguided. The problem arises because Paul's famous description of himself in Romans chapter 7 as subject to the 'law that is in his members' appears to present his sinful actions as not in accord with the determinations of his will. But Augustine's word for will, 'velle', is ambiguous; and despite Paul's own conclusion that 'I do not even acknowledge my own actions as mine' (Rom. 7:15 NEB) it is open to us to construe 'nolens ago', 'I do it, willing not to', as meaning no more than 'I do it unwillingly', a sense which certainly allows the sinful action to be *also* voluntary, done in accordance with the will, and so conformable to the definition of sin in *De Duabus Animabus* (Augustine must surely have thought so when he wrote that book, and see *Sp. Lit.* 31.53, quoted on p. 88). There is therefore no need to see Paul's confession of weakness as a reason for admitting a special kind of sin not entailing freedom in the second degree. Moreover, if this special conception is nevertheless introduced, Augustine's purposes will not be met by characterizing it as involving both sin and the penalty of sin. For one thing, the involved sin – whose presence is supposed to be a necessary but not sufficient condition of this new kind – will have to be understood as sin of Augustine's first kind, which *is* voluntary; therefore the new kind will be voluntary too, contrary to what is required for solving the supposed problem. Furthermore, the general difficulty which Paul's predicament was intended to elucidate is not eased in the slightest degree by regarding some sins as penalties. For that general difficulty was how to attribute original sin to any man except Adam, who committed it. The claim that newborn children are under a penalty of sin can indeed be made sense of, if the sin is Adam's; but such an understanding makes the claim *assert* Augustine's theory, and so does nothing to remove the *difficulty* in the theory, which was how anyone can be under a penalty of sin if he himself is not a sinner.

The problem therefore remains of justifying God's alleged anger against those who have done no wrong – alike whether the anger is supposed to be expressed in making their lives miserable or their deaths eternal. Augustine has not yet destroyed the apparently strong reasons for rejecting what in the letter to Vitalis he describes Catholic Christians as knowing, that those who 'have done nothing in their own lives, good or bad . . . are not freed from the penalty of eternal death . . . imposed by just conviction'. We must now pass to consideration of two more serious attempts in his writings to defend this paradox, one of which questions the principle that it is unjust to punish one person for another's offence, while the other questions whether Adam's descendants need be regarded as distinct from Adam.

Transmission of guilt

What a magnificent way for the gods to be fair! Do you think any state would tolerate someone who enacted a law whereby a son or grandson could be convicted for a crime committed by his father or grandfather? (Cicero, *De Natura Deorum* 3.38.90)

The principle to which Cicero here appeals had won acceptance long before he wrote. Aeschylus (525/524–426 BC), in his plays about the curse on the family of Atreus, has the chorus hint at one point that Agamemnon activated that curse upon himself only by his own crime of sacrificing his daughter Iphigeneia to gain a fair wind for the expeditionary fleet against Troy (*Agamemnon* 218ff.; I owe this comparison of Greece and Israel to de Ste Croix 1977:146); and still earlier in the writings of Ezekiel, who flourished about 580 BC, and in Deuteronomy, often identified with the book of the law 'discovered' under king Josiah in 621 BC, we read two famous biblical passages:

Fathers shall not be put to death for their children, nor children for their fathers; a man shall be put to death only for his own sin. (Deut. 24:16 NEB)

What do you mean by repeating this proverb in the land of Israel:
  'The fathers have eaten sour grapes,
    and the children's teeth are set on edge'?
As I live, says the Lord God, this proverb shall never again be used in Israel. . . . It is the soul that sins, and no other, that shall die; a son shall not share a father's guilt, nor a father his son's. (Ezek. 18:2–3,20 NEB, cf. the perhaps slightly earlier Jer. 31:29–30)

Augustine knew these passages, of course; but unlike some other theologians – e.g. the healthy-minded John Taylor (1694–1761) (1741: Supplement p. 13) – he did not imagine that everything in the Old Testament could be squared with their apparent message. Instead he rejected Cicero's implication that God should be judged by the standards appropriate to human legislators, citing Deuteronomy 5:9 as proof that 'The authority of divine law wills that sons should not pay penalties for their parents in human judgements, but does not do so in divine judgements' (*C. Sec. Jul.* 3.15). The verse of Deuteronomy on which this is a comment represents God as promising punishment on the children 'for the sins of the fathers to the third and fourth generations of those who hate me'.

At this point one may be tempted to hold up one's hands in horror, echoing Julian's sentiment that Augustine's teaching on divine justice is 'beneath argument', although for a reason Julian himself would not have approved of: his willingness to rely on the *authority* of such vindictive sayings in the Old Testament. But that would be too quick, for there are analogies which pose a rational challenge to the Cicero–Ezekiel principle. No one doubts that it is possible to transmit *debts*. In a well-run society Adam's death would leave Adam's estate; and Adam's estate would pass by due process of law to Adam's legal heirs. If Adam had contracted a debt to God, it would then be due from those heirs, and presumably from their heirs in turn so long as it remained unpaid. Many thinkers have been willing to extend this notion of transmissibility to *obligations*, for example of white Americans to black Americans, arguing that mistreatment of blacks by whites in one generation imposes an obligation on heirs of those whites to compensate the heirs of those blacks, in a later generation. And here we move one step nearer to Augustine's doctrine, because the heredity now invoked is by blood, not law: it is racial. From the idea of racial obligation it is then not a great further step to the idea of racial culpability: perhaps the whites inherit blame for their ancestors' misdeeds, from which they may be presumed still to profit at the blacks' expense.

I submit that this last step makes a bad analogy, or in other words a confusion, which can be described equivalently as confusion between compensation and punishment, or between debt and guilt. So long as the imposition of disadvantages on a new generation is intended as recompense to others who suffer what one might call an 'original disadvantage' it might – though only might – be justified; but as punishment it is not justified, because punishment requires guilt which cannot be transmitted. This was Julian's complaint: since God is just

> It is plain . . . that no one can be held ‹by him› guilty of another's sin, nor therefore is there any way of convicting the innocence of the newborn for the faults of their parents; because it would be an injustice if guilt were transmitted through semen. (*C. Sec. Jul.* 3.11)

In the case of guilt before a human court, we have seen that Augustine agrees with this; but what difference can the court make? When Donatists imputed the supposed guilt of certain African bishops during the Great Persecution to their Catholic successors down to Augustine's day, Augustine did not scruple to quote against them the view of their common hero Cyprian of Carthage (d. 258), that 'no one can be stained by someone else's [alienis] sins' (*Ep.* 93.10.36); and he has this to say in humane reassurance to the victims of rape at the sack of Rome in 410: 'The fear is that even someone else's [aliena] lust will defile. It will not defile if it is someone else's; if it defiles, it will not be someone else's' (*City* 1.18). Only unreasoning adherence to authority, surely, could have brought him to think that the judgements of God are exempt from this rule.

We were Adam

The judgements of God will not need to be exempt, however, if we humans on whom they are passed are not really *distinct* from our ancestor Adam. For in that case guilt for Adam's sin will need no transmission: as Adam's, it is already ours. Augustine makes several attempts to develop this idea. An early one occurs in his response to Simplicianus' request for exegesis of Romans 9:10–29:

> But carnal lust [carnalis concupiscentia] is dominant now, from the penalty of sin, and has lumped all the human race together as it were into one whole conflux, permeated in every part by original guilt [originali reatu]. (*Simp* 1.2.20)

The image is Paul's of God as a potter moulding clay (Rom. 9:20–3, see p. 147 below), which Augustine finds anticipated in Ecclesiasticus (33:13; cf. Jer. 18:5–10) and uses often elsewhere (for example 'the convicted lump of all humanity', 'totius humani generis massa damnata', *Ench.* 27.8). Here guilt is racial and collective: it belongs to the 'conflux' of men, and thereby to every man in that conflux. Moreover the conflux arises from 'carnal lust' (compare 'being born carnally following Adam', in the Vitalis letter), and this hints at Augustine's bizarre theory that we contract original sin from the manner of our generation, in particular from the fact that our parents must have been moved to the intercourse which starts the process off by an urge that affected their bodies involuntarily (see pp. 195–6).

Alongside this crude account of corporate culpability is another with rather more respectable credentials. It is based on the text of Romans 5:12, in which Paul says four things: first, that sin entered the world through Adam, that is, through Adam's act of disobedience in eating the forbidden apple; second, that death entered through that sin, that is, God punished Adam's disobedience by withdrawing the presumptive gift of eternal life on earth (Gen. 3:19); third, that this mortality was transmitted to Adam's progeny (compare 'the contagion of an ancient death' in the Vitalis letter); and finally that the reason justifying such transmission is that all the progeny are sinners too. The Pelagians drew Augustine's attention to the Greek expressing this final point, '*eph' hōi pantes hēmarton*', 'in that all have sinned'; but Augustine dismissed their interpretation as 'a sense both novel and distorted, at variance with the truth' (*C. Jul.* 6.75). Instead he stuck to his ambiguous Latin version 'in quo omnes peccaverunt', and explained its 'quo' as having for antecedent either Adam's sin (impossible in the original because of gender) or – his standard interpretation – Adam (impossible in the original because of the preposition '*eph*' ', i.e. '*epi*'; see *Pecc. Mer.* 1.10.11, *C. Du. Ep. Pel.* 4.4.7). Starting from this misconstrual he then faced the problem of understanding 'in'. The natural comparison would be with such Pauline phrases as 'In you [Abraham] all nations shall be blessed' (Gal. 3:8, quoted by Augustine, *Pecc. Mer.* ibid.) or 'As in Adam all die, so in Christ shall all be made alive' (1 Cor. 15:22), where the force is 'through'. But Augustine thinks that we sinned 'in' Adam because we *were* in Adam, present in his 'loins', i.e. genitals (*C. Sec. Jul.* 1.48). Furthermore, to be in Adam is to *be* him:

> But the man, having been corrupted by his own act [sponte], and justly convicted, produced offspring who are corrupted and convicted. For all of us men were in that one man when all of us were that one man. . . . There were not yet individual forms created and assigned to us to live in as individuals; but there was a seminal nature from which we were to be propagated. (*City* 13.14)

> Such ‹original› sin is not called someone else's in the sense of being wholly unrelated to the infants, since [si quidem] everyone sinned in Adam at the time when, in his nature, by the power residing in him which made him able to produce them, they still all were that one man; it is called someone else's because they were not yet living their own lives, but contained in the life of one man was everything in his future progeny. (*Pecc. Mer.* 3.7.14)

Augustine is likely to have shared the widespread ancient misconception that animals grow only from their fathers' semen, the mother contributing nothing beyond a receptacle and a channel for nourishment. Given the misconception it is not implausible to hold that each animal is already present in its father's genitals, or even, as part of a part, in its paternal grandfather's, and so on backwards. On such a basis Augustine is in a position to defend the claim that God 'completed all his work on the sixth day' of creation ('consummaverit omnia opera sua in die sexto', Gen. 2:2 LXX) by taking God to have created each subsequent man in

– literally as a part of – the first man. However, this will need qualification: God made the birds and beasts

> In one sense *then*, namely potentially and in cause [causaliter], as fitted the work of simultaneous creation from which he rested on the seventh day, but in another sense *now*, as we see them created by him over the course of time, in his 'activity up to the present' [Jn 5:17]. (*Gen. Lit.* 6.5.7; see Sorabji 1983:302–3)

> For all things have already been created in their origins and beginnings [originaliter ac primordialiter], in a web of elements as it were; but they reveal themselves when they get their opportunities. Like mothers pregnant with their children, the world itself is pregnant with the causes of things which come to birth. (*Trin.* 3.9.16)

The 'potential' and 'primordial' creation produces what the Stoics had called seminal reasons (*spermatikoi logoi*; seminales rationes, *Gen. Lit.* 9.17.32). For Augustine, each man's seminal reasons must be not merely something which has the potentiality for becoming him but also something which in a way is him.

But we have still to ask whether this 'way' is firm enough to justify the imputation of Adam's guilt to every later human being. It is not, for two reasons. First, even if the seminal reasons concreated with Adam include one which *is* me, not just later to become me, that will make me identical not with Adam but only with a tiny part of him; and the human race as a whole, of which Augustine says 'We were that one man', will have occupied no more than one member of Adam. It is merely ridiculous to extend to the members of a human body the principle that may often properly be applied – changing the senses – to the 'members' of a 'body' of humans, that each such member shares culpability for the body's misdeeds.

Secondly, even if Augustine had been able to make out that each of us is identical with Adam, he would have had to face Locke's objection that

> If the same *Socrates* waking and sleeping do not partake of the same *consciousness* . . . to punish *Socrates* waking, for what sleeping *Socrates* thought, and waking *Socrates* was never conscious of, would be no more of Right, than to punish one Twin for what his Brother-Twin did, whereof he knew nothing. (*Essay* 2.27.19)

The problem here is that time can affect guilt: although it is valid to argue 'Adam was guilty; I am Adam; therefore I was guilty', it is not valid without further premises to argue 'Adam was guilty; I am Adam; therefore I *am* guilty'. Locke thinks that guilt for a past offence survives only so long as memory of the offence is not lost 'beyond a possibility of retrieving' (ibid. 20). Others have judged that view too lenient, among them Augustine who challenged Julian to say of the sinner:

> What if he forgets that he has offended, and is not pricked by consciousness [conscientia] of it, where will his guilt be, which as you concede survives the passing of his sin, until its remission? It is certainly not in his body, not being one of the accidents that can belong to a body; and it is not in his mind [animus], because his memory of it has been destroyed by his forgetting; yet it is. Where is it, then. . . ? (*C. Jul.* 6.19.62)

The answer Augustine proposes – 'in the hidden laws of God, inscribed somehow on the minds of angels' – is not to the point. The answer he should have given, conformably to a standard ancient conception which he shared, is 'in the soul [anima]'; for guilt is a property not of bodies but of souls, or at least not of soulless bodies but of ensouled, animated, ones (Augustine had not outlived the conception of soul as that which animates *all* living things, or at any rate all animals – thus flies have souls, *Du. An.* 4.4). So if my identity with Adam is to justify imputing Adam's long-ago guilt to me now, it is not enough that Adam should survive to be me: his soul must survive to be mine. Now the criterion of identity of souls is (as Locke also pointed out) both obscure and not necessarily connected with memory. But whatever it takes to secure that Adam's soul is mine, at least we can deduce from this argument that my soul must have *existed* at the time of Adam's sin; and it is therefore the seeds of that soul, not (merely) of my body, which Augustine must postulate in the first man if he is to prove original guilt by this route.

Such an objection had been put by Pelagius (see *Pecc. Mer.* 3.3.5); and Augustine, puzzled about the origin of the soul, made it the subject of a number of letters and tracts, one to Jerome in 415 (*Ep.* 166, see p. 68–9), one to a certain bishop Optatus in 418 (*Ep.* 190), and three to Renatus, Peter and Vincentius Victor which he subsequently collected as *De Anima et ejus Origine* (420–1). One view on the matter, traducianism, had been elaborated by an earlier African theologian, Tertullian of Carthage (*c.*160–*c.*225), but Tertullian's version lacked appeal to the Platonist in Augustine because it made the soul material (*Retract.* 2.56, *An. Orig.* 1.5.5, 2.3.7, 4.12.18). Nevertheless Augustine himself speculated to Jerome whether the soul was a tradux:

> Since, therefore, we cannot say of God either that he compels souls to become sinners or that he punishes the innocent, and since there is no question for us of denying that souls, even those of babies, which leave the body without Christ's sacrament are consigned to be convicted [damnari], no less, I beg you to tell me how we are to defend the opinion which holds that all of them come into being

not from the one soul of the first man but each for each man, as his did for him. (*Ep.* 166.10, cf. *An. Orig.* 1.13.16)

It had been put to Augustine that the difficulty (which we have already encountered) of reconciling Genesis 2:2 LXX with 'my father is active up to the present' (Jn 5:17) was an argument for the view that God fashions new souls out of old ones, specifically out of Adam's, and transmits Adam's guilt in that way (*Ep.* 166.11). But Augustine himself felt that even new creation at birth was consistent with Genesis, as not being creation out of nothing (ibid. 12). This letter, we recall, elicited no reply from Jerome, and whether or not for that reason Augustine, as he relates at various places in his anti-Pelagian writings (e.g. *Pecc. Mer.* 2.36.59, 3.10.18, *An. Orig.* 1.15.25), settled into scepticism 'on the origin of souls'. But he should not have done so, if he was to rely at all on every man's being 'in' Adam as the ground for imputing Adam's guilt to the whole human race. That argument *requires* traducianism – the pre-existence of each individual soul, or of a stem or root or seed which can at need be identified with it; the later history of Adam's semen is nothing to the purpose.

Hell

Original sin was supposed to explain the phenomenon of infant suffering. I have argued that the explanation fails, both because original sin's very existence remains unproven in view of the fact that other explanations of the phenomenon are available, some open even to Christians, and also because a necessary step in the explanation by way of original sin cannot be justified, the step, namely, which imputes guilt to those who bear this kind of sin. In the course of our discussion the motivating theme of infant suffering has begun to be overshadowed by another supposed consequence of original sin, damnation. For Augustine additionally, in the words of his letter to Vitalis, takes the Catholic Christian to 'know' that unborn children 'are not freed from the penalty of eternal death . . . unless through grace they are reborn in Christ' (*Ep.* 217.5.16). This rebirth is to be attained by baptism, according to the saying of Jesus applied by Augustine to life after death: 'Unless one is reborn out of water and spirit, one is not able to enter into the kingdom of God' (Jn 3:5; the Greek has just 'born', but cf. 3:3). Finally, the outlines of Augustine's eschatology are completed by adding that the sole post mortem alternative to the kingdom of God is hell, 'everlasting wretchedness' as he wrote to his Hipponese congregation during an absence in the countryside convalescing from an illness, 'the dreadful pains [poenae] of eternal fire' (*Ep.* 122.1). This comes from Jesus' reported description of the Last Judgement:

When the Son of Man comes in his glory . . . he will separate men into two groups, as a shepherd separates the sheep from the goats. . . . Then he will say to those on his left hand, 'The curse is upon you; go from my sight to the eternal fire that is ready for the devil and his angels. . . .' And they will go away to eternal punishment, but the righteous will enter eternal life. (Mt. 25:31–46 NEB)

Jesus' curse was on those who have neglected their positive duties in this life. When the curse is extended to all who have not received God's grace, including all who die unbaptized, the question arises, Why? Punishment of man's first disobedience begins in this theology to seem to engage a disproportionate part of the divine attention. As Donne was somewhere to plead:

If we shall say, that Gods first string in this instrument [i.e. his plan], was Reprobation, that Gods first intention was for his glory to damn man; and that then he put in another string, of creating Man, so that he might have some body to damn; and then another of enforcing him to sin, that so he might have a just cause to damne him; and then another, of disabling him to lay hold upon any means of recovery: there is no musick in all this, no harmony, no peace in such preaching.

I do not suggest that all this is Augustine's preaching: he would deny that damnation preceded creation in God's purpose, or that Adam was 'enforced' to sin. But still, one would like to know why eternal fire is a suitable penalty on all of us for having issued, by way of sexual appetite, from the seed of someone who did not do what he was told. Through inclusion of the threat of hell Augustine's preaching on original sin becomes, as Williams says, a 'terrific dogma'.

The reason doubtless is that Augustine felt himself more closely constrained by the words of Jesus as reported in Matthew than by Paul's proclamation of a redeemer and saviour 'who wills that all men should be saved' (1 Tim. 2:4), which we have already seen him consequently struggling to explain away (p. 128). Against the complaints of more tender souls, like Julian, his response was always to seek justification of these divine arrangements: proof of them seemed to him needless (an exception is *City of God* 21.17–24, all exegetical; and he does insist, whenever the occasion arises, that the suffering of babies who die unbaptized will be 'extremely mild', 'mitissima poena', *Ench.* 93.23, cf. *Pecc. Mer.* 1.16.21).

Predestination

To this eschatological doctrine Augustine applied the Pauline idea of predestination. Paul had written:

> For God knew his own before ever they were, and also ordained [*proōrisen*, praedestinavit] that they should be shaped to the likeness of his Son, that he might be the eldest among a large family of brothers; and it is these, so fore-ordained [same Greek and Latin], whom he has also called. And those whom he called he has justified, and to those whom he justified he has also given his splendour. (Rom. 8:29–30 NEB)

In the parallel passage at Ephesians 1:2–14 choice (electio) is inserted before predestination, and the promise to these elect is inheritance when the time is ripe, presumably a reference to the imminently expected second coming of Christ. Thus Christian exegesis has always assumed that the elect are those who at the Last Judgement will be set at the right hand of the Son of Man and will enter eternal life. Predestination likewise: although the word merely means 'foreordaining', theological usage commonly applies it only to God's decisions fixing each man's final destination, heaven or hell.

It would be possible to hold that God makes these decisions in advance only for the heaven-bound, the saints. So thought Augustine's champion Prosper of Aquitaine, who was followed in this by the Councils of Orange and Trent (controversy over Augustine's teaching on the matter was acute in the sixteenth century, as it had earlier been in the ninth). Prosper complained that Augustine's opponents, such as Vincent of Lérins, accused him of saying:

> It is the will of God that a great number of Christians neither will to be saved [salva] nor can be. . . . God wills that a great number of saintly people should topple from their intention of sanctity. . . . Adulteries and seductions of consecrated virgins take place because God has predestined these people to fall. (*Contra Vincentium* 7,9,10)

Thus in praying 'Thy will be done' these unfortunates are praying for their own downfall (ibid. 16). Prosper responds to the accusation by citing the Augustinian distinction we have already encountered (p. 117) between divine will and divine foreknowledge (*Responsiones contra Gallos* 15): although God foresees the destiny of the damned, 'there is no question of ascribing to ⟨him⟩ the cause of their downfall' (*Contra Vincentium* 13); 'God is on no account going to make them topple and fall' (ibid. 16).

These replies conform with Augustine's teaching about God and bad, but it is not obvious that they are available to him. In *De Anima et ejus*

Origine he wrote: 'To those whom ‹God› has predestined to eternal death, he pays out punishment with total justice [justissimus retributor]' (*An. Orig.* 4.11.16). If this and a few similar passages (e.g. *Ench.* 100.26, *City* 15.1, 21.24) in support of 'double predestination' should be brushed aside, there is another Augustinian thesis, plainly intended seriously, from which an argument can be developed to the same conclusion that not only the saved but the damned are predestined. It is the thesis of the numerus clausus, which states that the number of the saints is closed by God's predestination, so that no one will be saved *unless* his salvation has already been predestined. In the *City of God* Augustine speaks of the original (or rather conditional) will of God that, had Adam not sinned, his progeny would have multiplied 'until the number of predestined saints was completed' (*City* 14.10). The case is similar in God's actual will:

> I am speaking of those who are predestined to the kingdom of God, whose number is so determined [certus] that nobody can be added and nobody subtracted from them. . . . That the number of the elect is determined, not subject to increase or subtraction, besides being hinted by John the Baptist . . . is stated more overtly in the Apocalypse, 'Keep hold of what you have, in case someone else should get your crown' [Rev. 3:11]. For if it is not to be got by someone else without the first one's losing it, the number is determined. (*Corr. Gr.* 13.39, cf. ibid. 9.20, *Don. Persev.* 8.19)

To be certus, I argued on p. 100, is to be resolved or decided on. If, then, not only the size but also the composition of the set of saints is decided in advance by God, all the saints are predestined saints.

From this premise there is an argument leading to the conclusion that, likewise, all the damned are predestined to damnation, or rather, what is no less worrying, are damned of necessity and so lack the power of avoiding hell. Since the argument employs principles (of modal logic) that are not altogether perspicuous, I shall set it out with a running commentary.

(1) All who are saved are predestined to salvation.

This states the numerus clausus.

(2) All who are predestined to salvation are necessarily saved.

Here already Augustine might object; but we have examined in chapter 6 (p. 124ff.) the case for judging that he is committed to the view that *God's* will imposes necessity, and we have found it a strong one.

(3) All who are not necessarily saved are not saved at all.

This follows straightforwardly from (1) and (2).

(4) All who *necessarily* are not necessarily saved, *necessarily* are not saved at all.

This involves assuming that (1) and (2), and hence (3), are themselves to be accepted not just as true but as necessary truths. There is room for challenge here too, perhaps especially in the case of (1); but neither (1) nor (2) seem to be the kind of proposition one could readily embrace as contingent. If (3) is necessary, then (4) follows from it by what I have called Edwards' Theorem (p. 122), that 'Those things that are indissolubly connected with other things that are necessary, are themselves necessary.'

(5) All who are not necessarily saved, *necessarily* are not necessarily saved.

This is an instance of the theorem of modal logic that whatever is *un*necessary (i.e. possibly not so) is necessarily unnecessary. That theorem also can be challenged, and can be avoided: it belongs only to systems of modal logic containing the system called S5. But S5 has powerful credentials (see my *Logic and Argument*, 1978:228–30).

(6) All who are damned are not saved, and conversely all who are not saved are damned.

The first half is obvious and the second, rejecting extinction (see *Doct. Christ.* 1.21.20) or a permanent limbo, accords with Augustine's reading of Matthew 25.

(7) All who *necessarily* are not saved, *necessarily* are damned.

This follows by Edwards' Theorem from the second half of (6), provided once again that we are allowed to assume that the latter is a necessary truth if true at all.

(8) All who are not saved, are not necessarily saved.

What is not so is, a fortiori, not necessarily so. The conclusion can now be reached. For assume someone damned; by applying in succession the first half of (6), and then (8), (5), (4), and (7), we can infer that he is necessarily damned. Therefore:

All who are damned are damned necessarily, QED.

God's favouritism

Whether or not the inhabitants of hell were predestined by God to their everlasting torment, God could have saved them from it. True, they did not deserve salvation. But then no one deserves it, and yet by grace, that is, as a favour, some get it; and these do not. Two questions arise: why does God's grace alight where it does? and isn't it unfair?

Why are others not saved? Why not more? Why not all?

> Didn't my Lord deliver Daniel, Daniel, Daniel?
> Didn't my Lord deliver Daniel?
> Then why not every man? (Negro Spiritual)

Augustine's reply is that he does not know. Quoting the peroration of Romans chapter 11 he says:

'How inscrutable are his judgements, and untraceable his ways! Who knows the Lord's mind [sensum]? Who has been adviser to him?' Hence we have very limited minds [sensum] for analysing his gratuitous grace, which is not unfair [iniquum] because we have no merits in advance, though it disturbs us less when offered to the undeserving than when denied to others equally undeserving. (*Pecc. Mer.* 1.21.29)

It is the same with the distribution of God's co-operative aid (ibid. 2.5.6). Against Julian's charge that Augustine makes God 'eager for us to become more just than he is, indeed not *more* just, but us fair and himself unfair', he blandly answers: 'What are you saying, you ignorant man? Just as much as divine justice is loftier than human, so it is more inscrutable, and so too it is remoter from human' (*C. Sec. Jul.* 3.24), and he cites God's practice, unjust in a man, of permitting crimes which he has power to prevent.

But as this reply makes clear, we can resign ourselves to concluding that God's motives are undetectable without calling into doubt whether his conduct is just; and the latter Augustine, stout champion of theodicy, will not do. His chief proof-text is once more from Romans, discussing God's partiality between the twins Jacob and Esau. Paul asks:

What shall we say to that? Is God to be charged with injustice? By no means. For he says to Moses, 'Where I show mercy, I will show mercy, and where I pity, I will pity' [Ex. 33:19]. Thus it does not depend on man's will or effort, but on God's mercy. For Scripture says to Pharaoh, 'I have raised you up for this very purpose, to exhibit my power in my dealings with you, and to spread my fame over all the world' [Ex. 9:16]. Thus he not only shows mercy as he chooses, but also makes men stubborn as he chooses. . . . Surely the potter can do what he likes with the clay. Is he not free to make out of the same lump two vessels, one to be treasured, the other for common use? (Rom. 9:14–21 NEB)

'Therefore', Augustine commented to Simplicianus in 395, 'All men . . . are as it were a single lump of sin [massa peccati], owing [debens] punishment to the divine, supreme justice; and whether it is exacted or remitted, there is no unfairness [iniquitas]' (*Simp*. 1.2.16). But is there really no unfairness? I shall argue to the contrary, basing my argument on a distinction of Joel Feinberg's between comparative and noncomparative justice.

Augustine seems to use the words 'iniquus' and 'injustus' interchangeably (cf. *Qu. An.* 9.15), as we may with equal propriety interchange the English 'unfair' and 'unjust'. But in both languages there are – naturally – differences of nuance between the members of the pair, and the connection of etymology between 'aequus' and 'aequalis' (noted in *Qu. An.* 9.15) suggests that the former's opposite 'iniquus' will be specially suitable for expressing a comparative idea of injustice. Be that as it may, it certainly can express that idea, which Feinberg (1974:298) explains as follows:

> In all cases, of course, justice consists in giving a person his due, but in some cases one's due is determined independently of that of other people, while in other cases, a person's due is determinable *only* by reference to his relations to other persons. I shall refer to contexts, criteria, and principles of the former kind as *noncomparative*, and those of the latter sort as *comparative*.

Kinds of act which typically invite judgements of comparative injustice include awards of prizes, where injustice is done when the prize is withheld from the *best* candidate, who merits it not from the intrinsic character of his performance but from its character in comparison with the performance of the other competitors. On the other side, typical acts of noncomparative injustice include frauds and slanders, where the victim is denied some good that is due to him absolutely, not because of his position in relation to other potential recipients of it. As well as these, however, there are also cases in which the very same kind of act, or even the very same individual act, can be just or unjust both comparatively and noncomparatively, or just in one of the two ways and unjust in the other. Punishments are an example: whenever mercy is shown to one of a pair of malefactors and not to the other, then unless this discrimination of treatment responds to some relevant difference in their circumstances (one is a first offender, say, or has children to support, or has suffered a recent calamity), a comparative injustice is done to the one from whom mercy is withheld. All the same, this unlucky one may have got no worse that his due, when his due is assessed by some standard such as a penal code or the calculation of a policy of deterrence, independently of the actual treatment of others like him. If he complains of his worse treatment in comparison with his accomplice, the sentencing judge may be able to reply that though worse than what the accomplice suffers it is no worse than what the complainant deserves; for the accomplice, granted mercy, has got better than he deserves.

From a judge in court we might be content with such a reply, since it would be possible to conceive the task of a judge as being limited to dispensing noncomparative justice. Nevertheless it seems to me that there is something incomplete about the reply if it fails to acknowledge that in another way the complainant is right: it *is* unfair if someone else is shown mercy when he, *ex hypothesi* no less pitiable or pathetic, is not. This man is treated justly *and* unjustly: justly in that the treatment matches his deserts, unjustly in that it ranks him below another whose deserts are no greater than his. A conception of justice which ignores the latter, comparative, dimension of assessment is a defective one.

Augustine has this defective conception. We have seen him claim that 'Whether the punishment is exacted or remitted, there is no unfairness'; and so far as I can discover he is always deaf to the suggestion that there might be a comparative unfairness in the vast discrimination between God's final awards to the saint and the damned, both of whom are, according to the doctrine of original sin, parts of the same 'lump of sin'. The most we get are some reasons – not very edifying – intended to explain why God should have exacted the penalty of hell from *some* of his creation instead of remitting it to all. Commenting on God's statement in Exodus, quoted by Paul, that he had raised Pharaoh up in order to exhibit his own power and spread his own fame, Augustine says:

> This exhibition [demonstratio] of the power of God and proclamation
> of his name in all the earth is useful [prodest] for implanting fear
> in those who are suited to that manner of invitation [vocatio], and
> for correcting their ways. (*Simp*. 1.2.18; Augustine's experience
> was that nearly all applicants for Christian instruction were motivated
> by fear, *Cat. Rud*. 5.9)

After the Last Judgement, when this deterrent purpose will no longer be served by hell, a different 'usefulness' will come into play; for the saints will then enjoy gazing on the spectacle of what they have themselves escaped.

There is a precedent for Augustine's narrow view of justice, in a passage of Matthew that he cites in his exposition to Simplicianus of Romans chapter 9. It is Jesus' parable about the vineyard, telling of a landowner who hired successive groups of labourers through the day. In the evening all were summoned to be paid off:

> When it was the turn of the men who had come first, they expected
> something extra, but were paid the same amount as the others. As
> they took it, they grumbled at their employer: 'These latecomers
> have done only one hour's work, yet you have put them on a level

with us (*isous epoiēsas*), who have sweated the whole day long in the blazing sun!' The owner turned to one of them and said, 'My friend, I am not being unfair (*ouk adikō*) to you. You agreed on the usual wage for the day, did you not? Take your pay and go home. I choose to pay the last man the same as you. Surely I am free to do what I like with my own money. Why be jealous because I am kind?' Thus the last will be first, and the first last. (Mt. 20:10–16 NEB)

It is an important truth that indignation should not be confused with envy ('jealousy'). Nevertheless it seems to me (as it has since I first met the story in childhood) that those who bore the burden and heat of the day had a just grievance; they were treated badly. A part of Julian's complaint about Augustine's use of original sin to justify eternal damnation is essentially of the same kind: that a truly just God would not show favouritism, extending favour (grace) beyond their (alleged) merits to some but not all of those he judges. I side with Julian.

Further reading

Williams (1927) is learned, critical and judicious. Warfield's introduction to *NPNF* 5 summarizes the controversy with Julian.

VIII

Meditations on
beginnings

Creation

Augustine wrote the *Confessions* in his early 40s, when he had been bishop for about five years. In the Latin usage of his time a confessor was not – as we oddly apply the word – one who hears confessions, but one who makes them; and there are two ways of making them, by acknowledgement of sins and declaration of allegiance. Augustine sees the latter as praise:

> Confession can be understood in two ways, either in our sins, or in praise of God. Confession in our sins is well known, so well known to people that they beat their breasts whenever they hear the word 'confession' in a reading, whether it is meant in praise or whether of sins. (*Enarr. Ps* 141.19)

'The former', he says in another place, 'expresses sorrow, the latter joy; the former shows the wound to the doctor, the latter says thank you for curing it' (*Enarr. Ps* 110.2). What these passages ignore is that a confession of praise must be advertised: it is an act by which a Christian – particularly in earlier penal times a persecuted Christian – proclaims his Christianity, takes sides, 'comes out'. This, as much as confession of sins, is the theme of Augustine's *Confessions*; and although the work is addressed as a prayer to God, it is essentially a public document.

It begins with nine books of autobiographical self-examination, in which Augustine traces his development through infant delinquency, acquisition of speech, idleness at school, the fascination of lewd stories from the classics, the episode of stealing pears (see p. 133 above). Then at Carthage we detect behind the somewhat prudish language an able, bumptious, popular, and rather conceited undergraduate growing serious-minded as he joins the Manichees, takes on domestic duties, and applies himself to (vaguely portrayed) academic pursuits. He remembers his affliction at the death of a dear man friend (see p. 187 below), and reflects on the differences of love towards man and God. Books 5 to 9 tell in fuller detail the story of his years in Italy, culminating with baptism at Milan and the death of his mother Monica at Ostia in 387. The theme of confession then reasserts itself, for the work does not end with this end of its autobiographical part. Book 10 is a disquisition on human powers (especially memory) and human weaknesses. At the start of book 11 Augustine proclaims his longing to spend every hour free from unavoidable refreshment of self and service to others in 'meditating on your law, confessing to you my knowledge and incompetence in it, the inklings of your illumination and the residue of my darkness, until infirmity is swallowed up by strength' (*Conf.* 11.2.2). 'Meditating on your law' quotes Ps 118 [Heb. Bib. 119]:18, and accordingly Augustine's meditations begin with Genesis, the first Book of the Law, which he also treated in his two earlier and one later commentary, *De Genesi contra Manichaeos*, *De Genesi ad Litteram Imperfectus Liber* and *De Genesi ad Litteram*. But in the remainder of the *Confessions*, books 11 to 13, this examination reaches no further than the creation, and then only the so called 'Priestly' account of it in Genesis 1 (part of a biblical stratum dated by modern scholars to the period of the Babylonian Exile, 586–538 BC, or slightly later, and distinct from the more ancient strata to which are assigned the independent creation story, telling of Adam and Eve, in Genesis 2:4–3:24).

Augustine starts his enquiry into Genesis chapter 1 by asking God to give him understanding 'How in the beginning you made heaven and earth' (*Conf.* 11.2.3, quoting Gen. 1:1). Taking Moses, in the traditional way, as author of the five Books of the Law, he says that he would have turned to Moses himself for elucidation, had Moses been still alive and able to speak Latin; that authority would have been sufficient, since something 'in the domicile of my thought' would have told Augustine that the answers he received were true. Lacking such access to the author, he must be content to rely on the fact that heaven and earth 'proclaim' their creation, 'clamant quod facta sint' (cf. 'proclamat', *City* 11.4.2); by which I take him to mean that clarification of the biblical account is available by the use of reason and argument:

> They proclaim that they have been made. For they undergo change and variation; whereas if anything has not been made, and yet is, there are not things in it that were not in it before (which is what it is to undergo change and variation). They proclaim also that they did not make themselves: 'We are there,' ‹they say,› 'because we have been made; therefore we were *not* there, before we were there, so as to be able to be made by ourselves.' And the voice of the speakers

is the evidence of the fact. It was you therefore, Lord, who made them. . . . (*Conf.* 11.4.6)

This argument is partly drawn from Plato's *Timaeus*. Plato had argued from four premises to the conclusion that 'the whole heaven or cosmos' is divinely made (*Timaeus* 27d–28c):

(1) The cosmos is perceptible;
(2) everything perceptible comes into being;
(3) everything that comes into being does so by the agency of (*hupo*) some cause;
(4) every cause that is an agent must be a craftsman (*dēmiourgos*); therefore the cosmos comes into being by the agency of a craftsman.

To this Platonic argument Augustine makes three amendments. First, he suppresses the reference to perception, substituting as first premise that the cosmos is subject to change. Secondly he amalgamates the second and third premises into the claim that everything which changes must have been made or, equivalently, what has not been made never changes. Thirdly, he varies Plato's doctrine of the divine craftsman by putting creation in place of fabrication. This is because Plato conceives a craftsman as necessarily working with pre-existent entities: the Platonic demiurge proceeds by 'looking to' forms that were not of his own making (28a) and imprinting them on matter that was not of his own making either (49a). Augustine's God, by contrast, has no such materials available for working on: 'For what is if not because you are?' (*Conf.* 11.5.7). The divergence between Judaeo-Christian and Platonist cosmogony in this respect was a commonplace of which Augustine shows himself aware:

‹God did not act› as a human craftsman forming body from body by a decision [arbitratu] of his soul, which is able somehow to impose on a form [speciem] that it sees in itself by its internal eye. (*Conf.* 11.5.7)

Christians on the contrary have to believe that God created the cosmos ex nihilo, since anything else derogates from divine omnipotence:

For the builder does not make the wood, but makes something from the wood, and so it is with all other craftsmen of this kind. But almighty God needed the help of nothing that he had not made himself for carrying out his will. For if he was helped in making the things he willed to make by some other thing that he had not made, he was not almighty: and to believe that is blasphemy [sacrilegium]. (*Gen. Man.* 1.6.10)

Elsewhere Augustine concedes that God made the heaven and earth 'from unformed matter', citing Wisd. 11:18; but he also made the matter, since to be almighty 'he who furnishes things with their form [formam] must furnish also the possibility of their being formed' (*Fid. Symb.* 2.2).

This reasoning of Augustine's is surely unsatisfactory both in its reliance on Plato and in its departures from him. It is well known that there are pervasive arguments in Plato for the thesis that everything perceptible is subject to *change*; but these, whatever their merits, will not serve the purpose of the *Timaeus* without the further claim, explicit in Augustine, that everything subject to change has a *beginning*. The claim is neither plausible in itself nor substantiated by Plato or Augustine. We are given no reason for thinking that what is mutable must have had an origin in time and what is everlasting must be changeless; even if coming into existence is counted as itself a kind of change, it needs to be demonstrated why the cosmos, or anything else, has to have that kind as a consequence of having others, and want of any such demonstration destroys the force of Plato's and Augustine's argument.

There is a second, and familiar, weakness in the move made by both philosophers from 'the cosmos began' to 'someone made it'. Why should the beginning of each thing have a cause? Why, if it does, should the cause be an agent? Why a single agent? The last of these questions (though not the other two) does attract Augustine's attention, and in order to examine his response to it we must at this point ask how much is supposed to have been created at the creation. In the passage we are examining Augustine uses the biblical description 'heaven and earth'; elsewhere the word is often 'universe', 'mundus' (e.g. *City* 11.4.2). Now if the mundus includes literally everything, then Augustine's own argument shows that it cannot all have been made, since nothing can make itself. But if the mundus excludes God, why should it not also exclude other beings – good or bad angels, say – who might then share God's creative activity? Such was the Manichaean cosmology, which had God as the power of light in contest with uncreated powers of darkness, and creation as a weapon used by each of these superpowers in its struggle to master the other (according to the Manichees Adam was made by Satan); we have already in chapter 4 considered Augustine's objections to this dualism. As to the good angels, Augustine considers their candidature as creators in the *City of God* 12.25–7 (or 24–6 – there are two chapter-numerations from 12.11 to the end of book 12, and I give both), but only under the assumption that they are also creatures, acting with God's 'permission or command' (*City* 12.25 (24)). Against the Platonist (if not Plato's) view that such lesser gods created mortal animals, or at least the bodies of mortal animals (*City* 12.27 (26)), he replies feebly that creatures cannot create because their supposed creative power is given from elsewhere and could be withdrawn by its giver:

Consider then the form [specie] which builders impose on bodily things from outside. We say that the cities of Rome and Alexandria were founded not by builders and architects but by their kings, Romulus and Alexander, by whose will and plan and command they were built. How much more then ought we to call none but God the founder of natures [conditorem naturarum], who neither makes anything from matter that he has not himself made nor uses workmen whom he has not himself created; and if he were to withdraw from things what we might call his 'building' power, they will no more be than they were before they were made. (*City* 12.26 (25))

But what if there were uncreated good angels? Perhaps Augustine would bring to bear his conviction that God is the lord, dominus. In *City* 12.16 (15).1 he uses that to show that God must always have creatures to dominate, and I suppose it could also be used to show that there cannot be other uncreated beings, such as would be needed according to the above reasoning if God's creative work were to be shared.

Finally, when we turn to Augustine's specifically Christian idea that the making of the cosmos had to be *ex nihilo*, creation rather than fabrication, we find that he rests this dissociation from Platonism on the authority of the Bible and not on argument. Whereas Plato can anticipate the Aristotelian doctrine that every change, including coming into existence, imprints pre-existing form on pre-existing matter, Augustine feels compelled by his reading of Genesis to assert that God 'held nothing in his hand from which to make heaven and earth' (*Conf.* 11.5.7). It remained for later Christian philosophers to respond to Parmenides' challenge, evidently heeded by Aristotle, that nothing will come out of nothing (Parmenides, fragment B8 lines 7–9).

I conclude that Augustine's attempt at a proof of what is said in the first verse of Genesis 1 is not a success.

Creation a finite time ago

The doctrine of creation had been the target of many attempted refutations in the centuries before Augustine wrote, refutations that had been found convincing by the majority of ancient philosophers, Plato seemingly excepted (see Sorabji 1983: chs 13–15). What the philosophers objected to was not so much creation itself, but beginning: they could accept, that is, that the universe came into being, and even that it had a maker or makers who brought it into being, but they jibbed at the idea of there being a first moment of its being, a moment with the property that nothing – except perhaps gods – existed before then.

Augustine was aware at least vaguely of this weight of pagan opinion, perhaps through the Platonists who had come to share it and to interpret Plato's own account as metaphorical (Sorabji 1983:271–2); and he responded in books 11 and 12 of the *City of God*. These books, from which I have already drawn some citations, introduce the second half of the work in which, having replied to the enemies of the city of God, he says (11.1.1) he will now speak of the origin, progress, and due destination of the two cities, commencing with an account of how their origins were laid in a dispute among the angels. In fact he starts further back with the very beginning of the universe, and at once diverges into philosophy. In chapter 4 he reminds us of the first verse of Genesis, 'In the beginning God created the heaven and the earth', and asks:

> Why did God decide to make heaven and earth then, which he had not made previously? (*City* 11.4.2)

The question is put by people who wish it to be thought that the universe was not made by God at all, but is eternal and without beginning. These people

> turn their backs too much on truth, and are infected by the fatal disease of disrespect [impietas]. For even if the words of the prophets are set aside, the universe itself as it were silently proclaims, by the wonderful organization of its changes and movements and the wonderful beauty of form in all that is visible in it, that it has been made by none other than God. . . . (*City* 11.4.2)

Here another argument for creation is glanced at, the argument from design. But without pausing to expatiate on it Augustine goes on:

> There are those who acknowledge that it was made by God, but are willing to allow it only a beginning of its creation, not a beginning of time, so that in some scarcely intelligible way it has *always* been made [semper sit factus]. (ibid.)

What do these new opponents mean by 'has always been made'? A weaker and a stronger interpretation are possible: either that there was no time at which the universe was not yet created, or that at all times it had been created earlier – equivalently, that all times in the one case *are*, or in the other case *are preceded by*, times at which it is true that the universe has already been created. Now it will turn out that Augustine himself accepts the truth of this claim in the weaker of the two interpretations; for he will argue both that time began with the universe (see p. 162) and that creation was instantaneous (see pp. 164–5), from the first of which it follows that 'is being created' is true of the universe at the first moment of time, while from the second it follows that 'has been created' is true of it so soon as 'is being created' is. The stronger interpretation, however, places creation an infinite time ago, and that is the one which Augustine next proceeds to examine.

He does not need argument, for it is enough that the thesis of creation at an infinitely remote epoch conflicts with the plain implications of the Bible; and he is willing to accept the chronology in Jerome's translation of Eusebius' (*c.*260–*c.*339) *Chronicon* according to which 'we [Christians] calculate that 6,000 years have not yet elapsed since man's creation' (*City* 12.11). Thus the puzzlement conveyed in his comment that the thesis is 'scarcely intelligible' receives no further notice, and Augustine passes to the question why his opponents should have been attracted by it.

The theory of cycles

The view that the universe was created infinitely long ago had attracted philosophers, Augustine suggests, because it promised to solve a problem; however, he will maintain, the promise fails and anyway there is a different solution. The problem is this: if God made a universe which previously he had not made, then God must have changed his mind, which is impossible in an immutable being. Champions of a beginningless universe

> are saying something which, they think, defends God from the charge
> of acting on random impulse, and avoids the need to believe that
> it suddenly came into his mind, having never done so before, to
> make the universe, and that a new will arose in him although he is
> in every way quite immutable. (*City* 11.4.2)

The thought underlying this charge is that if there is a time when any of God's acts has not yet been done, then there is a time when he has not yet decided to do that act, so that between then and the act his will changes. Now this is a crude thought, and the problem it gives rise to is easily solved by distinguishing between willing a change and changing the will. In the formula 'X decides to do A' there is room for two time references, one for 'decides' and one for 'do'; and these references do not have to be the same in order for the formula to come out true (see p. 178f below). So it is possible for God's will to be immutable, in the sense of there being no time when he has not yet willed it, or in the stronger sense here supposed of there being no first time of his willing it, even if there are times at which the effects of his will – whether creation of the world or indeed later happenings such as miracles – have not yet taken place.

The solution which thus distinguishes willing a change from changing the will was already known before Augustine's time, going back at least to Philo (*c.*20 BC–AD *c.*50); and it reappears as Augustine's own solution to the problem he has raised:

> Though ‹God› himself is eternal and without beginning, nevertheless
> he was starting from a beginning when he made times and man in

157

time, whom he had never made before – but by an immutable and eternal plan, not a sudden new one. (*City* 12.15 (14), cf. 12.18 (17), *Conf*. 11.10.12, 12.28.38)

We say 'it will happen when God wills' . . . not because God will then have a new will which he did not have before, but because what has been prepared in his will from eternity will then be. (*City* 22.2, cf. *Ench*. 102.26, *Enarr. Ps* 101.2.14, *Gen. Lit*. 6.17.28, *Ord*. 2.17.46)

For reasons which I do not understand, Augustine seems to have found this solution somewhat mysterious (it displays the 'altitudo' of God, *City* 12.15 (14); the question it solves is 'very difficult', *City* 12.22 (21)); certainly in the passage we are considering from *City of God* book 11 he goes to it roundabout. His route is via a theory of cycles, which from the fuller treatment in book 12 we know he regarded as Platonist, although he was aware that Porphyry had repudiated it (*City* 12.21 (20).3); we associate it particularly with the Stoics (von Arnim 1903–5:1.109, 2.624). According to the theory, 'nothing new happens which has not happened at a fixed [certis] interval of time previously' (*City* 12.21 (20).3). Its proponents

> think that the same revolutions of time and of things in time are repeated. For example, at a certain period the philosopher Plato taught his pupils in the school called the Academy in the city of Athens. Just so in countless earlier periods, separated by very long but fixed intervals, the same Plato, city, school, and pupils were repeated, as they are due to be repeated in countless later periods. (*City* 12.14 (13))

The same chapter 14 (13) of *City of God* book 12 contains two criticisms of the theory of cycles. It is inconsistent with the Christian beliefs that 'Christ died once [semel] for our sins' and that since his resurrection 'death has no more dominion over him [Rom. 6:9]'; and it is also inconsistent with the assurance that the saints will after the general resurrection be 'always with the Lord [1 Thess. 4:17]'. Later in his discussion in book 12 (12.21 (20)) Augustine supplements this appeal to authority with an argument which has already appeared as follows in book 11:

> They will be quite unable to explain where any new unhappiness [miseria] comes from, which has never previously come to the soul through all eternity. For if they have said that unhappiness has always alternated with happiness [beatitudo], they must also say that these always will alternate. From which they will be led into the absurdity that the soul is certainly *not* happy even in the times when it is said

to be happy, if it foresees its own future unhappiness and befoulment [turpitudo]; while if it does not foresee the coming befoulment and unhappiness, but counts on being happy for ever, it is happy in a false belief, which is as stupid a thing as could be said. (*City* 11.4.2)

The argument is:

(5) No one is happy who fears future misery;

(6) no one is happy who is ignorant of his future misery;

(7) everyone for whom future misery is in store fears it or is ignorant of it;

therefore no one is happy for whom future misery is in store.
But

(8) future misery is in store for everyone in this era;
    while

(9) some men will be happy in some era;

therefore this era will not recur for ever.

We have already in chapter 2 seen the young Augustine setting high standards for human happiness; but here they are higher still, for premise (6), with its echoes of Solon's dictum that one must see a man's end before calling him happy (Aristotle, *Nicomachean Ethics* I.10; also Ecclus. 11:28, see *City* 13.11) expressly rules out happy ignorance. The weakness of the argument surely lies in its combination of (6) with (9). For if a fool's paradise is no paradise as (6) asserts, we may wonder at the confidence which expects paradise at all.

For a cycle-theorist who is content to accept the above argument there remains only one further recourse, to suppose that the alternation of happiness and misery in the endless past will end some time in the future. But that, says Augustine, 'will amount to an admission that something new happens to the soul, a glorious outcome which has never happened earlier through all eternity' (*City* 11.4.2). And in this way the cycle theory too is forced to lay God open to the charge of mutability.

The upshot is that Augustine has not disproved the thesis of a beginningless universe, but has claimed to show that the thesis does nothing to solve the problem of divine mutability which it addressed. The problem calls for the different solution – difficult though this seems to Augustine – that God can will change without changing his will; and that solution leaves Augustine free to embrace the biblical chronology of creation.

A delayed start?

Both in the *Confessions* and elsewhere Augustine raises the question why God created the universe when he did and not at another time. We have examined one response, presented in chapter 4 of *City of God* book 11, where he tells us that the question was asked by thinkers – Platonists, he evidently supposes – who concluded, from the difficulty of answering it, that the universe had no beginning and consequently was not created, though under pressure they substitute 'created an infinite time ago' for 'not created'. Augustine sees these thinkers as stumbling on the idea that God should have changed his will. Once it is acknowledged that a change does not have to be willed at the time it happens, but can be willed earlier (or even perhaps outside time – see chapter 9), Augustine thinks that the Platonist objection to creation a finite time ago will collapse: for it will be possible for God to have willed the creation without forming a new will; his will to create can have been always in existence, immutable.

The fact is, though, that while this theory of the will answers one of the Platonist objections to creation a finite time ago, it does not answer the objection with which *City of God* book 11 chapter 4 begins. For granted that the creation occurred at the time implied by biblical chronology, and granted that God's decision to create was not formed then but had always been in existence (or exists outside time), we may still demand to know why his changeless will was a will *to* create at *that* time, and not sooner or later. There is particular reason for asking why the creation was not sooner. For a superficial view appears to suggest that the sooner it had occurred the shorter would have been the gap between God's forming his decision to create and its implementation, and the gap is an embarrassment because it postulates a time during which God was idle, a wasted time. So the same problem as emerged through the question 'Why did God create when he did?' can also be brought out by asking 'What was God doing before he created?'

The people who ask this latter question are given a hearing in book 11 of the *Confessions*:

> They say to us: What was God doing [faciebat] before he made [faceret] heaven and earth? If he was idle and inactive, they say, why did he not abstain from activity ever afterwards, as he had done earlier? ‹His will could not change, but› if God's will that there should be a creation [creatura] was everlasting, why is the creation not everlasting? (*Conf.* 11.10.12)

Here the objectors argue that nothing except a new will could explain God's change from idleness to creative activity. It is not that God has to be busy, as some pagan philosophers had thought (Sorabji 1983:250); for the God of Genesis rested on the seventh day. The problem is rather that if he had been idle all that long – through infinite ages – there is no reason for his ceasing to be so: he must continue in idleness unless a new cause intervenes. The standing cause, that he has decided to create, is not enough; there would have to be a triggering event also, which makes the decision operative. But, of course, no triggering event can precede the beginning of the universe, if God himself is changeless. So behind the question 'What was God doing?' lies a serious difficulty for the view that the universe had a beginning.

Kant (1724–1804) stated the difficulty as the antithesis of the First Antinomy of Pure Reason:

> For let us assume that the world has a beginning. Since the beginning is an existence which is preceded by a time in which the thing is not, there must have been a preceding time in which the world was not, *i.e.* an empty time. Now no coming to be of a thing is possible in an empty time, because no part of such a time possesses, as compared with any other, a distinguishing condition of existence rather than of non-existence; and this applies whether the thing is supposed to arise of itself or through some other cause. In the world many series of things can, indeed, begin; but the world itself cannot have a beginning, and is therefore infinite in respect of past time. (Kant, *Critique of Pure Reason* B 455, Kemp Smith 1929:397)

Empty time is time in which nothing happens. Kant assumes that the beginning of the world would be preceded by a time, and argues that the time would have to have contradictory properties: it would be both empty, as preceding the world and its happenings, and also occupied by a happening which triggers the world.

It is clear from this that the difficulty behind the question 'What was God doing before the creation?' is the same as that behind Augustine's earlier question 'Why did he create *then* and not sooner?' The sixth-century pagan philosopher Simplicius (fl. *c*.530), commenting on Aristotle, was to bring out the connection. As Sorabji paraphrases him,

> Normally we explain why something is delayed, by pointing to earlier causal sequences, in order to show that the time is not yet ripe. Socrates could not have been born that much sooner, because his parents had not yet met. When we are inquiring about the whole universe beginning, however, there is no earlier causal sequence by reference to which we can explain why things have to wait. (Sorabji 1983:232, commenting on Simplicius, *In Aristotelis Physica* 1176 and 1177.29, *In Aristotelis de Caelo* 137–8)

At least three kinds of response are possible to the problem posed by Kant and Simplicius, and earlier by Augustine's unnamed opponents: (a) there was no triggering event; the creation happened when it did without a cause of its happening *then*; (b) although there was no triggering event, nevertheless the timing of the creation has an adequate *reason* or explanation, viz. that it could not have happened earlier or later; (c) it could have happened at a later time, but not at an earlier time because there was none; when the universe began, time began with it.

Augustine seems averse to the first kind of response. At any rate he represents opponents who postulate an infinite time before the creation as claiming in their own defence that 'it does not follow that we must suppose that God's establishing the universe at that time rather than a prior one was something random [fortuitum] that happened to God' (*City* 11.5). The second kind of response, which is that of Leibniz (1646–1716), seems not to have occurred to Augustine. More precisely, Leibniz was to distinguish two hypotheses: God might have extended history backwards, by tacking on extra events before the actual beginning (a trial universe, for example, which he subsequently abolished); or God might have advanced the beginning without disturbing actual events and their order. The first, according to Leibniz, is a possibility but one which God had no need or reason to actualize (Leibniz–Clarke correspondence, Alexander (ed) 1956: 75–6); the second is not a distinct possibility at all, for 'instants . . . consist only in the successive order of things: which order remaining the same, one of the two states, *viz.* that of a supposed anticipation, would not at all differ, nor could be discerned from, the other which now is' (ibid. 27). This verificationist attitude to dates chimes with Augustine's psychological analysis of time, which we shall examine in chapter 9. But he did not exploit it in solving the puzzle about God's idleness.

His own solution is stated in the *Confessions*:

Here is my reply to the person who says, 'What was God doing before he made heaven and earth?' I keep off the facetious reply said to have been given by someone wriggling out of a serious answer, 'He was preparing hell for people who ask awkward questions [scrutantibus gehennam parabat]'. . ‹Those who› cannot understand why you were idle through countless ages should wake up and pay attention, because the thing they cannot understand is a fiction. How would countless ages have passed if you had not made them, since you are the author and creator [conditor] of all ages? What times would there have been if they had not been created by you? How could they have passed without ever having been? Therefore since all times are your work, if there was any time before you made heaven and earth, why is it said that you were idle, not at work? You had made time itself; times would not pass before you made them. Whereas if there was no time before heaven and earth, why is it asked what you were doing then? For there was no then, where there was no time. (*Conf.* 11.12.14–11.13.15, cf. *Gen. Man.* 1.2.3, *City* 11.6)

This solution does not entirely rule out time 'before heaven and earth'; but Augustine evidently means that there cannot be time before the *creation*, since time was made by God and so is part of the created universe.

The beginning of time

What arguments are there in favour of Augustine's thesis that time began? A theological one can be framed by combining God's immutability with Simplicius' point that there can be no delay without a reason:

(10) There was no time at which God had not *yet* decided to create;
(11) creation could not be delayed once decided on;
therefore there was no time at which God had not yet created.

Augustine cannot easily accept premise (10), for his solution to the delay problem goes on:

There was no then, where there was no time. But you do not precede times *in* time, otherwise you would not precede *all* times. You precede all the past in the eminence of ever-present eternity. (*Conf.* 11.13.16)

I shall return to this passage in the next chapter; at the moment it is enough to remark that there would at least be a difficulty in reconciling its doctrine with the idea that God's decisions are at all times either present or past, as (10) supposes.

Augustine's own argument for the thesis that time began is not theological. Before creation, he says,

there could have been no past, because there was no created thing by the changing motions of which the past could carry on [ageretur]. (*City* 11.6)

For if there were no motion of either a spiritual or a bodily creature by which the future succeeded through the present to the past, there would be no time at all (*Gen. Lit.* 5.5.12, cf. *Conf.* 12.8.8, 12.11.14, *Gen. Lit. Imperf.* 3.8).

The argument is:

(12) There was no change before the universe;
(13) time requires change;
therefore there was no time before the universe.

Premise (13) goes back to Plato (*Timaeus* 37e–38a) and Aristotle (*Physics* 4.11 218b 21–219a 1), although Aristotle drew the opposite conclusion that since there has always been time there has always been change (*Physics* 8.1 251b 10–28, *Metaphysics* Λ.6 1071b 5–10). Later in antiquity the connection was crystallized into a definition of a time (*chronos*) as 'a stretch of change in the cosmos', '*diastēma tēs tou kosmou kinēseōs*', which we find attributed to the Stoic Chrysippus (von Arnim 1903–5: 2.510, 520). Philo anticipated Augustine's combination of this connection with the biblical creation story, and drew Augustine's conclusion:

> For there was no time before the cosmos, but it came into being either with it or after it. For since a time is a stretch of change of the cosmos, and change could not have come into being earlier than what is changed but was necessarily established later or simultaneously, it is therefore necessary that time too is either coeval with the cosmos in its coming into being or younger than it; to venture the claim that it is older would be unphilosophical. (*De Opificio Mundi* 7.26, cf. *De Sacrifiis Abelis et Caini* 18.65)

God, says Philo elsewhere, is the grandfather of time, for the cosmos is its father (*Quod Deus Immutabilis Sit* 6.31).

I shall digress for a moment to consider an oddity in Philo's version of the thesis, its suggestion that time might be younger than the cosmos. Probably he was influenced here by a problem in the Genesis story noticed also by Augustine in *Confessions* book 12, the apparently double creation of heaven and earth. God's work on the first 'day' of creation includes what we read in verses 1 and 2 of Genesis 1: 'In the beginning God created heaven and earth. And the earth was without form and void' (Gen 1:1). Yet on the second day God made the firmament and called *it* heaven (vv. 7–8); and on the third day he made the dry land, calling it earth (vv. 9–10). Both Augustine's Latin and the original Hebrew repeat the same word for 'heaven' and the same word for 'earth' at these different places. Augustine is characteristically shy of committing himself to any particular solution of the exegetical problem (*Conf.* 12.20.29); but his preference is to read into verse 1 the Platonist distinction between intelligible and perceptible beings. 'Heaven', he suggests, refers at that first occurrence to angels, 'a certain intellectual creature' which was never to fall (*Conf.* 12.9.9), 'earth' to the whole visible creation (*Conf.* 12.17.25); whereas the references in the later verses are of course to sky and dry land respectively. Augustine then notes that neither angels nor the visible creation initially change, even though both are changeable. Angels 'repress their mutability in the luxury of their blissful contemplation' of God (*Conf.* 12.9.9); while the visible world begins formless and, as Augustine argues, 'there is no variation where there is no form' (*Conf.* 12.11.14). It appears to follow, then, that the first 'day' passed without change, and therefore without time if time requires change. Unlike Philo, Augustine is rightly unwilling to embrace this consequence. Encouraged by the text: 'He who lives in eternity created everything at once' (Ecclus 18:1 Vg), he solves the problem by making the second 'day', when time began, simultaneous with the first.

In this respect Genesis is allegorical: creation was actually instantaneous, and God's creative acts are ordered by 'connection of causes', not 'intervals of time' (*Gen. Lit.* 5.5.12, cf. 4.1, 7.28, *City* 11.9, 11.30, 11.31). As a corollary he has to maintain that the first words of the Bible, 'In principio', do not refer to temporal order; and he interprets them with reference to the *logos* in the first chapter of the gospel of John as meaning 'In his word' (*Conf.* 12.20.29; the allusion is to the means – 'and God said' – by which creation was effected).

Mathematical time

In any case the principle used in solving this particular crux of biblical interpretation, that time requires change, seems likely to have been Augustine's main inducement to postulating a beginning of time, which postulate he could then neatly invoke to solve the problem of God's idleness. Yet the principle is not obviously true. Aristotle inferred it from the premise that experience of time requires experience of change (*Physics* 4.11 218b 21–219a 1), but the premise has been challenged (Lucas 1973:12–13), while the inference from it is fairly plainly invalid. Although time has sometimes been regarded as a measure, essentially divisible into days or years which in their turn require the existence of periodic changes, Augustine for his part repudiates that view, as we shall see in chapter 9.

Moreover the principle, although popular in the history of thought, has not gone quite undisputed. Newton (1642–1727) rejected it when he wrote: 'Absolute, true, and mathematical time, of itself, and from its own nature, flows equably without relation to anything external [absque relatione ad externum quodvis]' (*Principia*, scholium to definition VIII). A modern argument in defence of the Newtonian view is given by S. Shoemaker as follows (see Shoemaker 1969:363–81, and cf. Newton-Smith 1980:19–24). Suppose a universe of three regions, in which the observers in each region notice periods of complete changelessness in the other two. The periods of standstill appear at first to be regular, lasting in region A for one year out of every three, in region B for one year out of every four, and in region C for one year out of every five. Thus if the periods *are* regular, there will be changelessness throughout the universe for one year out of every sixty. We can concede (with Aristotle, see above) that this total standstill will not be noticed by anyone; but unless it is postulated, the regularities which preceded it will have to be judged temporary. A theory of total standstill therefore affords the simplest and best explanation of the other, partial standstills which the observers do severally witness, and that fact justifies their accepting it as true. Since it is true in their universe, and their universe is possible, such total standstill is possible.

Shoemaker's argument is by no means irresistible because, like many an attempt to prove a possibility, it depends on another possibility not very much more evident. The hypothesis of total standstill is indeed simplest; but it will only be judged best if it is judged possible, and a determined champion of the principle that time requires change will find little difficulty in doubting the possibility. Nevertheless the story of the three regions may well weaken our confidence that the claim of Philo and Augustine that time had a beginning gets support from their premise that the universe, and so change, had a beginning.

There are, on the other side, arguments against the beginning of time (see e.g. Swinburne 1968:207), but this is not the place to examine them; it is enough to say that they have been challenged (see e.g. Newton-Smith 1980: ch. 5). Newton-Smith, drawing his data from modern science rather than the Bible, concludes his discussion of the subject with the Augustinian sentiment that 'it is difficult to envisage within our current scientific framework any viable theory that involves positing both a first event and time before that event' (p. 110). On the other hand, he adds, 'it appears that the prospects for ever having evidence for a genuine first event are remote'; hence he can infer, unlike Augustine, that 'the prospects for ever being warranted in positing a beginning of time are dim' (p. 111).

Further reading

For an examination of ancient philosophical views about time see the excellent book by Sorabji (1983), in which chapters 13–17 are relevant. Chapters 2 and 5 of Newton-Smith (1980) give a modern perspective.

IX

More meditations on time

Eternity

Augustine must pay a price for his ingenious solution to the problem of God's idleness, that time began when the universe began. According to his Christian conception the universe does not comprise everything, because it does not comprise God. God did not create himself; nor did he come into existence without a creator, for Christians cannot admit that God came into existence at all. But if time had a beginning, must there not be a beginning of God's existence at the first moment of time? Otherwise, surely, he would have existed before that moment, so that it would not have been the first. To combine a God without beginning and time with a beginning seems like self-contradiction.

Augustine is aware of the danger of self-contradiction in this general area. For example he notes (perhaps with Cicero's *De Natura Deorum* 1.9 in mind) that one natural way of predicating a beginning of something, as in 'There was a time when Rome did not exist', cannot be used for predicating a beginning of time: 'When we say that there was a time when [quando] there was no time, we speak as incongruously [inconvenienter] as if someone were to say, "There was a man when there was no man" ' (*City* 12.16.2). Does Augustine himself avoid such incongruity? Some translators make him slip into it at the end of *Confessions* 11.13.15, which they translate 'For there was no then, *when* there was no time' (cf. Plotinus, *Enneads* 3.7.11.5, 'time did not *yet* exist'); but Augustine's Latin has 'ubi', literally 'where' (as I translated it), only secondarily 'when', and here surely bearing the meaning 'in the case in which', neither locative nor temporal. When similarly in other passages he says that God is 'before times' (*Gen. Lit.* 1.2.4, *Conf.* 12.15.20) and 'precedes all the past' (*Conf.* 11.13.16, quoted on p. 163), the sense of 'before' and 'precedes' is also non-temporal, as his remarks surrounding the latter text make clear: God precedes time not *in* time

167

but in 'the eminence [celsitudine] of ever-present eternity'. He is above it, or outside it.

The thesis that God is outside time reconciles time's having a beginning with God's not having one, but it is not the only way in which the reconciliation could be achieved, if we take 'God did not begin' to mean merely 'there was no first moment of God's existence'. For on the assumption that time is dense, there could be a first moment of time without a first moment of God's existence, if God existed at every moment *except* the first moment of time. In that case every moment of God's existence would have a predecessor at which he also existed, so that his existence would in the sense given be without a beginning; but the backward course of these infinitely many predecessors would approach the first moment of time without reaching it, so not endangering its status as first. However, this alternative reconciliation lacks appeal because it compels us to understand the claim that God did not begin as compatible with there being a moment at which he did not exist before every moment at which he did exist.

To avoid the unwelcome compatibility it is better to interpret 'God did not begin' in a more complex way, as including both the two following propositions:

(1) There is no first moment of God's existence;
(2) no moment at which God did not exist lies before any moment at which he did exist.

The thesis that time began is:

(3) there is a first moment.

From (1) and (3) it follows that God did not exist at the first moment. But by (2) he would have to have existed at the first moment in order to exist at any moment. So (1), (2), and (3) yield:

therefore there is no moment at which God exists.

The reasoning shows that nothing less than placing God outside time will reconcile time's having a beginning with God's not having one, if the latter is understood in the complex way as combining (1) and (2).

There is no indication that Augustine himself saw the force of this reasoning, unless we may infer that he did from the fact that one of his statements of its conclusion immediately succeeds premise (3) in the passage from the *Confessions* quoted on p. 163. In full, the passage runs:

There was no then, where there was no time. But you do not precede times *in* time, otherwise you would not precede *all* times. You precede all the past in the eminence of ever-present eternity, and you surpass all the future because it *is* future and will be past when it has come, whereas you are always yourself the same, and your years shall not fail [Ps 101 [Heb. Bib. 102]:28]. Your years neither go nor come, but these years of ours both go and come, in order that all of them may come. Your years stand simultaneously, because they stand; those that go are not pushed out by those that come, because they do not pass, whereas these of ours shall all be when they shall all not be [i.e. all will have come only when all are gone]. Your years are one day, and your day is not any day [cotidie] but today, because your today does not give way to tomorrow; for neither does it succeed yesterday. Your today is eternity. (*Conf.* 11.13.16)

This 'ever-standing eternity', Augustine thinks, is something whose 'splendour men might briefly snatch' (*Conf.* 11.11.13), as he and Monica in the ecstasy at Ostia had 'for one instant with all the power of the heart touched eternal wisdom' (*Conf.* 9.10.24).

Two ideas are prominent in Augustine's perplexing account of eternity: God's years *stand*, and all of them are *present simultaneously*. Both ideas had been anticipated by Plotinus (*Enneads* 3.7.3.16–20) and recur in the more famous and more influential definition of eternity by Boethius (*c.*480–*c.*524) a century later (*Consolatio Philosophiae* 5.6 ll.25–38, cf. ll.9–11, *De Trinitate* 4 ll.64–77). According to Plotinus and Boethius everything eternal is alive; and although that requirement is not explicit in Augustine, it is clear that for him an eternal being must have, if not life, at least duration. Yet if God's life has endless duration, and all parts of it are simultaneous, then his calendar, as I write, shows not only 1987 but every other year. This has seemed to some impossible:

For simultaneity as ordinarily understood is a transitive relation. If A happens at the same time as B, and B happens at the same time as C, then A happens at the same time as C. . . . But on [this] view, my typing of this paper is simultaneous with the whole of eternity. Again, on this view, the great fire of Rome is simultaneous with the whole of eternity. Therefore, while I type these very words, Nero fiddles heartlessly on. (Kenny 1969:264, quoted in Kenny 1979:38–9).

The criticism assumes that parts of eternity – God's 'years' – are simultaneous not only with each other but with *times* – our years; and such does indeed seem to be what Augustine is claiming when he says that God's day is 'today'. It is natural that he should claim it, since the point of attributing *duration* outside time to God's existence is presumably to match his existence to the temporal durations of our own lives and other events. Given the assumption it is therefore important for Augustine to be able to evade Kenny's criticism by invoking an understanding of simultaneity which is not 'ordinary' but makes the relation both non-transitive and capable of holding between a temporal and an eternal event or thing. Such a special understanding has been proposed by Stump and Kretzmann (1981). According to the definition which they give, it will be true, for example, that each of the years 1987 and 1988 is simultaneous with (the whole of) God's life only if there are temporal observers in each year each of whom observes God's life as 'eternally present'. But this account will not help us to understand the kind of simultaneity that avoids Kenny's criticism unless we already understand what it is for an event to be 'eternally present'. Since Augustine's explanation goes in the other direction, Stump and Kretzmann's analysis does not help towards its clarification.

Augustine says that God's years stand simultaneously 'because they stand'; by contrast, time passes. This feature of time has often been regarded as mysterious and contentious, but it really only collects together a number of commonplaces about the temporal relationships of being earlier than and later than, for example that what happens earlier than a time happens earlier still than every later time. The failure of these commonplaces, by Augustine's account, to carry over to eternity simply classifies eternity as not a species of time, that is, classifies eternal beings and events as not temporal, not 'in' time. So it is a purely negative point that does nothing to explain how a being or event which lacks the temporal attributes can endure or persist, or have anything that might be called a life.

In view of these difficulties we might be tempted to drop the idea of duration and interpret Augustine's eternity as mere atemporality, i.e. timelessness. There is no problem about understanding this simpler notion: an atemporal occurrence or thing is one for which the question 'When did it happen or exist?' has no answer; the thing possesses neither temporal duration nor temporal location. Abstract objects such as numbers, and truths about them such as 'root two is irrational', come to mind as plausible examples, even though there appears to be no knockdown objection to the rival view that in such cases the answer 'always' is, however unnatural, correct. Yet it seems clear that Augustine's definition of the eternal could not reasonably be applied to an abstract object.

I conclude that he does not succeed in providing an adequate explication of the sense in which God is eternal. In what follows therefore I shall confine my attention to the more modest negative thesis, which is certainly also Augustine's and which we can certainly find sense in, that God's existence and his acts are atemporal.

Change of time

We have already seen that part of the thesis of divine atemporality, 'There is no moment at which God exists', can, whether Augustine recognizes the fact or not, be derived from premises about beginnings to which he is committed. There is another line of argument to atemporality which he certainly does recognize and use, from God's immutability.

Psalm 101, the beautiful lament *Domine exaudi*, contains the verse: 'As for thy years, they endure throughout all generations' (Ps 101 [Heb. Bib. 102]:24). In his commentary on it Augustine wrote:

> For the years of God are not one thing and himself another, but God's years are God's eternity; eternity, the very substance of God, which contains [habet] nothing mutable. There nothing is past, as if no longer being; nothing future, as if not yet being. There nothing is except what *is*: *was* and *will be* are not there, because what was is no longer and what will be is not yet; but whatever is there, only *is*. (*Enarr. Ps.* 101.2.10)

The argument is:

(4) If a thing has a past or a future, it is not what it was or will be;
(5) if a thing is not what it was or will be, it changes;
(6) God does not change;
therefore God has no past or future.

Both of the general premises are open to serious challenge. In the case of (4) we can object that a *changeless* object which passes from the past or to the future, i.e. from earlier to later times, does not come to be anything that it was not, or come not to be anything that it was; changelessness ensures that what it was or will be it *is*. Augustine can meet this objection only if he can treat temporal location as itself a property of things, or as part of the individuation of properties of things. He must be willing to argue that, for example, if God is omnipotent on Tuesday and survives into Wednesday, then *omnipotent on Tuesday* is something that God no longer is on Wednesday. But the reply saves (4) at the cost of falsifying (5): for whereas loss of the property of *omnipotence* between Tuesday and Wednesday clearly constitutes a change, loss between Tuesday and Wednesday of the pseudo-property of *omnipotence-on-Tuesday* equally clearly does not constitute change. Furthermore, (5) can be challenged even if temporal location does not come into the individuation of properties, as we shall see later.

A stronger argument occurs in the treatise *Ad Simplicianum* which Augustine addressed to his Milanese friend in response to exegetical questions about two biblical passages from Paul and five from Kings (i.e.

Samuel and Kings). One of the passages is: 'Then the word of the Lord came to Samuel: "I repent of having made Saul king" ' (1 Sam. 15:10–11 NEB). Augustine deploys his standard reply to the charge that such ascriptions represent God as changing his mind: on the contrary repentance, a 'will that something should not be as he had made it to be', is 'a will of change', not a change of will (*Simp*. 2.2.4; see p. 157 above). On the way to this solution he has raised the question whether repentance is compatible with foreknowledge. He comments:

> For what is foreknowledge but knowledge of future things? And what is future to God who spans all times? For if God's knowledge grasps [habet] things themselves, they are not future to him but present, so that he cannot be said now to have foreknowledge but only knowledge. Yet if it is with God as in the order of temporal creatures, and the things that are future are not yet but he comes before them in knowing them, then he experiences them twice, in one way as foreknowledge of the future and in another way as knowledge of the present. Hence something accrues to God's knowledge with the passage of time; which is totally absurd and totally false. For . . . when what was formerly foreknowledge later becomes knowledge in God, he admits changeability and is temporal. (*Simp*. 2.2.2; cf. Plotinus, *Enneads* 4.3.15.20–4, discussed by Mignucci 1985: 235)

A foreknows that *p* only if *a* knows that *p* at a *time* earlier than the time at which *p*; so foreknowledge is one of various casualties of God's atemporality, something he cannot do because it has to be done in time (we shall consider later the length of the casualty list overall). This passage therefore calls for Augustine to retract the incautious remark in the *De Libero Arbitrio* that denial of God's foreknowledge would be 'crazy disrespect' (*Lib. Arb*. 3.2.4, see p. 102 above); or rather, since divine foreknowledge continues to appear in his later works – for example when he claims in the *City of God* that 'anyone who lacks foreknowledge of all the future is not God at all' (*City* 5.9) – we should perhaps impute to him a distinction rather than a retraction: God foreknows the future in the attenuated sense of knowing what, at any time, happens later than that time, not in the proper sense of knowing, at any time, what happens later than that time.

We can see in the passage just quoted from *Ad Simplicianum*, surrounding its denial of divine foreknowledge, another argument from immutability to atemporality ('if it is with God as in the order of temporal creatures . . . he admits changeability') which can be set out as follows:

(7) If God is temporal, he knows as present some things which he foreknew as future;

(8) if someone knows as present what he foreknew as future, he changes;

(9) God does not change;

therefore God is not temporal.

There is more theology here than in the previous argument; for now we have to assume not only that God is immutable but, in premise (7), that he has knowledge of temporal events. More than that, (7) claims that such knowledge (at least some of it) would persist through time if its owner did. The basis for the new premise is, I suggest, a general conviction of divine omniscience: since God cannot be charged with any ignorance, it follows that if he were capable of knowledge at a time, he would have to have it at all times.

On the other hand premise (8) is pure philosophy; and it is false. Its appeal rests on what P. T. Geach has called

> the Cambridge criterion ‹of change› (since it keeps occurring in Cambridge philosophers of the great days, like Russell and McTaggart): The thing called 'x' has changed if we have '$F(x)$' at time t' true and '$F(x)$' at time $t1$' false, for some interpretation of 'F', 't' and '$t1$'. (Geach 1969:71–2)

According to the Cambridge criterion, anyone who foreknows that p, changes when it comes to pass that p; for if '$t1$' is interpreted as referring to the time at which it comes to pass that p and 't' is interpreted as referring to some arbitrarily close preceding time, then we have 'at $t1$ he foreknows that p' false (the knowledge is not foreknowledge any more) but 'at t he foreknows that p' true. Yet as Geach proceeds to say:

> ‹The Cambridge criterion› is intuitively quite unsatisfactory. By this account, Socrates would after all change by coming to be shorter than Theaetetus [even if Theaetetus grew while Socrates remained the same height as before; the allusion is to Plato, *Theaetetus* 155a–c]. . . .
> The changes I have mentioned, we wish to protest, are not 'real' changes. (ibid.)

Applying this critique to our case, we wish to protest that the 'change' from a's foreknowing that p to a's not foreknowing that p which occurs when the knowledge ceases to be *fore*knowledge through its coming to pass that p, is not a real change; and it is therefore consistent with God's immutability that a should be God.

Augustine's partnership in error with the 'Cambridge philosophers' is explicit in another passage about divine knowledge, where he writes (my emphasis):

> Nor does ‹God see› things in one way now, in another way earlier, and in another way later, since his knowledge of the three times,

present, past and future, is not, *unlike ours*, changed by the difference [varietate mutatur]; for with him there is no changing, or shadow of movement [Jas 1:17]. (*City* 11.21)

The same error is also implicit in the argument we previously considered from his commentary on Psalm 101; for premise (5) on which that argument relied is an alternative formulation of the Cambridge criterion.

Knowing what's happening

Although Augustine denies divine foreknowledge, he maintains, as we have seen, that there is an attenuated sense in which God knows all the future: with respect to any time, God knows (atemporally) everything that happens later than that time. We may also safely presume that in Augustine's view God knows all the past and present in the same sense, and that he knows all those general and abstract truths which cannot be tied to any date or period of time: in fact, Augustine's God is omniscient.

But can omniscience be combined with atemporality in the same being? Some modern philosophers have thought not, and have found here an objection against Augustine's thesis that God is atemporal, to add to the failure to find good arguments in its favour with which I have charged him in the preceding section. I shall next consider this objection, and after it another to the effect that it is also impossible to combine atemporality with agency. I shall argue that these objections against Augustinian theology are unsuccessful.

Here is a statement of the first objection:

An omniscient being must know all truths, and it is true that the Great War ended more than fifty years ago; so, seemingly, an omniscient being must know that the Great War ended more than fifty years ago. But someone can know that the Great War ended more than fifty years ago only if it did end more than fifty years ago, and so, seemingly, only when more than fifty years have elapsed since it ended. Therefore this truth can be known only at times, and so not by an atemporal being. Since, then, there is a truth which must be known by any omniscient being and cannot be known by any atemporal being, no atemporal being is omniscient.

'Ago' is one of the class of words called token-reflexive, whose truth conditions are relative to the circumstances – here the times – of their utterance. Temporal token-reflexives are definable in terms of the earlier-later relationship together with the present tense, or 'now' used as a mark of presentness: in this example, knowing that the Great War ended more than fifty years ago is the same thing as knowing that it is now more than fifty years since it ended.

Let us start by considering a temporal being, and ask whether, for example, Clemenceau knew in 1920 that the Great War ended more than fifty years ago. There seem to be three ways of understanding this question, yielding different answers to it. If we understand the question as asking whether in 1920 Clemenceau knew concerning 1920, his current temporal location, that it lay more than fifty years later than the war's end, the answer is no, because it did not. If, secondly, the question asks whether in 1920 he knew concerning now, my current temporal location, that it lies more than fifty years later than the end of the Great War, the answer will be yes or no depending how my current temporal location is identified to him: if, say, it is identified by its date 1987, he could easily have worked out that 1987 lies more than fifty years forward from the date at which (as he knew) the Great War had ended; but if it is identified as, say, the thirty-sixth year of the reign of Queen Elizabeth II, he would not have known concerning 1987 so identified that it lay more than fifty years later than the end of the Great War. Thirdly, the question might be understood as asking whether in 1920 Clemenceau knew, concerning my current temporal location, *both* that it was (is?) his own current temporal location *and* that it lay more than fifty years later than the end of the Great War, and in this case the answer again is no, because the two temporal locations do not in fact coincide.

Is the objector's argument right in asserting that knowledge that the Great War ended more than fifty years ago can be had only *when* more than fifty years have elapsed since it ended? On the second of our three accounts of what such knowledge amounts to, the answer to this question is no: knowledge concerning now, my current temporal location, that it lies more than fifty years later than the war's end, can be had at any time, and therefore for all the argument shows can be had at no time, by an atemporal knower. On this interpretation, then, the objection fails to display knowledge unattainable by an atemporal being but required of an omniscient being.

According to the first and third interpretations, however, knowledge that the Great War ended more than fifty years ago does turn out to be possessable only at certain times, and therefore not available to an atemporal being. On the first account, such knowledge can be had at any time lying more than fifty years later than the end of the Great War; while on the third account it can be had at one of those times, viz. now, and otherwise never. Therefore in neither of these two cases is the knowledge available to an atemporal being. Does that fact derogate from his omniscience? It is important at this point to remember that not every failure to know is ignorance. For example, the fact that Clemenceau failed in 1920 to know that his current temporal location was more than fifty years later than the end of the Great War does not convict Clemenceau of ignorance, and neither does the fact that he failed in 1920 to know that his current temporal location was 1987. He failed to know those things because those things were false, whereas ignorance is ignorance of truths. As for Clemenceau's failure in 1920 to know that the Great War ended more than fifty years ago, that is due, according to the first and third interpretations, respectively to one or other of these former failures, so that it too can hardly be blamed on him as ignorance. For an atemporal being the case is different but similar. We have to ask, according to the first interpretation, whether it is ignorance in such a being that he fails to know, concerning his current temporal location, that it lies more than fifty years later than the end of the Great War; or, according to the third interpretation, whether it is ignorance in him that he fails to know, concerning the same location, that it is 1987. Since he has no current temporal location, it seems to me that these failures likewise do not display ignorance or derogate from omniscience. (Stump and Kretzmann, it should be remarked, argue in their article 'Eternity' (1981) that we ought to be asking a different question about the atemporal being, concerning his *eternal* position – which is single – rather than his temporal position – which is non-existent; but they also argue that, taken that way, the atemporal being does not fail to have the requisite knowledge.)

It is possible to formulate the above reply to the objection from omniscience as a dilemma. The truth that the Great War ended more than fifty years ago is either an atemporal or a temporal truth. If as the second interpretation proposes it is atemporal, an atemporal being can know it. If as the other two interpretations say it is temporal, an omniscient being does not need to know it. In neither case is it a truth which both must be known by any omniscient being and cannot be known by any atemporal being.

Some philosophers have given a simpler argument to the conclusion that an atemporal being cannot be omniscient, from the premise that an atemporal being cannot know what the time is, i.e. where he is located in time. But this is like complaining about a bachelor that he does not know who he is married to. A man who does not know who he is married to is ignorant *or* unmarried; just so, a being who does not know what the time is is ignorant *or* atemporal.

Semi-dating

Change requires time; so an atemporal being cannot change. This excludes not only many sorts of bodily activity such as walking, winking, writing, which we should not in any case ascribe to a bodiless God, but also those mental activities which are similarly 'imperfect' in the sense that while we are doing them we have not yet done them (Aristotle, *Metaphysics* Θ.6 1048b18–35): for example, working out the solution to a problem, screwing up courage to rebuke someone, giving a course of instruction in ancient history. Nor, as we have seen, can an atemporal being be in such states as foreknowing or remembering which, though not changes, require a location in time. However, other activities do remain possible, as Stump and Kretzmann make plain:

> Considered as an atemporal mind, God cannot deliberate, anticipate, remember, or plan ahead, for instance; all these mental activities essentially involve time, either in taking time to be performed (like deliberation) or in requiring a temporal viewpoint as a prerequisite to performance (like remembering). But it is clear that there are other mental activities that do not require a temporal interval or viewpoint. Knowing seems to be the paradigm case. . . . Willing . . . unlike wishing or desiring, seems to be another. . . . And although *feeling* angry is impossible for an atemporal entity – if feelings of anger are essentially associated, as they seem to be, with bodily states – we do not see anything that prevents such an entity from *being* angry, a state the components of which might be, for instance, being aware of an injustice, disapproving of it, and willing its punishment. (1981: 446–7)

An atemporal being need not, then, be inactive. But it is another question whether he can intervene in the world, producing results such as the existence, skills, fortunes, successes, or deaths of creatures. According to Augustine's theology God does such things, and does them by his word, by saying 'let it be so', 'fiat'. How can he, if he is outside time?

This is the second of the two objections I shall consider against the idea that God is atemporal. Nelson Pike has stated it as follows:

> Let us suppose that yesterday a mountain, 17,000 feet high, came into existence on the flatlands of Illinois. One of the local theists explains this occurrence by reference to divine creative action. He claims that God produced (created, brought about) the mountain. Of course, if God is timeless, He could not have produced the mountain *yesterday*. This would require that God's creative-activity and thus the individual whose activity it is have position in time. The theist's claim is that God *timelessly* brought it about that yesterday, a 17,000 feet high mountain came into existence on the flatlands of Illinois. . . . [But] the claim that God *timelessly* produced a temporal object (such as the mountain) is absurd. (1970:104–5)

Pike's objection was anticipated by Augustine, who first adumbrates his reply to it like this:

> EVODIUS: . . . Things do not come to be [fiunt] in God, they are for ever [sempiterna].

177

AUGUSTINE: So God effects [operatur] nothing in his creation?
EV: He fixed once and for all the manner in which the order of the universe that he created should be carried on. He does not contrive anything by a new will.
AUG: Does he make no one happy?
EV: Indeed he does.
AUG: Then he definitely acts [facit] when the person becomes happy?
EV: Yes.
AUG: So if, for example, you are going to be happy a year from now, he is going to make [facturus] you happy a year from now?
EV: Indeed.
AUG: So he already foreknows today what he is going to do a year from now?
EV: He has always foreknown it. (*Lib. Arb.* 3.3.6, cf. *City* 12.15 (14))

By denying change to God's foreknowledge of his own future act this passage denies change to God's decision so to act (see pp. 117–18 above); and the materials are thereby present for denying time as well as change to the decision. But seemingly God's *actions* must still be in time – they are things he is 'going to do'. Augustine takes the next step in the *Confessions*:

‹With you, God› it is not that what has been spoken comes to an end and something else is spoken, in order that it should be possible for everything to be spoken; but everything ‹happens› simultaneously and for ever [sempiterne]. . . . You act [facis] in no other way than by speaking; nevertheless not all the things you make [facis] by speaking come into being [are made, fiunt] simultaneously and for ever. (*Conf*. 11.7.9)

Augustine gains useful generality from having at his disposal the single verb 'facere' for 'act' and 'make' and its passive 'fieri' for 'be made' and 'happen, come to be'. Part of the same effect can be achieved in English by recasting assertions of acting and making into forms such as '*a* brings it about that *a* is victorious', '*a* brings it about that *b* is victorious', '*a* brings it about that *b* exists'; in general, '*a* brings it about that *p*'. Let us stipulate that '*p*' in the general formula always marks a place for a sentence that neither contains nor implies a particular time-specification. Then the formula displays – better indeed than Augustine's Latin – the feature which Augustine uses to rebut Pike's conclusion, the feature of containing two verbs each of which can have a time-specification added to it, not necessarily the same in the two places. The opportunity is created to date an action doubly.

Double-dating of actions is sometimes the only way out of a puzzle.

Suppose I stab someone and he dies of the wound 365 days later. In English law I am answerable to a charge of murder. But *when* did I kill my victim? On the day of the stabbing, or on the day of his death, or (but surely this is absurd) on some day in between? There is in truth no single answer to the question; we must say 'a year ago I brought it about that today he died'. The same move should be made against Pike, for if an ordinary human act can have two dates, the act of an atemporal God can shed one of the dates without shedding the other: God *can* timelessly produce a temporal object or result. Commenting on the story of Babel where we are told: 'Then the Lord came down to see the city and tower which men had built' (Gen. 11:5), Augustine wrote:

> He who is unable ever to be ignorant of anything does not find out at a time [ad tempus], but he is said to see and to realize at a time what he makes to be seen and realized. Thus that city had not previously been seen in the way that God made it to be seen when he showed how much it annoyed him. (*City* 16.5)

The interpretation is specious, and Augustine was to retain a sense that 'the way in which ‹God›, being eternal, effects temporal things is a puzzling one [miro modo]' (*City* 22.9). But he should not have worried; the tool he used is a good tool, and was to be put to use more confidently by Aquinas (*Summa Contra Gentiles* 2.35) and his successors.

Puzzles about time

We have now examined, in this chapter and the last, the first half of Augustine's discussion of time in *Confessions* book 11. Down to 11.13.15 he has considered the idleness problem and defended his solution that time began at the creation. In 11.13.15 he has asserted and briefly explained God's eternity. The remainder of the book propounds the thesis for which Augustine is probably best known among philosophers, that times are affections of the mind. The thesis emerges from his struggles with two new questions: how can times be long? and how can their length be measured? These questions are themselves introduced by means of a prior one which evokes Augustine's famous description of the analytic philosopher's predicament (cf. *Conf.* 11.22.28, 11.25.32):

> But what is time [or, a time]? Who can explain it easily and briefly, or even, when he wants to speak of it, comprehend it in his thought? Yet is there anything we mention in our talking that is so well known and familiar? And we certainly understand when we say it, as we understand when we hear it said by someone else with whom we are talking. So what *is* [a] time? If no one asks me, I know; if they ask and I try to explain, I do not know. (*Conf.* 11.14.17)

He starts the new inquiry by dividing time into past, future, and present. At first it is not obvious why there is any special interest in that particular division as opposed, for example, to the division between antediluvian and postdiluvian time, or between the time of Christ, the time before Christ's birth, and the time after the Resurrection. The reason emerges when we find that the past, present and future *move*: 'If the present were always present and did not move [transiret] into the past, it would not now be a time, but eternity' (*Conf.* 11.14.17). The nature of this movement is important, because it reveals which of two ways Augustine adopts of individuating times. According to one possible conception a single time, called the present, moves *forward* through successive dates, so that once it lay at AD 387 and before long it will lie at AD 2000. But that is not the way Augustine thinks. He treats times as moving *backwards* into the past, so that as the present moves it ceases to *be* present and becomes a part of the past. The word 'present', then, is for Augustine a temporary name of a time, describing a property which each time holds successively, and discards as it assumes the property of being past. The word names a time only relative to a time; it names that time which, relative to any time, is present *at* (and so is the same as) it. Similarly 'the past' and 'the future' name times which, relative to any time, are past *to* (i.e. earlier than) it or future *to* (i.e. later than) it respectively. We must notice that there are also non-relative uses of 'past', 'present', and 'future', even on Augustine's conception of times as flowing backwards into the past rather than forwards through successive dates: these are the token-reflexive uses, in which 'present' names the time of naming it (as 'now' usually does), and 'past' and 'future' name times earlier and later than that. But of course Augustine does not intend such particularity in *his* discussion of time in *Confessions* book 11, where he is writing philosophy and not autobiography. Even if he had used the word 'now', we should have understood it in these chapters as like a philosopher's use of 'I' in an example meant to be generalized.

Another property of times is length, but Augustine proceeds to argue that no time is long. The past and future cannot be long, because

> How on earth can anything be long, or short, which *is* not? But the past is not, any more, and the future is not, yet. So we ought not to say in this way 'it is long'; about the past we ought to say 'it was long' and about the future 'it will be long'. (*Conf.* 11.15.18)

Neither can the present be long, because

> The present century . . . ‹cannot› be present. For if its first year is occurring [agitur], that is present and ninety-nine are future. . . . ‹Similarly with years, days, minutes›. . . . Only that much time, if

such can be understood, as cannot be divided into even the tiniest parts of minutes can be called present. And that flies across from the future to the past so hurriedly that it extends over no pause whatever. (*Conf.* 11.15.20)

The argument can be set out as follows:

(10) When a time is not present, it does not exist;
(11) when a time does not exist, it is not long;
(12) when a time is present, every part of it is present;
(13) when a time is divisible, not every part of it is present;
(14) no indivisible time is long;
therefore no time is long.

This argument is valid, but I shall contend in the next section that two of its premises, (10) and (12), are false. Meanwhile the present section will survey Augustine's reflections on it in the remaining chapters of *Confessions* book 11.

His immediate response is twofold: somehow the fact that we experience (sentimus) times, and the fact that we measure them, must be reconciled with the argument (*Conf.* 11.16.21); and the argument itself should not be accepted without further scrutiny (11.17.22). He then questions premise (10): perhaps the past and future exist after all, the latter 'issuing out of some hiding place' to become present, and then retreating into some hiding place when it becomes past. That would account for the apparent fact that some who 'hymn the future' see it, and for the apparent fact that some historians report the past truly (11.17.22). But Augustine turns his back on this alternative, preferring to think that we draw from our memories only 'images of things', and that we see only present 'causes or signs' of, for example, a coming sunrise (11.18.23–4), mysterious though this process is (11.19.25). Properly speaking what exists is not past or future but a present of past which is memory and a present of future which is expectation; and the present of present is viewing (contuitus, 11.20.26).

As to the fact that we measure time, we must measure it 'over some extent' (in aliquo spatio, 11.21.27); but no existing time has extent. Time cannot be identified with the movement of the heavenly bodies, because they could speed up, or stop as the sun did for Joshua at the battle of Ajalon (11.23.29–30, alluding to Josh. 10:12–14; cf. Plotinus, *Enneads* 3.7.9.31 5); and anyhow bodies move *in* time (11.24.31).

The duration of an event, such as someone's recital of a poem, can be measured by counting its parts; so perhaps we measure times as they are passing (praetereuntia). Here 'the truth begins to dawn' (albescit veritas, 11.26.33–27.34). But no: a noise, for instance, can be measured only when it has ended: 'Therefore we measure neither future nor present nor past nor passing times, and yet we measure times' (*Conf.* 11.27.34). In scanning the first line of Ambrose's evening hymn *Deus Creator Omnium*, one can only measure

> something in the memory that stays imprinted [infixum]. I measure times in you, my mind. What I measure is the affection [affectionem] which passing things make in you and which stays when they have passed; that, which is present, I measure, not the things, which have passed in the making of it. . . . So either these things [he means the affections] are times, or I do not measure times. (*Conf.* 11.27.36)

You can memorize a space of time and then match a performance to its length. What you then attend to is your present memory of the segment that has passed and your present expectation of the segment still to come. Therefore

> A past time is not long, because it is not; but a long past is a long memory of the past. (*Conf.* 11.28.37)

A treatment of Augustine's puzzles

In the chapters just surveyed Augustine has faced an easy problem and a hard one, both of them concerning stretches of time (Latin uses the same word 'tempus' for stretches and points of time, being in this like English but unlike Greek; Augustine is aware of the divergence from Greek, *Ep.* 197). The hard problem is, 'How do we measure time-stretches?', and Augustine's solution is that we do so by comparing memories of them, which he calls affections of the mind. He infers that time-stretches *are* these affections. He then applies the inferred consequence to the solution of his easy problem, 'How can time-stretches have any length?', that is, how can they really stretch? I shall argue that his solution to the hard problem is brilliantly right, but the consequence is fallaciously inferred from it, and is false. The easy problem needs to be solved differently.

Let us first see how the easy problem ought to be solved. Augustine has attacked the proposition that some times are long with a two-pronged argument in which one prong denies length to past and future times, the other to present times. A fault in either prong will destroy the argument; in fact both are faulty.

He ought to have been more persistent in questioning his assertion that past and future times do not exist, premise (10) in the reconstruction I offered on p. 181. His suggestion that perhaps the present retreats 'into hiding' as it passes is meant to be ironic, but actually there is nothing much wrong with the spatial analogy which it conveys. Admittedly past times, such as the eighteenth century, are not in hiding *now*, for that implies that the eighteenth century exists now, which in turn could only mean that now is the eighteenth century. But I think there is a misunderstanding embodied in even raising the question 'when?' about an assertion of the existence of a time, just as it would betray misunderstanding to raise the question 'where?' about an assertion that a place exists. In the case of a time, to exist is, merely, to lie within time, as a part of time; and that is something which times do timelessly. Therefore the eighteenth century does exist, but timelessly. It has to be admitted also, secondly, that past and future times are not literally hidden; and this fact does, I suspect, reveal a genuine difference between spatial and temporal *presence*. Whereas as we have seen the latter is normally relative to a time, the former is normally relative to a place-occupying observer (e.g. 'in *his* presence') rather than a place. So the past and the future are in hiding only in the attenuated sense of being absent; but absence, not non-existence, is the true contradictory of being present.

Although I conclude from the above that, contrary to Augustine's opinion, the 'coming out of hiding' view of the future ought to be adopted, and similarly for the past, I do not think that any weight should be given to the considerations which Augustine himself offers in its favour. He maintains that without a currently existing past or future it would not be possible for a currently existing memory to have the past for its object, or a currently existing expectation to have the future for its object, if the memory and the expectation are true. The issue belongs to Augustine's philosophy of mind, which is beyond the purview of this book. Nevertheless it is worth remarking here that what he says misunderstands the relationships between (true) memories, or prophecies, and the objects they recall or prophesy. The objects in question are in any case not past or future times, but past or future events, which it is much more plausible to exclude from (present) existence; but the relationship holding towards them is intensional, in the sense of being a relationship that can hold towards something at a time when the thing does not exist. It is therefore open to Augustine to banish past and future events from present existence without adopting the consequence which he does proceed to adopt, that the objects of present memories and expectations are not those events but present images and signs of them.

Even if this criticism of premise (10) is mistaken, Augustine's argument against times being long can be faulted in its other prong, because he is wrong to say that all present times are wholly present, premise (12). He needs the premise, for otherwise there will be present times, such as the twentieth century, which are divisible into parts and so escape his objection against their having length. Moreover he sees the need for it when he states and argues for an instance of it as follows:

Therefore the current [qui agitur] year is not present as a whole [totus praesens]; and if it is not present as a whole, the year is not present. For a year is twelve months, some one of which, the current one, is present, whereas the rest are past or future. (*Conf.* 11.15.19)

Expressed in terms of parts, the supplementary argument is:

(15) A year is twelve months;
therefore if a year is present, twelve months are present;
therefore if a year is present, every part of it is present.

This argument fails through equivocation, because 'twelve months' must be taken collectively in its first step, distributively in its second. That is: the step to the final conclusion is valid only if the intermediate conclusion means 'if a year is present, *each* of its twelve months is present'; but that would follow from premise (15) only if (15) meant 'a year is *each* of its twelve months' (e.g. 1987 is January 1987, and 1987 is February 1987, and . . .). Although there is no way of defending the supplementary argument against this objection, some philosophers (e.g. Aristotle, *Physics* 6.3 234a16–21) have agreed with its conclusion, and more generally with Augustine's premise (12), on the different ground that if what is present need not be wholly present, then the present will be able to overlap with the past and future, as we say that the present century includes past decades; but I do not myself see why this consequence of rejecting (12) should be thought embarrassing (as it is e.g. by Sorabji 1983:26).

Since there is the above alternative solution to Augustine's easy problem, we can conclude that his identification of times with affections of the mind, which he uses to solve it, is not needed for that purpose. Moreover the identification is not sufficient for the purpose either, since Augustine's own faulty argument against long times can be transformed into an argument against long affections. Augustine sees that the kind of times he is talking about (periods of time as we should call them) are stretches or extensions (distentio, presumably translating the Greek *diastēma* which we found in Chrysippus' definition, pp. 163–4); and he seems also to see that his theory of affections involves making them stretches of the mind (*Conf.* 11.26.33, and cf. Plotinus, *Enneads* 3.7.12.1–3 for a similar view: a time is a stretch of a life). But the stretches proposed by Augustine, which are expectations and memories, must exist, and so by the earlier argument must be present and cannot *be* long; while they cannot when existing be expectations *of* a long future or memories *of* a long past, because by the earlier argument again, no future or past will be able to *be* long at the time of the expectation or memory of it, as Augustine's assumption of the extensionality of these relations requires it to be. Therefore according to Augustine's own argument, expectations and memories neither are stretches nor are of stretches; which will rightly disqualify them in his eyes from being times. (J. F. Callahan has proposed that the 'distentio animi' is an 'inextended distention', but I do not see how this can avoid being a contradiction in terms; Callahan 1978:177.)

The outcome is that nothing in Augustine's argument recommends his conclusion that times are affections of the mind. The falsity of the conclusion can be seen well enough by reflecting that, even if one were to concede (contra Shoemaker, p. 165 above) that time cannot pass when nothing changes, it would still be necessary to admit the obvious fact that time can pass when no one is paying it any attention – and the atheist who thinks that it *did* pass for many millions of years in a mindless universe cannot be refuted on grounds of inconsistency.

Let us now turn to the hard problem, how time is measured. All measurement is by reference to a standard. The problem in measuring time is not how to choose a standard but how to use it. A standard weight will be used by balancing it against the object to be measured by it, a standard rod by applying it alongside the object to be measured by it. But if we choose, for example, New Year's Day 1987 as a standard time-stretch (duration), how are we to determine whether another time, e.g. tomorrow, or next week, is of the same duration or less or more? Augustine arrives at his answer from considering the scansion of *Deus Creator Omnium*:

> Going by plain experience [quantum sensus manifestus est], I measure the long syllable by the short, and my experience is that it lasts twice as long. But one of them is uttered after the other; and if the earlier is short and the later long, how shall I hold on to the short one and apply it in measuring the long one, so as to discover that the latter lasts twice as long, in view of the fact that the long one does not begin to be uttered until the short one has ended? (*Conf.* 11.27.35)

His answer is contained in the following insight:

> If someone has willed to make an utterance of some modest length and decided by thinking in advance how long it is going to be, he first spends precisely that space of time in silence and then, committing it to memory [memoriae commendans], he begins to make the utterance, which goes on [sonat] until it reaches the end set. (*Conf.* 11.27.36)

As I put it in the last section: you can memorize a space of time and then match a performance to its length. Thus it is a brute fact of mentality that durations can be *remembered*; and on that fact depends our ability to measure times (cf. *De Musica* 6.8.21, which explains that only what is present, and so durationless, can be *heard*).

185

Augustine does not develop the implications of this fundamental insight, but the materials for developing it are provided in his remarks about the battle at Ajalon when the sun stood still. The battle is supposed to have lasted longer in fact than it did by sun-reckoning; and if so, it refutes the theory that the sun measures time. It refutes this well-regarded theory because, at the battle, predictions by the theory of equal durations will have failed to accord with the memories of the participants. Conversely, as we can now add on Augustine's behalf, a recurrent phenomenon such as the revolution of the sun *will* commend itself to us as a measure of time, provided that it does not conflict with the deliverances of our memories (and 'we' must be in general accord with one another if the time-measure is to be a common one). A time-measure is a clock. Augustine has shown, in all essentials, how clocks are possible.

When he says that what he measures is the affection which passing things make in his mind and which stays when they have passed (*Conf.* 11.27.36), the truth in this remark is that time-measures depend on retained memories of stretches of time. He was wrong to infer that the measured time *is* the memory; but then, as we have seen, he did not need that inference.

Further reading

For a brief comparison of Augustine's treatment of time with Aristotelian and Stoic views see O'Daly (1981). On the question whether it can be known only after 1968 that the Great War ended fifty years ago, see, *pro*, Sorabji (1983:259), Prior (1967 and 1962), and Kenny (1979:46–7); *contra*, Pike (1970: ch. 5), Stump and Kretzmann (1981), Castaneda (1967), and Swinburne (1977:162–7). On time and the mind see Findlay (1964). On Augustine's precursors see also Callahan (1948).

X

A priestly life

Love was the great good that Augustine found in Christianity. Had he
not loved and felt loved by God, it is hard to imagine that he would
have been steadfast in his acceptance of the Christian creed.

We need to remember that when in Milan he recovered his faith
('recuperatae fidei meae', *Conf.* 10.33.5), he was by his own account a
miserable man; and the main thing which held him back from conversion,
he says, was fear of losing or not regaining sexual comfort. He loved
Adeodatus' mother; the wound made by her departure would not heal
(6.15.25); the girl to whom he was now engaged, still not old enough
for marriage (6.13.23), must have been nearly twenty years his junior.
He dilates on grief not at this place in the *Confessions* but earlier, when
he recounts the death of a childhood acquaintance with whom he had
grown into close friendship during his year teaching rhetoric at Thagaste.
Augustine had chaffed this young man for accepting baptism in a bout
of serious illness, and been rebuffed. When the friend relapsed and died,

> My own country became a torment and my own home a grotesque
> abode of misery. All that we had done together was now a grim
> ordeal without him. My eyes searched everywhere for him, but he
> was not there to be seen. I hated all the places we had known
> together, because he was not in them and they could no longer
> whisper to me 'Here he comes!' as they would have done had he
> been alive but absent for a while. (*Conf.* 4.4.9, trs. Pine-Coffin)

Augustine's reflections on this episode are so important for understanding his later choice of life that they deserve lengthy quotation:

> Time never stands still, nor does it idly pass without effect upon our
> feelings or fail to work its wonders on the mind. It came and went,
> day after day, and as it passed it filled me with fresh hope and new

thoughts to remember. Little by little it pieced me together again by means of the old pleasures which I had once enjoyed. My sorrow gave way to them. But it was replaced, if not by sorrow of another kind, by things which held the germ of sorrow still to come. For the grief I felt for the loss of my friend had struck so easily into my inmost heart simply because I had poured out my soul upon him, like water upon sand, loving a man who was mortal as though he were never to die. My greatest comfort and relief was in the solace of other friends who shared my love of the huge fable which I loved instead of you, my God, the long-drawn lie which our minds were always itching to hear [2 Tim. 4:3], only to be defiled by its adulterous caress.

But if one of my friends died, the fable did not die with him. And friendship had other charms to captivate the heart. We could talk and laugh together and exchange small acts of kindness. We could join in the pleasure that books can give. We could be grave or gay together. If we sometimes disagreed, it was without spite, as a man might differ with himself, and the rare occasions of dispute were the very spice to season our usual accord. Each of us had something to learn from the others and something to teach in return. If any were away, we missed them with regret and gladly welcomed them when they came home. Such things as these are heartfelt tokens of affection between friends. They are signs to be read on the face and in the eyes, spoken by the tongue and displayed in countless acts of kindness. They can kindle a blaze to melt our hearts and weld them into one.

This is what we cherish in friendship, and we cherish it so dearly that in conscience we feel guilty if we do not return love for love, asking no more of our friends than these expressions of goodwill. This is why we mourn their death, which shrouds us in sorrow and turns joy into bitterness, so that the heart is drenched in tears and life becomes a living death because a friend is lost. Blessed are those who love you, O God, and love their friends in you and their enemies for your sake. They alone will never lose those who are dear to them, for they love them in one who is never lost, in God, our God who made heaven and earth and fills them with his presence, because by filling them he made them. (*Conf.* 4.8.13–9.14, trs. Pine-Coffin)

I believe that the pain at Milan must have been similar, even though Augustine chooses not to lay it bare – similar, but probably worse, for then his yearning was obscure and undirected, and nothing (so far as we know) forced him to abandon his previous life; what is more, the partnership he lost was sexual.

He understood the mixture of selfishness and gratitude in love, how we love people both because we have received their love and in order to keep it; he writes the *Confessions*, he says, for love of God's love (*Conf.* 11.1.1). He also understood insecurity, the fear of loss of good things, and especially of friendship by rejection or death. He would surely have seen force in Kant's dictum: '[Man's] own nature is not so constituted as to rest or be satisfied in any possession or enjoyment whatever' (Kant, *Critique of Judgement* (1928:93)). Peace, says Augustine,

> is an uncertain good, since we do not know the hearts of those with
> whom we wish to be at peace, and if we can know them today,
> there is no doubt we are ignorant how they are going to be tomorrow.
> (*City* 19.5)

Yet many people seek that peace, and Augustine was one of those who sought and found it in God, 'who is never lost'. From Cassiciacum in 386 he wrote to a friend:

> All the time that I miss someone who is away, I want to be missed
> by him. But I watch out for this as much as I can, and try hard not
> to love anything that can be away from me against my will. (*Ep.* 1)

Some years later, justifying Christian morals against the Manichees, he said of the summum bonum:

> It must be the sort of thing that cannot be lost against one's will.
> For no one can trust a good thing that he is aware can be removed
> from him even if he wants to keep it and hold it in his arms. If you
> do not trust the good that you enjoy there is no way you can be
> happy [beatus], when the great fear of losing it hangs over you.
> (*Mor. Cath.* 3.5, cf. *Divers. Quaest.* 35.1)

This attitude can be parodied, as we find it parodied, either in the living or the telling, in a traveller's comment written during Augustine's lifetime about the monks of Caprera, an island near Elba:

> They fear the gifts of fortune, from the apprehension of losing them,
> and, lest they should be miserable, they embrace a life of voluntary
> wretchedness. How absurd is their choice! how perverse their
> understanding! to dread the evils, without being able to support
> the blessings, of the human condition. (Rutilius, *Itineraria* i 439–48,
> quoted by Gibbon, *Decline and Fall* volume 3 p. 235)

But the attitude has a long and respectable history before Augustine. Aristotle had said, 'We have an intuition that the summum bonum is a person's own property and hard to remove from him' (*Nicomachean Ethics* I.5 1095b 25–6, cf. Cicero, *Tusculan Disputations* 5.41); and it was a commonplace among Greek philosophers that truth and knowledge are specially valuable because no one can lose them against his will.

Augustine advised the nuns of his sister's convent that 'it is better to want less than to have more' (*Ep.* 211.9, the so called Rule). He surmised that fear of loss might spoil the happiness even of someone who had all that he desired (*Beata Vita* 2.11, see p. 19 above); this was one of the reasons that had led Stoics to recommend 'apathy', i.e. not minding what happens to you, as a means of becoming untroubled. Since everyone must have aims and make choices, the wise man will set his heart on things within his control.

It is special to Augustine's place in this tradition that he formulates the question about the summum bonum in terms of love rather than, say, value or desire or aims. The formulation is well adapted to his own answer, which demands a relationship to a person, God, not to any abstraction such as truth or honour or virtue. But the Latin words 'amare' and 'diligere' (synonymous according to *City* 14.7) can quite easily be extended, as in English (and Greek), to cover relationships to the abstractions and to other inanimate things; with the difference, of course, that such loves cannot be reciprocated nor, therefore, sustained by the desire for reciprocation.

On what Augustine loves depends what Augustine does:

> A body inclines by its weight to its own place. . . . When things are out of order [minus ordinata] they are restless; they come into order [ordinantur] and settle to rest. *My* weight is my love. To whatever place I am taken I am taken by love. (*Conf.* 13.9.10)

The passage in which this well-known remark appears is deeply personal. Nevertheless it seems that Augustine would have been willing to generalize it into the thesis that all people are drawn by love to do what they will to do; at any rate that is the message of: 'A right will is therefore good love and a perverted will is bad love' (*City* 14.7.2). If he does mean the point generally, he is departing from an Aristotelian tradition which distinguishes acting voluntarily from acting in accordance with a settled inclination; for only the latter would exhibit love of an object which the agent aims to achieve or benefit, while the former is consistent with contrary inclinations which he manages to master and control. Augustine's psychology of action seems to leave no room for this distinction. Self-mastery, Aristotle's *enkrateia*, is 'continentia' in Augustinian Latin, a word which he normally reserves for sexual abstinence, following Paul:

> I say to unmarried women and widows, It is good in them if they stay that way, just as I do. But if they are not continent, they should marry. It is better to marry than to be inflamed. (1 Cor. 7:9)

We shall see in the next section that such continence demonstrates 'good love' in Augustine's eyes, not the lesser merit of right action in despite of loving and valuing the wrong things. Thus Aristotle's valuable contrast between voluntary actions that accord with, and those that conflict with, an agent's character and settled inclinations was through Augustine lost to the philosophical tradition, till it came to be reinstated, somewhat awkwardly, by Aquinas (see p. 86 above). Augustine could have used it with advantage in accounting for the will which is free but enslaved (pp. 89–90 above).

On the other hand, Augustine concurs with the main thesis in Aristotle's conception of the good *man*, that a good man's actions must flow from the right inclinations and must be done gladly:

> A man lives in justice and sanctity if he values things soundly [rerum integer aestimator]; and he does that if his love is well ordered, so that he neither loves what ought not to be loved, nor fails to love what ought to be loved, nor loves more what ought to be loved less, nor loves equally what ought to be loved either less or more, nor loves less what ought to be loved more or equally, (*Doct. Christ.* 1.27.28)

> And when realization comes of what ought to be done and what ought to be striven for, unless that gives delight and is loved, it [sc. right action] is not done, not undertaken, not lived well (*Sp. Lit.* 3.5).

Elsewhere, reflecting on the Watchers story in Genesis 6:1–8, Augustine quotes the opening of his own Easter poem *De Anima* and comments: 'In my view a brief but correct definition of virtue is: ordering of love [ordo amoris]' (*City* 15.22, cf. 14.10). It is because of this conception that he can say 'Love, and do what you will' (*Ep. Joh.* 7.8, on 1 Jn 4:9). We have seen similar thoughts in his commentary on the Sermon on the Mount (pp. 75–6).

The passage just quoted from *De Doctrina Christiana* has in mind mainly love of persons, even though it speaks more generally of things (rerum). Its continuation shows just how much in personal relationships Augustine is willing to sacrifice out of 'fear of the gifts of fortune':

> But since you cannot benefit everyone, you ought to care most for those who are most closely bound to you by fitness of place, time, and circumstance, just as if you were choosing at random. (*Doct. Christ.* 1.28.29)

Here love is divorced from passion and even affection. It is the love you should feel for your neighbour (Lev. 19:18), indiscriminately so far as time and strength allow; and everyone is your neighbour, as the parable of the Good Samaritan teaches (Lk. 10:29–37; see *Doct. Christ.* 1.30.31–3). Augustine's model for human love is thus the neighbourliness of a community, the kind of relationship which he inculcates in his

191

influential Rule for the Hipponese nunnery where his sister had been abbess (*Ep.* 211).

He had loved music, but that love too must now be tempered:

> I confess that I still find a certain satisfaction [acquiesco] in music which is imbued with the glorification of you, when it is sung by melodious and well-trained voices. . . . This sensual [carnis] delight, by which I ought not to allow my mind to be paralysed, often tricks [fallit] me, when sense accompanying reason is not content to be in second place but tries to rush ahead and take the lead, only because it deserves to be admitted for reason's sake. So I sin in this way without realizing [sentiens], though I realize later. (*Conf.* 10.33.49)

Men and women who live by Augustine's prescription will to some extent live as in a monastery, not necessarily renouncing 'the world' of business and family and power and property, but renouncing intimacy, ardour, sensual delights, all special loyalties. Augustine had known these good things, none better. But he gave them up, and he asks the rest of us to do the same. He had known their price too: jealousy, that intractable and humiliating emotion, and the 'suspicions, fears, bad temper, and rows' which also beset him as a young lover in Carthage (*Conf.* 3.1.1). In place of these flawed goods he offers one supreme nourishment to the human spirit, the love of God. Here are the breathtaking words in which he describes the life of his own choice:

> But what do I do when I love my God? . . . a light of a certain kind, a voice, a perfume, a food, an embrace; but they are of the kind that I love in my inner self, when my soul is bathed in light that is not bound by space; when it listens to sound that never dies away; when it breathes fragrance that is never consumed by the eating; when it clings to an embrace from which it is not severed by fulfilment of desire. This is what I love when I love my God. (*Conf.* 10.6.8, trs. Pine-Coffin)

Sex

Not only its transience shapes Augustine's attitude to sex. He also thinks that sexual activity is, in itself, wrong and shameful and degrading.

There was a fashion for sexual abstinence among upper-class fourth-century Christians such as Pelagius and Jerome and their disciples and admirers – and not only among Christians, for we find, for example, the pagan historian Ammianus Marcellinus (c.330–c.391) praising the pagan emperor Julian (332–63) for choosing celibacy at the age of 28 when his wife died (*Res Gestae* 25.4.2). But celibacy in the sense of sexual abstinence is not the same as bachelorhood, and two of Augustine's writings were actually in defence of matrimony: *De Bono Conjugali* which sought to remove the misconception that the Catholic church disparaged the married state, and the later *De Nuptiis et Concupiscentia* (the work whose first book provoked Julian of Eclanum into controversy), refuting its disparagement by some of the Pelagians.

Marriage according to Augustine is a good thing:

> not only for the sake of procreation of children but for the sake of fellowship with the other sex, which is itself natural. (*Bon. Conj.* 3.3)

> The fact that incontinence is bad does not prevent a marriage from being good, even one in which the partners are not continent but have sexual intercourse. (*Gen. Lit.* 9.7.12)

In the letter which he sent to a certain Valerius, count of Africa, enclosing a copy of book 1 of *De Nuptiis et Concupiscentia*, Augustine praised the marital continence which Valerius had adopted (*Ep.* 200.3). But to another count, Boniface, who was to lead the unsuccessful defence of Hippo against the Vandal siege during which Augustine died, he explained that a married man may adopt continence only with his wife's consent, and conversely (*Ep.* 220.12, cf. *Bon. Conj.* 6.6); to do otherwise is not sound doctrine (*Ep.* 262.2). Exploring what he calls the labyrinths (multos sinus, *Retract.* 2.57) of Christian teaching on divorce, he argues that 1 Corinthians 7:11 is not meant to sanction a wife's leaving her husband except on grounds of his adultery (*Conj. Adult.* 1), and that only death dissolves a marriage (*Conj. Adult.* 2); the same remarriage rules apply to men and women (*Bon. Conj.* 7); it is permissible to regularize an extra-marital liaison by marriage (*Bon. Conj.* 5); unnatural sexual acts, using 'a part of a woman that is not allowed', are worse towards one's wife than towards a prostitute (*Bon. Conj.* 11.12, a rule perhaps meant for the protection of reluctant wives).

However, marriage is a second best (*City* 16.36, *Conf.* 10.30.41). Although Augustine would not have ventured the erotic imagery, drawn from the Song of Songs, with which Jerome commended virginity to the daughter Eustochium of his friend and monastic neighbour Paula in Bethlehem (Jerome, *Ep.* 22), he writes in lavish praise to the rich and splendid mother and grandmother of that other virgin protégée of Jerome, Demetrias (see p. 105 above): 'It is a more fruitful and fertile happiness to have purity in the heart than milk in the breasts' (*Ep.* 150). Not that virginity makes up for other faults:

> One knows many dedicated virgins who are garrulous, inquisitive, drunken, disputatious, greedy, and proud, all of which things go against their rules and involve them in the offence of disobedience, as Eve was involved. For this reason not only should the obedient

be preferred to the disobedient, but a more obedient married woman to a less obedient virgin. (*Bon. Conj.* 23.30)

Nevertheless Augustine expresses regret that Boniface chose to remarry after being widowed (*Ep.* 220.4).

Marriage is a lesser good than celibacy because sexual intercourse is bad. When continence beckoned Augustine in the garden at Milan (*Conf.* 8.11.27), the inner voices that tried to hold him back whispered:

'From this moment we shall not be with you ever again. From this moment you will not be allowed to do this thing or that, ever again.' And what were they putting into my mind, which I call 'this thing or that', what, my God, were they putting into my mind? Filth, that's what they were putting into my mind, foulness, things that I pray you, in your mercy, to keep from the soul of your servant. (*Conf.* 8.11.26)

True to his 'brief definition' of virtue, Augustine holds that the badness of sexual acts makes desire for them bad also. Thus it is that writing in the 390s, some ten years after the events recorded, he laments that memories of old bedmates still come to him in dreams (cf. Donne, *Sermons* X 56), and he looks forward to the time when 'subjected in sleep to these degrading temptations ‹my soul› not only will not succumb, to the point of bodily secretion, but will not even give its consent' (*Conf.* 10.30.42). Victims of rape, he ludicrously advises, should try not to enjoy the experience (*Mend.* 19.40); and a lecherous person 'makes good use of a bad thing when he curbs his lust [concupiscentia] in matrimony' (*Pecc. Mer.* 1.29.57).

We have seen that Augustine thinks procreation a part of the justification for marriage; he thinks it the *only* justification for sexual intercourse. Sex not aiming at children is a fault, though venial in a married couple (*Bon. Conj.* 6.6). Referring to the polygamy recorded in Genesis he says:

Those to whom the apostle allowed bodily intercourse with a single spouse as pardonable on account of their intemperance are on a lower step towards God than the ‹patriarchs› who, though each had more than one, aimed in intercourse with them only at the procreation of children, as a wise man aims only at his body's health in food and drink. (*Doct. Christ.* 3.18.27)

And many other texts carry the same message (e.g. *Pecc. Mer.* 1.29.57, *City* 16.25, *Gen. Lit.* 9.5.9).

Not every Christian in Augustine's day shared this attitude. Augustine was shocked to read in Julian of Eclanum the opinion that pleasure had been attached by God to copulation for the purpose of encouraging people to go to the trouble of reproducing their kind (*C. Sec. Jul.* 3.212). According to Julian there is nothing wrong with sexual desire; it is natural and innocent (ibid. 1.71, 3.209); it existed before the Fall (1.70); if what went wrong after Adam had been our sexual proclivities, that is what Christ would have put right (2.137). But Augustine even considered castration, rejecting that course (unlike Origen) on the ground that he was not among those who 'have the power to take it' ('potest capere', *Conf.* 8.1.2, quoting Mt. 19:11, where the Greek translates 'to whom it has been given').

We must now ask *why* Augustine thought that sex is bad. Mainly, of course, he hoped to rely on scriptural authority. Although it would surely defy any interpreter to extract a general disapproval of sexual activity from the Old Testament, Paul, inheriting a newer strain of asceticism which undoubtedly existed already in the civilized world of his time, and not only in the Jewish part of it, provides Augustine with a more promising source. It is interesting that the text, Romans 13:13, which Augustine 'picked up and read' at his conversion (p. 4 above) is singled out by him only a few years later, in a letter to his metropolitan Aurelius (the letter of a young priest in a hurry), as *not* harping exclusively on sex. Of the three objects of Paul's condemnation in it, he complains,

> lechery and lewdness [NEB: debauchery and vice] are considered so
> great an offence that no one who has defiled himself with that sin
> is thought fit to take communion, let alone to hold office in the
> church. Rowdiness and drunkenness are considered so permissible and
> tolerable that they are practised not only on holy days in honour of
> the most blessed martyrs – a lamentable sight to anyone who looks
> on such festivities with more than a carnal eye – but on any and
> every day. . . . At least let such a disgraceful practice be removed
> from the cemeteries where the bodies of the saints are laid, and from
> the place where the sacraments are celebrated, and from the house of
> prayer. (*Ep.* 22.1.3 after Baxter)

More important for our purpose, the Romans text does not condemn sex as such. Against Julian Augustine cites (*C. Sec. Jul.* 3.212) Paul's doctrine of the two laws: 'Flesh lusts against spirit, spirit against flesh. Each opposes the other, to prevent you doing what you will' (Gal. 5:17). Yet the continuation shows that neither does this passage object to sex as such, but only to a list of vices including fornication (verses 19–21).

Augustine has also his own objection against sexual activity: it depends on erection of the penis which is not subject to the will. He supposes that erection was the embarrassment which caused Adam and, apparently, Eve to cover their nakedness (*Pecc. Mer.* 2.22.36, alluding to Gen. 3:7); and on the basis of the supposition he constructs the theory that involuntary erection is a result of the Fall:

> Without ‹bodily lust, concupiscentia carnalis› there cannot be . . .
> intercourse for the purpose of obtaining children; but it would have
> been possible without it if human nature, by not sinning, had
> remained in that state in which it was created. The sex organs . . .
> could have been responsive to the bidding [nutu] of the will, instead
> of being roused by a surge of physical attraction. (*Ep.* 184A, cf. *Ench.*
> 28.105, *C. Sec. Jul.* 2.45, 6.22, *City* 14.24 – some people can wiggle
> their ears)

Adam's and Eve's genitals became disobedient in punishment for Adam's
and Eve's disobedience; that is why they covered them (*City* 13.15,
14.23).

But the theory that sexual activity became disgraceful because of the
Fall does not explain why the involuntariness of erection is a disgrace:
it assumes that. A recent writer has proposed the contrary, that this
feature is what makes erection attractive to its object (Scruton pp. 63–8);
and while the suggestion seems to me implausible – since it is also
attractive to have someone *make* themselves ready for you – it reminds
us that the involuntariness of erection does not have to be seen as a flaw
in the human condition (wouldn't Augustine have done better to cite
menstruation, traditionally detected in the curse of Genesis 3:16?).

To my mind the mystery why Augustine regarded sex as bad is only
exceeded by the mystery why Christian culture for so long agreed with
him.

Lying, utility, sin, and fault

In the remainder of this chapter I have selected two further topics, lying
and suicide, which illustrate the tenor of Augustine's moral convictions
and on which his views have been influential.

> But here arises an extraordinarily difficult and intricate question
> about which I once, when I felt the need for an answer, wrote a
> big book: whether it is ever required [officium] of a just man to
> lie. . . . My own opinion is that every lie is a sin, but it makes a great
> difference with what mind [animo] and about what matters one lies.
> Someone who lies with an intention to be of use [consulendi . . .
> voluntate] does not sin so much as someone who lies with an
> intention of harming; and the man who by lying sends a traveller
> on the wrong road does not do so much harm as the man who
> perverts a course of life by a deceptive lie. (*Ench.* 18.6)

The *Enchiridion*, or handbook of Christian doctrine, from which this
summary is taken, was written in 421 at the request of an upper-class
Roman called Laurentius. The big book to which Augustine refers in it

(only one 'book' in the ancient sense, so a small treatise) is *De Mendacio*, 'On Lying', dating from the late 390s; and in 422 he was to cover much the same ground in his *Contra Mendacium*, 'Against Lying'.

The latter work had a special purpose, to dissuade its Catholic addressee Consentius from lying about his religious allegiance in order to infiltrate the heretical Spanish sect of Priscillianists, currently under persecution but showing no signs of demise (its founder Priscillian, bishop of Avila, had been executed by the civil powers in 386 for sorcery, to the dismay of some leading Catholic churchmen). Augustine does not have much difficulty in demonstrating to Consentius the folly of his proposed course, which, despite the fact that Priscillianists were likewise in the habit of passing themselves off as Catholics, would sow distrust where respect was sought. He takes the opportunity of broadening his theme into a general defence of the position taken by the *Enchiridion*.

The earlier *De Mendacio* had defended the same uncompromising position, but was prefaced by a discussion of the definition of lying. Augustine realizes that not every falsehood is a lie nor every lie a falsehood (*Mend.* 3.3), and that one may lie without being believed (ibid.). Jokes are not lies (*Mend.* 2.2, *Quaest. Hept.* 1.145), nor is metaphor (*C. Mend.* 10.24), nor fiction (*C. Mend.* 13.28). The psalmist's praise of him 'who speaks truth in his heart' (Ps 14:3 [Heb. Bib. 15:2]) is not a licence to speak falsehood in the mouth (*C. Mend.* 6.14); Augustine would have had no time for the doctrine later called 'mental reservation' by which, for example, an errant husband can say 'I haven't ever slept with her' and save himself from a lie by silently adding 'since last Wednesday' (see Bok 1979:37–9). Definition becomes problematic when we consider a speaker who expects to be disbelieved, and exploits the expectation. There are two things this speaker may do:

(i) say what he thinks is true with the purpose of inducing belief in what he thinks is false, or

(ii) say what he thinks is false with the purpose of inducing belief in what he thinks is true.

The former purpose is deception (fallere); and Augustine shows that the question which of these two performances is a lie turns on two candidate conditions for lying:

(a) 'an utterance with the will to utter a falsehood'
(b) 'an utterance with the will to deceive' (*Mend.* 4.4).

He tacitly assumes that at least the disjunction of these conditions is necessary, and that no further condition is necessary, and under those assumptions he derives the following results about performances (i) and (ii). If condition (a) is necessary but (b) is not, the second performance only is a lie; if condition (b) is necessary but (a) is not, the first performance only is a lie; if both conditions are necessary, neither performance counts as a lie; while if merely the disjunction of them ('a will to some sort of falsity') is necessary, then both of the performances will have to be reckoned lies. Augustine notes that whichever of these four accounts of the conditions for a lie is correct, it is possible for anyone to avoid lying if he avoids both (i) and (ii), and chooses instead to:

> (iii) say what he thinks is true without the purpose of inducing belief in anything other than what he says.

Therefore, he concludes, 'there is no need to be afraid of any of these definitions' (*Mend*. 4.4). So his recommendation is to assume for safety's sake that the disjunction of (a) and (b) is enough for a lie, and act accordingly. He does not seem to notice that although this policy may be suitable for someone choosing how to act, it is inadequate for his own purpose, which is critical, not practical. How can he discuss whether any lie is required without having decided what a lie is? His actual procedure in the ensuing discussion appears to assume that (a) and (b) are both necessary (as at *Ench*. 22.7), and to ignore the special case of the counter-suggestible audience in which the two conditions cannot be satisfied jointly.

If he is to sustain an interdict on lying Augustine must take account of numerous biblical texts in which lies appear to be condoned. Consentius had doubtless reminded him of the story told of Jehu king of Israel, who compassed the deaths of the priests of Baal by pretending to favour their god, declaring, 'Ahab served Baal a little; but Jehu shall serve him much' (2 Kgs 10:18 AV). Augustine's response is that the Bible does not set up Jehu as a model; on the contrary he 'departed not from after ‹the sins of Jeroboam›, to wit, the golden calves that were in Beth-el, and that were in Dan' (2 Kgs 10:29 AV, see *C. Mend*. 2.3). He deals differently with Jacob's lie, 'I am Esau your firstborn', in the episode where Jacob's mother dressed her son in a goatskin to trick a blessing out of his old, blind father Isaac (Gen. 27:19). This is 'not a lie but a mystery' (mysterium, *C. Mend*. 10.24); for since the blessing of Jacob prefigures the proclamation of Christ among all nations, Jacob did not know what he was doing! (velut a nesciente, *City* 16.37, cf. *Quaest. Hept*. 1.74, *Serm*. 4.16–24). Augustine also has a third, simpler tactic, deployed in his first letter to Jerome (see p. 11 above) reproving the older man for having suggested that Paul lied in his account at Gal. 2:11–14 of the quarrel with Peter over eating in the company of gentiles:

> It is one question whether it is ever right for a good man to lie, another whether there can have been good reason [oportuerit] for a writer of holy scriptures to lie; or not really another *question*,

because there is no question of it. Admit even one required lie [officiosum mendacium] into such a pinnacle of authority, and no smallest part of those books will remain which, if it appears difficult for morality or incredible for faith, will not be attributed by the same pernicious rule to a purpose in the author, and a requirement on him, to lie. . . . Speaking for myself, I shall use every strength the Lord gives me to show that in all the texts which are adduced to clothe lies with utility, there is good reason to understand them differently, and so to maintain their undeviating veracity throughout. (*Ep.* 28.3.3,5)

However, non-biblical lies do pose a 'question'; as he had said to Laurentius, an 'extraordinarily difficult and intricate' one. On the one side, Augustine has a clear perception of the *dis*utilities of lying, some of which apply even to a policy which admits lying as an option. The liar is liable to bias in estimating the consequences of his action (*Mend.* 18.38), which are likely to be uncertain (*C. Mend.* 5.8). The practice is habit-forming, so that even one honourable lie may lead by insensible steps to a lack of respect for truth (*C. Mend.* 18.37, *Mend.* 12.19, *Ep.* 28.3.5). Above all, a liar who is discovered loses credit, which may be very hard to recover (*C. Mend.* 4.7); and without credit, the purpose of speech is subverted: 'I know this, that even someone whose teaching is that there is good reason to lie, wishes it to appear *true* teaching' (*C. Mend.* 18.37, cf. *Mend.* 8.11).

On the other hand Augustine (unlike Kant, see Bok 1979:40) readily concedes that lies are not all equally heinous, and *De Mendacio* expands the distinctions of the *Enchiridion* summary into eight different grades of them (*Mend.* 14.25). The 'difficult' question is whether any of these grades deserve the name of 'officious', or 'required', lie. Augustine often gives the appearance of seeing this as a question about 'utility' (e.g. *Mend.* 4.5), viz. whether the utility of a lie ever outweighs its disutility, thereby constituting 'good reason' (oportere) to tell it. But his own solution turns out to be non-consequentialist, and to rest on the concept of sin.

Like the preacher, Augustine is against sin, on first appearance unconditionally:

It does indeed make a very great difference for what cause and what end and with what intention [intentione] a thing is done; but nothing established as a sin [quae constat esse peccata] may be done on any pretext [obtentu] of good cause, or for any supposedly [quasi] good end, or with any would-be [velut] good intention. (*C. Mend.* 7.18)

Is this principle really unconditional? Its qualifications 'quasi' and 'velut', and the opprobrious tone of 'obtentu', might be thought to imply that sin can be justified by genuinely good ends; though on the other hand there is no sign of that in the ensuing text, and Augustine often quotes with approval the Pauline ban on 'doing evil that good may come' (Rom. 3:8). More telling against the unconditionality of Augustine's principle is his restriction of it to sins that are 'established' – i.e. fixed, or agreed, or both – which suggests that there is some other kind of sin to which the prohibition does not apply. Once more the context fails to indicate what this other kind might be; but elsewhere in his two books on lying Augustine makes use of the notion of a compensative, or redeemed, sin, peccatum compensativum, and it is in terms of that notion that he examines the hard cases without which no discussion of lying would be serious.

A compensative sin is a bad act from which enough good consequences flow to counterbalance the badness in the act itself (we have to assume that the distinction between acts and their consequences can be drawn with sufficient precision). Someone who wishes to defend the thesis that it is sometimes 'required of a just man to lie' will need to do more than show that some lies are compensative sins, since it might be that no one is ever required to commit a compensative sin. It might even be that no one is *permitted* to commit a compensative sin, however good the consequences flowing from it. I shall argue that this last is the conclusion at which Augustine is aiming. From that general conclusion about sin he will then be in a position to counter-attack. However, it is important to recognize from the start that his counter-attack will depend on his being allowed to assume that every lie *is a sin*. I take it that the notion of compensative sin is introduced against the background of that assumption: lies are sins because there is badness 'in' lying, and Augustine sees his task as that of determining whether the goodness 'outside' any lie can be such as to require a good man to tell it. (But it has to be admitted that this is not the only way in which he pictures the relationship between sin and badness, even in the two books on lying; often – like Aquinas on lying – he assumes that a lie will be permissible only if it is not a sin at all.)

Having set up this framework we are now in a position to inspect Augustine's treatment of the hard cases. Some of those he considers come from the Old Testament: e.g. the midwives who lied to Pharaoh in order to save male Hebrew babies, and whom God made to prosper (Ex. 1:19–20); and Rahab the Jericho prostitute who lied to her king that the two Israelite spies staying with her had departed, and was spared when Joshua took the city (Josh. 2:5, 6:25; both stories are discussed in C. Mend. 15.32–17.34). He also describes an imaginary case:

> But because we are men and live among men, and I confess I am not yet in the number of those who are untroubled by compensative

sins, I am often overcome in human affairs by human feeling. . . .
Suppose a man is dangerously ill with a serious disease, and would
not have the strength to bear it if told of the death of his only and
much loved son. He asks you whether the boy is alive, and you know
his life has ended. What answer will you make, given that, if it is
anything but these three, 'He is dead', 'He is alive', and 'I don't
know', the man will believe that his son is dead, and that you are
afraid to tell him and unwilling to lie? It will come to the same
thing if you keep quite silent. Of these three two, 'He is alive' and
'I don't know', are false and cannot be said by you without lying. But
if you say the one true one, 'He is dead', and the man is so upset
that his own death ensues, the cry will go up that you have killed
him. (*C. Mend.* 18.36)

If we survey Augustine's two books on lying we can, I think, separate
three responses to this plea on behalf of the officious lie. One, not very
telling in the example of the dying man but a good point in general, is
that anyone who shows himself willing to do wrong for the sake of
avoiding greater evil puts himself in the power of wicked men (*C. Mend.*
9.20). The other two, I shall argue, fail.

In his comment on the example of the dying man Augustine asks
rhetorically how Consentius would think it right to respond if a woman
said to him, 'Come to bed with me, or I shall die' (*C. Mend.* 18.36).
This comparison with sexual wrongdoing, which is frequent in both
books, correctly displays the problem of compensative sins as a general
one, not special to lying. On the other hand Augustine's own doctrine
of the gradation of lies, to say nothing of the metaphor contained in the
word 'compensativum', should remind us that the case for required lying
does not depend on there being also a case for required extra-marital
intercourse – or, to take another example, required murder, substituting
our own for Augustine's moral prejudices. It might be possible to justify
some lies by their compensation, even if it were not possible to justify
any murders that way.

The third and major Augustinian argument against the existence of
officious lies has to be gathered from other passages in *De Mendacio* and
Contra Mendacium. It contains three main stages, the first of which goes
like this. The accusation in the example, 'you have killed him', must be
rejected. The choice at the dying man's bedside is not between lying and
killing someone, but between lying and acquiescing in someone's death.
And this makes a moral difference. Discussing the dilemma of a Christian
in penal times who is ordered to sacrifice to the heathen gods on pain
of rape (stuprum, being debauched), he comments:

If [the victim], when that condition was proposed to him . . . had
replied, 'I choose neither; I hate them both', then in his uttering

these and suchlike words, which certainly, because they were true, would not constitute any consent or approval on his part, acquiescence in being wronged [injuriarum acceptio] would be imputed to him, whatever he suffered at their hands, but commission of sins would be ascribed to *them*. . . . If the question is, which of [these two outcomes] ought someone rather to avoid who could not avoid both but could avoid either one, then I shall answer, His own sin rather than another's, and a lesser sin of his own than a graver sin of another. (*Mend.* 9.14)

We have already seen on p. 75 that in Augustine's eyes consent makes a full sin. Here he argues that consent can always be avoided, and that without it a man is not implicated in what he fails to prevent, even if he was able to prevent it. It follows from this that no one is ever faced with a choice between two sins: in avoiding the one sin he can always ensure, by withholding his consent, that what happens in consequence, if a sin at all, is someone else's. Moreover, it is not possible to prevent someone else's sin by yielding to his threats (or more generally thwarting his proposed action), since the sin is in the threat itself (or more generally the proposal, *Mend.* 9.13 – but the text is doubtful). The upshot is, though Augustine does not make it explicit, that no compensative sin compensates for another *sin*; and this ends the first stage of his major argument.

One of Augustine's grades of lie is the polite lie, 'told for charming people, in a desire to please' (*Mend.* 14.25). Aquinas, commenting on the question whether 'light-hearted' lies (jocosa mendacia), of which this grade is a species, are sins, says that the answer depends on whether the audience for the lie understands it as intending what it says: if so, it is a sin, if not, it is not a lie (*Summa Theologiae* 2.2.110.3). Augustine, perhaps assuming the former kind of case, treats it as beyond question that lies of politeness should be 'completely shunned and rejected' (*Mend.* 14.25). This severe view may rest, I suggest, on the principle that no good consequence can justify a bad act unless failure to secure the consequence would be culpable, a fault; or in other words (on the conception of sin which we are attributing to Augustine), every permissible sin compensates for a fault. At any rate it appears that Augustine needs this principle, over-severe though it surely is, as the second stage of his major argument.

At the third stage he needs to maintain that every fault is a sin; from which it follows according to his conception of sin as requiring consent, that mere acquiescence is never blameworthy. But now he is being over-generous: it might be your fault, for example, that the wind blew your vase over, because you should not have put the vase in such a silly place; but you did not consent to its being blown over, which is therefore not your sin. Similarly it might be partly your fault that a thief stole your raincoat from your car, because you should not have left the car unlocked; but in leaving the car unlocked you did not consent to the theft, which is therefore not your sin but the thief's alone. Again, if Rahab in Jericho had told the king that the Israelite spies were still in her house, and they had been found and killed, their death would not have been her sin but only the king's; yet the fact that she acquiesced in it by not using her opportunity to conceal them might expose her to blame, even though the acquiescence does not constitute consent. These examples seem to me to demonstrate that 'no fault without sin' is too narrow a doctrine of fault, if it is founded on Augustine's perfectly reasonable conception of a sin as requiring consent. But that narrow doctrine of fault is Augustine's, implicit in his treatment of the Christian threatened with rape. Augustine espouses what might be called *Pilatism*, the view that one can absolve oneself of blame for a course of events by washing one's hands and 'hating' it. (His opinion about Pilate himself, however, is that Pilate does bear a small part of the blame for Jesus' death; but he bases that judgement on the ground that Pilate, despite saying that he would not act in the matter, 'nevertheless acted', *Enarr. Ps* 63.4 on Mt. 27:24–6.)

The three foregoing stages furnish Augustine with the following argument:

(1) No compensative sin compensates for a sin;
(2) every permissible sin compensates for a fault;
(3) every fault is a sin;
therefore no compensative sin is permissible.

His conclusion now follows, given the assumption, discussed above, that

(4) every lie is a sin;

For the following two extra premises are acceptable:

(5) no sin is required unless it is compensative;
(6) only what is permissible is required;

and from (4), (5), and (6), together with the conclusion of the previous argument, we can infer

therefore no lie is required.

I think that Augustine feels insecure in this conclusion (cf. Bok 1979:44). On Rahab, for example, he reassures us that if she had refrained from lying and her house had been searched, God might have prevented the search from succeeding (*C. Mend.* 17.34). Perhaps if Augustine had given more than passing attention to the example of Pilate he would have found a way to escape from what is clearly for him an uncomfortable dogma to be saddled with. And then his Christian successors might have abstained from some of the sophistry by which, too often awed by his authority, they contrived (see Bok 1979:37–9) to persuade themselves that what could not be permitted if it were a lie, was not a lie *really*.

Suicide

Although Augustine was not the first Christian thinker to oppose suicide (see Clement, *Stromateis* 4.13.71,76, referred to by Chadwick in Armstrong 1967:173), it is due to him more than anyone that suicide came to be officially condemned by the western church, and to be made illegal in many Christian states. It had not always been so. Early Christianity thrived on martyrs, and many martyrs courted death, some of them in ways that came close to self-killing. In fourth- and fifth-century Africa Donatism sustained this tradition. According to Gibbon's account:

> Many of these fanatics were possessed with the horror of life, and the desire of martyrdom; and they deemed it of little moment by what means, or by what hands, they perished, if their conduct was sanctified by the intention of devoting themselves to the glory of the true faith and the hope of eternal happiness. Sometimes they rudely disturbed the festivals and profaned the temples of paganism, with the design of exciting the most zealous of the idolaters to revenge the insulted honour of their gods. They sometimes forced their way into the courts of justice, and compelled the affrighted judge to give orders for their immediate execution. They frequently stopped travellers on the public highways, and obliged them to inflict the stroke of martyrdom, by the promise of a reward, if they consented, and by the threat of instant death, if they refused to grant so very singular a favour. When they were disappointed of every other resource, they announced the day on which, in the presence of their friends and brethren, they should cast themselves headlong from some lofty rock; and many precipices were shewn, which had acquired fame by the number of religious suicides. (Gibbon, *Decline and Fall* volume 2, pp. 389–90, based on *Corr. Don.* 3.12)

The Donatists and others who agreed with them in defending the practice of religious suicide could plausibly maintain that, in Hume's later words, 'There is not a single text of scripture which prohibits it' ('On suicide' in *Essays*, p. 595 note). The Old Testament records four suicides, of Abimelech (who ordered his servant to kill him, Judg. 9:53–4), Samson (Judg. 16:23–31), Saul (1 Sam. 31:4) and Ahitophel (2 Sam. 17:23). A character from the Apocrypha called Razis was the Donatists' favourite, a Jerusalem elder whose spectacular suicide is recounted at 2 Macc. 14:37–46. In the New Testament Judas, seized with remorse for betraying Jesus to the chief priests, went out and hanged himself (Mt. 27:3–5, but according to Acts 1:18 he died of a sudden hernia). Finally, some Christians, including Tertullian and Origen, had likened the death of Jesus himself to a suicide, on the ground that it could not have happened without his consent: 'our *B: Sauiour* . . . chose that way for our redemption to Sacrifice his Life and profuse his blood' (Donne, *Biathanatos*, part 1, distinction 3, section 2).

Augustine comments on three of these seven examples, exonerating Samson but condemning Razis and Judas. When Samson pulled down the temple on himself and the Philistines who were gathered inside it:

> the death which they had soon been going to inflict on him he wanted to share with them, since he was not able to escape it. Indeed, he did not act of his own accord [sponte sua]; the act must be ascribed to the spirit of God which was using him by its presence to do what he could not do when that same spirit was lacking. (*C. Gaud.* 1.31.39, cf. *City* 1.21)

Unfortunately the biblical account mentions neither that Samson was threatened with execution nor that the strength returning to him as his hair grew was the spirit of God acting in him. As Donne complained:

> Therefore to iustify this fact in *Samson*, *St Augustine* aequally zealous of *Samsons* honor, and his own Conscyence, builds still vppon his old foundation *That this was by the speciall inspiration from God* Which because it appeares not in the *History*, nor Lyes in proofe, may with the same easinesse be refusd, as it is presented. (Donne, ibid., part 3, distinction 5, section 5)

By contrast Razis *is* reported as having had no escape from death at the hands of his enemies. Augustine notes that fact, and adds that the chronicler does not praise this suicide, that the 'nobility' commended in it by Donatists is a pagan virtue, and that in any case Jews did not rank the (Apocryphal) books of Maccabees within 'the Law and the Prophets and the Psalms' (*C. Gaud.* 1.31.36–8, quoting Lk. 24:44). With his comment on the death of Judas he begins to reveal his own objections to suicide:

> In the case of the traitor Judas it was not so much the offence he committed that brought him to utter destruction, as despair of being pardoned [indulgentia]. He did not deserve mercy; and that is why no light shone in his heart to make him hurry for pardon from the one he had betrayed, as those who crucified him were to do. In that despair he killed himself. (*Serm.* 353.3.8, cf. *City* 1.17)

When Rome was sacked in 410 certain dedicated virgins were reported to have taken their own lives in order to avoid rape; and these reports are the occasion of Augustine's extended discussion of the morality of suicide in book 1 of the *City of God*. It is a strangely unsatisfying passage. He starts by remarking that anyone who blames the other virgins, those who preferred rape, is a fool, for rape without their consent was no sin of theirs (*City* 1.17). Accordingly, a suicide such as Lucretia's ought to be seen as self-punishment of someone who is *innocent*, and ought to be condemned as such; even supposing Lucretia did secretly consent, penitence not death was her correct course (*City* 1.19). Augustine stresses that suicide is killing, and as such banned by the Sixth Commandment. To be sure, that commandment has exceptions: other animals than men are not covered, and only (Manichean) idiots think it applies to bushes (*City* 1.20); in addition there are such persons as 'God commands to be killed either by an enacted law or by express command referring to some person at some time' (*City* 1.21) as Abraham was commanded to sacrifice his son Isaac. Such a decree ad personam might in principle enjoin suicide, as we must suppose in the case of Samson. Otherwise 'anyone who has killed a man, whether himself or someone else, is involved in a charge of murder [homicidia]' (*City* 1.21). Pagans who find greatness of soul (animi magnitudo) in the man who kills himself in adversity should rather have called it weakness, 'in not managing to bear whatever comes to him of hardships or others' sins' (*City* 1.22; in this Augustine agrees with Aristotle, inventor of the virtue of magnanimity, see *Nicomachean Ethics* 1116a 12–15, 1138a 10, 1166b 11–13). It would be more reasonable to describe as great-souled the philosopher Cleombrotus (Augustine calls him Theombrotus), who on reading Plato's proofs of immortality took his life for the sake of gaining a better one (ibid., cf. Cicero, *Tusculan Disputations* 1.34.84). Jesus advised flight from persecution, not death; Job and Regulus were more admirable than Cato (*City* 1.22–4). Augustine sums up this part of his discussion as follows:

> This we say, this we assert, this we approve in every way: no one ought to inflict on himself spontaneous death with the idea of escaping temporary troubles, in case he should fall into unending ones; no one ought to inflict it on account of someone else's sin, in case by that very act he should bring a really serious sin on himself, whereas he was not defiled by the other's; no one ought to inflict it on account of his own past sins, for which he needs more of this life to make possible their healing by repentance; and no one ought to inflict it out of yearning for a better life which he hopes for after death, because the better life after death is not available to those who are guilty of their own death. (*City* 1.26)

Finally, Augustine asks why it is not good for a Christian to commit suicide at the moment of baptism, rather than 'thrust his freed head back into all the dangers of this life' (*City* 1.27). No reason, he concedes, could be more just than this one; but this one is mad, a short cut (compendium) that merely substitutes one serious sin for the risk of many small ones.

What arguments can we find in these chapters and elsewhere for the doctrine that suicide is a sin? It is noticeable that although Augustine cites Plato he does not mention Plato's reasoning (of which he may have been ignorant). According to Plato the true philosopher, by cultivating those activities which, not depending on the body, will continue after death, 'practises dying and being dead' (*Phaedo* 64b). Yet he may not hasten his release, because he like all men is a possession of the gods, placed on earth at their will as in a prison or a garrison (the Greek word here is ambiguous); he must 'await another benefactor' (*Phaedo* 62a–b). Although Plato elsewhere condoned suicide as a response to calamity or disgrace (*Laws* 873c–d), the *Phaedo* passage has had the greater influence; and the suggestion conveyed by the word 'garrison', if that is the right translation, was to recur in the later formulation which Hume set up for criticism: ' "*But you are placed by Providence, like a sentinel, in a particular station*" ' (Hume, 'On suicide', *Essays* p. 592). Hume trenchantly criticized (ibid.) this implication that each person's life is God's to dispose of, not his own, though others including Kant ('Suicide' in *Lectures on Ethics* p. 154) have subsequently revived it. A hardly different idea is at work in Augustine's claim that homicide – even, he must mean, with the victim's consent – is permitted only by God's command. But this is vulnerable to another part of Hume's objection:

> Shall we assert that the Almighty has reserved to himself, in any peculiar manner, the disposal of the lives of men, and has not submitted that event, in common with others, to the general laws by which the universe is governed? . . . If I turn aside a stone which is falling on my head, I disturb the course of nature, and I invade the peculiar province of the Almighty, by lengthening out my life beyond the period, which, by the general laws of matter and motion, he has assigned it. (Hume, 'On suicide' in *Essays* pp. 589–90)

Two other arguments are contained in the passages of Augustine we have looked at: that suicide manifests cowardice, and that it manifests despair, both of which are vices. Neither of these reasons, I think, supports an absolute prohibition. A man may take measures to alleviate his own pain and affliction without cowardice, when the pain and affliction are not demanded for the sake of some valuable end; and the view that suicide is always cowardly must therefore show that the preservation of one's own life is always an end of such a kind, whatever the prospects for its future use. The objection from despair is a stronger one. Despair is a vice whenever it is unreasonable; and almost always it is unreasonable, for almost always a mood of melancholy will abate with time, into a mood in which the sufferer is glad once more to be alive. The Christian can indeed even profess that the unreasonableness of despair is absolute, but that conviction depends on there being a reason, in the death of Christ, for all men to hope for *salvation* – good after death. It cannot be reasonable in absolutely every case to hope for future good in one's earthly life; in the other cases 'sad Patience, too near neighbour of Despair' (Arnold) may be no better than its neighbour.

Augustine's view prevailed in western Christendom. At the Council of Orleans in 533, and again more strongly at the Council of Braga in 562, suicide was officially condemned; a still later council at Toledo in 693 extended the ban to excommunication of attempted suicides. Ronald Knox was doubtless not speaking in his own person when he made a character in one of his detective stories say:

I think it is a fine thing, very often, and the Christian condemnation of it merely echoes a private quarrel between St Augustine and some heretics of his day. (Knox 1960:43)

But I agree with the thrust of Donne's more measured verdict, so far as it concerns suicide:

[Augustine] was of so nice, and refind, and rigorous a conscyence (perchance to redeeme his former Licenciousnes, as it falls out often in such Convertites, to be extremely zealous) that for our direction in actions of this Life, *St Hierome*, and some others may be thought somtymes fitter to adhere vnto, then *St Aug*:. (Donne, *Biathanatos*, part 2, distinction 4, section 1)

Further reading

On lying see the excellent book by Bok (1979). Battin and Mayo (1980) collect useful articles on suicide.

XI

Christian society

Compel them to come in

On 1 June 411, during the summer following the first sack of Rome by Alaric the Goth, 570 African bishops met in conference (collatio) at the Garglian bath-house in Carthage under the presidency of count Marcellinus, a court official sent for the purpose from Ravenna by the western emperor Honorius (imp. 395–423; the *City of God* was to be addressed to Marcellinus). Two hundred and eighty-four of the bishops were Donatist, 286 Catholic, Augustine a 'spokesman' among them. Marcellinus' instructions were to suppress the Donatist 'superstition' and enforce all previous edicts against it (*Codex Theodosianus* 16.11.3). On 26 June, after listening to nearly four weeks of episcopal debate, he pronounced his sentence. The Donatists appealed to Ravenna. On 30 January 412 Honorius promulgated a fresh edict:

> The Donatist clergy were to be exiled and, separated one from another, dispatched to remote corners of the Empire. Donatism was henceforth a criminal offence, punishable by a scale of fines. . . . All Donatist property was to be handed over to the Catholics, but, as in previous edicts, the death penalty was not prescribed. (Frend 1952: 289, citing *Codex Theodosianus* 16.5.52)

Donatism struggled on. Indeed according to Frend (ibid.:229) its church 'had at least a century and a half of existence after Augustine died' in 430. But to the Catholic protagonists in these events, especially bishop Augustine of Hippo and the metropolitan bishop Aurelius of Carthage, the battle must have seemed to be won. Why had they fought it to such a bitter ending?

The three north African provinces of Africa, Numidia and Mauretania had for many years been in a state of tumultuous civil unrest. In November 409 Augustine wrote to a presbyter named Victorianus:

Indeed the whole world is so convulsed with disasters that there is scarcely a place in it without deeds like those you write of, and complaints about them. Even in the Egyptian desert, where the monasteries are seemingly secure in situations remote from bustle, some monks were killed by barbarians not long ago. I expect you have all heard about the atrocities in parts of Italy and Gaul; and now we are beginning to get reports of the same sort from a number of Spanish provinces which for a long while seemed untouched by these troubles. And why look far afield? Here round Hippo, where barbarians have not penetrated, the ravages of Donatist clergy and Circumcellions make havoc in our churches beside which the doings of barbarians are mild. What barbarian could have devised schemes like theirs, of throwing lime and acid into the eyes of our clergy and inflicting the most dreadful injuries on every part of their bodies? They pick on houses to loot and burn, granaries to rob, and store-barrels to drain, compelling many people to be rebaptized by the threat of more of the same. Only the day before I am dictating this, news came in of forty-eight rebaptisms in one locality due to this kind of intimidation. (*Ep.* 111.1, cf. *Corr. Don.* 7.30)

In any divided community where there are atrocities, there are atrocities on both sides, and we may be sure that this was true in north Africa in the fourth and early fifth centuries, even though our evidence, being mainly Catholic, does not tell us so, and even though the Donatists were the fanatical party, strongest in the less romanized country districts, their adherents the economically oppressed, their terrorist Circumcellion bands a menace on the country roads (Augustine once evaded death from such a band only as a result of having been misdirected).

The origin of the religious division, which we, like Augustine (*Ep.* 61), would call a schism, goes back to 311, exactly a century before Marcellinus' conference at Carthage and a few years after the end of the Great Persecution under the last great pagan emperor Diocletian. The primate of the province of Numidia had the right to consecrate the bishop of Carthage in neighbouring Africa; but in 311 a certain Caecilian was consecrated by three local bishops only, one of them, Felix of Apturga, regarded as a 'traditor' in the late persecution, that is, as having complied with the imperial command to hand over all sacred books for destruction. In 312, the year of Constantine's victory over the usurper Maxentius at the Mulvian bridge near Rome, a council of Numidians deposed Caecilian and elected Majorinus, chaplain to a certain Spanish noble lady Lucilla, whom Caecilian a dozen years earlier had ticked off for kissing the bones of an unauthenticated martyr. Following the deposition Constantine appointed an arbitrating commission under pope Miltiades (an African) which found for Caecilian. His opponents appealed, claiming that Miltiades had been seen sacrificing to the Roman gods ten years before. Constantine appointed another tribunal of thirty-three bishops to sit at Arles in Gaul, which again found for Caecilian, at the same time condemning the practice of rebaptizing reconciled heretics. The trouble continued, until eventually Constantine decided to give judgement in person. In fact he never went to Africa, but in 316 he confirmed Caecilian's position in a judgement at Milan, and the next year issued an edict against the rival party. By this time Majorinus had died and in his place Donatus of Casae Nigrae in Numidia had been chosen as schismatic bishop of Carthage; thenceforward the movement bore his name. In 321 Constantine abandoned his edict, when it was clear that the Donatists still had massive popular support. After that the main events were as follows. In 347 commissioners named Paul and Macarius were sent to north Africa by Constantine's successor Constans. They declared the unity of the two African churches and exiled Donatus to Gaul, where he appears to have died. When the pagan emperor Julian (imp. 361–3) succeeded, a policy of toleration prevailed briefly and all church exiles, including Donatists, were allowed to return. Of the years after Julian's short reign Jerome was able to write, doubtless with some exaggeration, that Donatism 'gained practically all Africa' (*De Viris Illustribus* 93; this would refer to all the north African provinces); and in the 370s when Augustine was a student, there was even a Donatist bishop in Rome.

Persecution was renewed following the suppression in 398 by Stilicho of a local revolt under Gildo against the western emperor. Augustine and Aurelius, then newly inducted to their bishoprics, seem to have seen this as an opportunity for reunification. A recent edict of the emperor Theodosius I in June 392 had turned the weight of the civil power against all heresy, subjecting heretical clergy to fines and their places of worship to confiscation (Frend 1984:640, *Codex Theodosianus* 16.5.21). Despite protestations of orthodoxy by the Donatists, the African Catholics laboured to bring Donatism under this ban, representing as a heresy its doctrine that the value of baptism was dependent on the merits of the minister, which the Donatists used in justification of their practice of rebaptizing converts from Catholicism (*C. Ep. Parm.* 1.10.16, 1.12.19, *Ep.* 93.11.46; Augustine is obliged to admit that unless the documents are forged the Donatists had the authority of the third-century African martyr–bishop Cyprian on their side in this serious doctrinal controversy, *Ep.* 93.10.35–6). The Catholic bishops' work bore fruit in 405 when Honorius issued an edict comprehensively outlawing Donatism as a heresy: its adherents were debarred from making contracts, bequests, or gifts, its church property was forfeit to the Catholic church, its meetings and services were banned and houses used for them confiscated, and its clergy were liable to exile. The climax, Marcellinus' judgement

211

and the edict of 412, did little more than confirm these severe measures. Only the death penalty was avoided, in an attempt to choke off the production of Donatist martyrs.

Religious coercion could hardly go further. Why did Augustine lend his support to this intrusion of the civil arm? He gives us his candid account in a long letter written in 408 to Vincentius, a Donatist from the moderate wing known as Rogatists, in answer to one which has not survived but must have pleaded against persecution (apparently represented by Vincentius as 'returning evil for evil', *Ep.* 93.1.2, 4.14). Augustine defends the coercion of Vincentius and his fellows in the following passage:

> So I imagine you can now see that what needs to be considered is not that somebody is forced [cogitur] but whether what he is forced to do is good or bad. Not that anyone can *be* good against his will; but if he stands in fear of suffering some treatment he does not want, he either renounces the prejudices [animositas] that were blocking his way, or is compelled [compellitur] to recognize the truth that he had overlooked. The fear either makes him repudiate falsehood which he used to defend or makes him search for truth of which he used to be ignorant, and what he used to be unwilling to hold he now holds willingly. Perhaps it would be a waste of time to go on asserting this, if there were not so many examples to prove it. (*Ep.* 93.5.16, cf. *C. Gaud.* 2.12.13)

The attitude here expressed had not always been Augustine's, and he proceeds with equal candour to explain why he had changed his mind:

> I have therefore yielded to these examples, which have been put to me by my colleagues. Originally my opinion was simply that no one ought to be forced into the unity of Christ, but words should be our instruments, arguments our weapons, reason our means of conquest, and we should avoid making enforced Catholics out of those whom we had known as open heretics. But this opinion of mine was overcome, not by the words of others controverting it but by the examples to which they pointed. In the first place, my own city was an argument against me, converted to Catholic unity by fear of imperial laws, from having been entirely on the Donatist side; the way your people's destructive prejudices are now hated here makes it hard to believe that those prejudices were ever among us. Then so many other cities were cited to me that I had to acknowledge on the evidence of the facts themselves that this was a case to which the scripture could rightly be applied: 'Give the wise man an opportunity, and he will be wiser' [Prov. 9:9 Vg]. We know for a fact that many individuals already wanted to be Catholics and were

212

impressed by the obvious truth, but dithered from day to day out of reluctance to offend their own people. Many were held back, not by truth – in which you never claimed sole rights – but by the heavy chains of force of habit, so fulfilling the divine saying: 'A hardened servant will not be corrected by words; even if he has understood, he will not comply' [Prov 29:19 LXX]. Many thought that the Donatists were the true church only because their undisturbed life [securitas] had made them too lazy or proud or dull to recognize Catholic truth. For many the way in was blocked by the slanders of detractors, who put it about that we placed I don't know what objects on the altar of God. And many used to think it did not matter to what party a Christian belonged, and so remained Donatists just because they had been born that way and nobody was forcing them to leave and join the Catholics. (*Ep*. 93.5.17, cf. *Corr. Don*. 7.29)

Before examining these passages we need to know why Augustine had earlier favoured toleration. Partly, he was naturally influenced by the traditions of the early Christian church. As the Donatists often emphasized, Christians were habituated to the role of victims, not agents, of persecution (*Ep*. 44.4.7, *Corr. Don*. 2.10); it took time to adjust to episodes like the execution of Priscillian (see p. 197). In particular the New Testament seemed to afford no instance of persecution by Christians of heretics, or of approval of it (*Ep*. 93.3.11). This tradition, as Augustine came to argue, was a consequence of the church's having been born into an age in which the worldly powers, prefigured by Nebuchadnezzar, had not yet been made available as instruments for the destruction of those 'who speak against the true God' (*Corr. Don*. 2.8, referring to Dan. 3:29). Yet even when persecution by Christians became possible, there were arguments against it which swayed Augustine during the early part of his episcopate, and which perhaps explain his lasting distaste for severity (*Corr. Don*. 7.25, 26, *Ep*. 93.2.8). In his first years as a presbyter at Hippo he had written (392) to Maximin the Donatist bishop of Sinaita with a proposal to read out in church both his own objections to rebaptism (for which, he argues, there is no more 'place' than for recircumcision, *Ep*. 23.4) and Maximin's reply, if one is forthcoming. But, he says,

I shall not do this in the presence of the military, so that none of you can think I have wished to act more excitably than the cause of peace demands. I shall wait until they have gone; then our hearers can realize that it is not part of my purpose that anyone should be forced against his will into a particular communion, but rather that people should think things through in complete tranquillity until the truth sinks in. On our side there shall be no fear of the secular [temporalis] power; on yours, let there be no fear of Circumcellion mobs. (*Ep.* 23.7)

A few years later, in 396, he appeals to Eusebius, a lay Donatist in Hippo, to bring pressure on his bishop Proculeianus against affording a refuge to miscreant Catholics. In return he assures this correspondent that 'God knows . . . that I am not in the business of forcing anyone into the Catholic communion against his will, but of declaring the truth openly to those who are in error' (*Ep.* 34.1); and a second letter expresses disapproval of the proposal by one of his tenants to force his daughter from her recent profession as a Donatist nun; she should not 'be received except by her own will and her love, in a free decision, of the better course' (*Ep.* 35.4).

There are two distinct principles at work in this forbearance: that in the search for truth the seeker should be free from fear, and that in choice of allegiance he should be free from coercion. Let us see how the principles fare as Augustine's mind moves away from toleration during the following decade, the first of the fifth century. In a much later letter, written in 417 to count Boniface and alternatively known as the tract *De Correctione Donatistarum* (*Corr. Don.* = *Ep.* 185) he acknowledges in favour of the first principle that compulsion to 'the Catholic truth' risks the production of 'false and pretended Catholics'. On the other hand it now appears to him that fear may have the beneficial effect of causing its victim to 'renounce the prejudices that were blocking his way' (*Ep.* 93.5.16 of 408), or at least to examine truths of which he had been contentedly ignorant (*Corr. Don.* 7.25; it 'shakes him up [excutiendi]' as *Ep.* 93.1.2 had put it). Seemingly, then, in deciding whether to impose sanctions on dissent a legislator or pastor ought to balance his hope of convincing the lethargic against the risk of harbouring the insincere. But things do not really stand like that, because such a balancing already presupposes that fear is being applied in the interest of *truth*, that the dissenter is in *error*. Augustine is aware of this, and in several places he states that it makes a difference whether the doctrines being inculcated by intimidation are true (*Corr. Don.* 2.8), so that Elijah was not at fault in killing false prophets although Jezebel was at fault in killing true ones (*Ep.* 93.2.6, on 1 Kgs 18:4,40). In so arguing Augustine merely overlooks what is nowadays a commonplace of liberal ideology, that in controversy the problem is always how to prove the truth not how to inculcate it; and in proving it there is no substitute for reason. As Mill said:

The beliefs which we have most warrant for have no safeguard to rest on, but a standing invitation to the whole world to prove them unfounded. If the challenge is not accepted, or is accepted and the attempt fails, we are far enough from certainty still; but we have done the best that the existing state of human reason admits of. (*On Liberty* ch. 2. p. 83)

Two things, however, must be added in mitigation. First, if Augustine neglects the need for proof to resolve dogmatic differences between Donatists and Catholics, that is not because of the numerical weakness of the Donatists (although he is scathing about *their* claim to be 'catholic', world-wide). The famous tag 'Securus judicat orbis terrarum' is only a half-sentence from his conclusion to one particular argument, against Donatist pretensions to be able to maintain by exclusiveness the moral purity of their own congregation: 'Accordingly the judgement of the world as a whole is safe, that those who separate themselves from that world, in whatever lands, are not good men' (*C. Ep. Parm.* 3.4.24). Secondly, Augustine also foreshadows a more limited contrary principle that was to prove attractive during the centuries of ascendency of Christian government, the principle that force can be justified in securing assent when the consequences of dissent are grave enough, and in particular when its alleged penalty is eternal damnation:

What then does brotherly love do? Does it, because it fears the shortlived fires of the furnace for a few, abandon all to the eternal fires of hell? And does it leave so many . . . to perish everlastingly . . . whom ‹others› will not permit to live in accordance with the teaching of Christ? (*Corr. Don.* 3.14, cf. 8.32, 10.43–4, *Ep.* 143.4–6)

This, the principle which later brought so many Christian heretics to death by burning, cannot as easily be overturned, it seems to me, by intellectual doubts about the possibility of proof. For ordinary utility theory will show that an *infinite* harm needs only to be minimally probable in order to be worth avoiding at great cost, including the cost of life itself. Rather, the proper objection against Augustine at this point is a theological one, questioning whether the harm can be avoided by the means he suggests: or putting it the other way round, if God will spare those whose faith is bought by a policy of oppression, will he not spare them anyway, saving the oppression?

The argument from hell-fire will seem to have no more force when applied against the second of the two principles of toleration that we find in Augustine's letters from the 390s, the principle which says that *allegiance* or communion should not be won by coercion. For although it may be easier to change someone's allegiance than convictions by threats, it is surely no more likely that a benevolent God will reward the former than the latter when so bought. This was Locke's opinion:

In vain, therefore, do princes compel their subjects to come into their church communion, under pretence of saving their souls. If they believe, they will come of their own accord; if they believe not, their coming will nothing avail them. . . . And therefore, when all is done, they must be left to their own consciences. (*Epistula de Tolerantia*, p. 141)

Locke's language alludes to Jesus' parable of the great supper, at which the host, snubbed by those he had invited, sends his servant to summon the poor and crippled and blind and lame. When there is still room for more he says: 'Go out into the highways and hedges, and compel them to come in' (compelle intrare, Lk. 14:23). Augustine had fatuously applied this text to his own anti-Donatist policy (e.g. *Corr. Don.* 6.24, *Ep.* 93.5, *C. Gaud.* 1.25.28, *Serm.* 112.7.8).

If, on the other hand, we leave aside the Last Judgement and attend to the social and moral harms in this life which Augustine saw the Donatist congregations as bringing on themselves, then paternalist arguments become available for imposing sanctions against them. Should someone who through habit or stupidity or ignorance is inflicting unnecessary harm on himself not be forced to desist? Augustine cites the case of one of his own correspondents, a Donatist presbyter himself named Donatus (the name in Africa was like Jones in Wales), who had tried to drown himself in a well in order to evade arrest under the penal laws (this was in 416). Surely, Augustine writes to him, the police did right to pull you out:

How cruel the servants of God would have been, if they had not delivered you from that death. Who would not deservedly have blamed them? Who would not rightly have judged them uncaring [impios]? And yet you threw yourself willingly into the water to die, and they pulled you out of it against your will to prevent you dying. (*Ep.* 173.4)

The correction of Donatists is like stopping a delirious man from running into danger (*Ep.* 93.1.2). We can see this in the many cases of ex-Donatists who bless their deliverers (*Corr. Don.* 2.7, *Ep.* 93.1.2, and *Ep.* 93.5.16 quoted above). Augustine's description of the reconciled Catholics as regaining spiritual health, and his description elsewhere of pastors as healers (e.g. *Ep.* 93.1.3), might also encourage many people to agree that reconciliation lies in an area in which the wishes of the patient should not be allowed to be decisive.

The presbyter Donatus had rejected paternalism. 'You say', Augustine writes to him: 'that God has given us free decision, and therefore no man ought to be compelled even to good' (*Ep.* 173.2). It is a curious argument, since freedom to make right choices does not ensure that right choices will always be made by the free. At any rate Augustine does not have any difficulty in constructing a case for the paternalist view that it is sometimes permissible to do good to a man against his will. That the

man is thereby persecuted does not make him a true martyr, since the
blessed are only those who are persecuted for their defence of the right,
'for righteousness' sake' (*Corr. Don.* 2.9, citing Mt. 5:10, cf. *Ep.* 89.2).
Coercion of the unjust is not only permissible but often good, as when
they persist in their false allegiance through indolence or fear: 'It is a
great mercy to them when these very imperial laws secure their rescue
against their wills' (*Corr. Don.* 3.13). And Augustine is willing to go
further still, representing the use of the civil power to make people just
as a positive duty on Christian rulers. In this he is picking up, though
without acknowledgement in any text I know, the common view among
pagan philosophers that the state should seek to make men good (e.g.
Aristotle *Nicomachean Ethics* 1103b 3–5). He says:

> For [a king] serves God in one way because he is a man, in another
> way because he is also a king. Because he is a man, he serves him
> by living faithfully, but because he is also a king, he serves him by
> enacting laws with suitable vigour which enjoin what is just and
> prohibit the contrary. (*Corr. Don.* 5.19, cf. *Ep.* 155.10, *City* 5.24,
> *C. Lit. Pet.* 2.210, *C. Cresc.* 3.56)

How much of a case does Augustine have here? I would agree with
him that there is nothing intrinsically disreputable about doing people
favours against their will, especially since, as he repeatedly stresses (*Ep.*
93.1.3, *Corr. Don.* 3.13, 4.15), the wills of many Donatists were shaped
by gross intimidation. But do you do people a favour when you forbid
their meeting for worship, confiscate their places of worship and the
property of their church, make their spiritual leaders liable to exile, and
threaten to debar them – laymen and clergy alike – from making bequests
and contracts? These are the measures which were in force against Donatists from 405 onwards, and therefore at the time of his writing his two
fullest vindications of coercion against them, *Ep.* 93 in 408 and *Corr.
Don.* in 417. In defence of these measures paternalist grounds are inadequate, for coercion by a parent should – as Augustine realized in his
less excited moments – be mild and discriminating (compare his remark
in *Ep.* 93.2.8 that the surgeon cuts carefully if he aims to heal).

I wonder whether Augustine really thought that the paternalist justification of the anti-Donatist edicts was adequate. Was the candour with
which he explained to Vincentius (*Ep.* 93) his change of heart between
the old century and the new really false candour, and did he prefer to
keep his true opinions on the coercive policy largely to himself? He
drops various hints – admittedly to correspondents who would think the
better of him for them – of having been overborne by more extreme
colleagues. Even if his support for the persecution was wholehearted, it
may have been motivated by reasons to which he does not see fit to
give much advertisement, for example the theological conviction that

Donatism was offensive to God (they 'speak against the true God', *Corr. Don.* 2.8), or the political conviction that Donatism was an enormity which demanded suppression for the sake of civil peace. This latter perhaps shows through both in the satisfaction he displays in *Ep.* 93.5.17, quoted above, that unity now (408) prevailed in Hippo, and in the little note he wrote in the *Retractationes* about a treatise since lost, *Against the Donatist Party.* In that work, he tells us, he had taken the view we have found expressed in others of his writings from the 390s, that 'schismatics should not be forcibly constrained into communion by the intervention [impetu] of any secular power' (*Retract.* 2.5). And he explains why:

> I was opposed to that then, because experience had not yet taught me either what outrages they would stoop to if unpunished or what improvements could be achieved by firm measures steadily applied. (*Retract.* 2.5, cf. *C. Jul.* 3.1.5, *C. Sec. Jul.* 1.10, *Ep.* 143.2–3)

Alone, I think, among notable philosophers Augustine was also a man of power, charged with a share of responsibility for the destiny of a populous region. Even had he conceded what Locke was to call the 'equitableness' of religious toleration, he may have been right in the circumstances of his time and place not to concede the 'practicableness of the thing' (Locke, *Epistula de Tolerantia*, p. 122).

The earthly city

Augustine has left us no blueprint for human society on earth, the 'terrena civitas'. We cannot suppose this an accident. We cannot doubt that he thought that human institutions must go on much as they always had: wars must be fought, slaves bought and sold, fallible judgements handed down, innocents subjected to judicial torture. No projects captivated him for economic or legal or administrative reform; even in church government he seems not to have been concerned about seeking improvements. Partly this was because the churchmen of his era were attracted to conservatism by the need, now that public affairs were run by Christians, to explain away various extravagant and antinomian tendencies in the gospels and the early church. Thus Augustine assures a correspondent that Jesus did not mean us literally to turn the other cheek; for he himself did not do so when struck by an officer of the High Priest (*Ep.* 138.13, alluding to Mt. 5:39, Jn 18:23). The warning that all who take the sword shall perish with the sword (Mt. 26:52) applies only to those who use arms 'without the command or permission of a legitimate superior power' (*C. Faust.* 22.70). (This is one of the key texts for the later Christian theory of just war; see Barnes in Kretzmann, Kenny, and Pinborg 1982, ch. 41.) Of course otherworldliness had never implied insubordination:

obedience to the civil power belongs in the roots of Christianity (Rom. 13:1–7, 1 Pet. 2:13–14, see *Serm.* 302).

Augustine could not fail to be aware that he lived in a troubled age, a 'tempus barbaricum' (the title of a possibly spurious sermon, *PL* 40 699–708); yet 'each generation, he remarked, thinks its own times uniquely awful' (Chadwick 1986: 101, on *Serm.* 25). The traditional recourse of pagan philosophy had been to recommend abstention from public life: a wise man, thought Plotinus, if he holds any offices will give them up (*Enneads* 1.4.14.21). Augustine repudiates such quietism. Commenting on the duties of magistrates required to torture prisoners and witnesses in the ordinary process of Roman criminal investigation, he asks:

Since there is this dark side to political life [in his tenebris vitae socialis], will a wise man sit on the judge's bench, or will he flinch from it? Plainly he will take his seat; for he is constrained and driven to the duty by his association with other men, which he would not dream of abandoning [humana societas, quam deserere nefas ducit]. (*City* 19.6)

Concluding the same chapter with the psalmist's cry 'Bring me out of my necessities' (Ps 24 [Heb. Bib. 25]:17 Vg) Augustine stresses the *necessity* of dirty hands. For him the imperative 'bring [erue]' has optative force: 'if only you could bring'.

As in the relation of God to man so in relations between men Augustine regards justice as the paramount virtue. He cites from Cicero's *Republic* a definition of 'republic', 'res publica' which, together with another definition, yields the theorem that no republic can exist without agreement on what is right and community of interest (juris consensu et utilitatis communione, *City* 19.21; at 19.24 he substitutes 'consensus on what is loved', 'rerum quas diligit concordi communione', cf. *Ep.* 138.10 quoting Sallust *Catiline* 6.2, and *Doct. Christ.* 1.30 on sharing admiration for an actor); and from this theorem he speciously infers that no republic can exist without the 'justice' of allegiance to the true God. There are, of course, societies without such justice. In a celebrated passage earlier in the *City of God* he says:

So if justice is off the scene [remota justitia], what are kingdoms but large-scale terrorist gangs? . . . There was truth as well as neatness in what the captured pirate said to Alexander the Great when Alexander asked him what business he had to infest the sea, and he defiantly replied: 'The same as you have to infest the world. Because I do it with one small ship I am called a terrorist. You do it with a whole fleet and are called an emperor'. (*City* 4.4)

Some have read this as asserting that justice makes the difference between gangs and states. But probably there is no irony in Augustine's description of the pirate's remark as true: justice *is* off the scene, and therefore only size makes the difference. The passage exposes the pessimism of a tired man in a tired world. It anticipates J. H. Newman:

> Earthly kingdoms are founded, not in justice, but in injustice. They are created by the sword, by robbery, cruelty, perjury, craft and fraud. There never was a kingdom, except Christ's, which was not conceived and born, nurtured and educated, in sin. There never was a State, but was committed to acts and maxims, which it is its crime to maintain and its ruin to abandon. What monarchy is there but began in invasion or usurpation? What revolution has been effected without self-will, violence or hypocrisy? What popular Government but is blown about by every wind as if it had no conscience and no responsibilities? What dominion of the few but is selfish and unscrupulous? Where is military strength without the passion for war? Where is trade without the love of filthy lucre, which is the root of all evil? (Newman 1843:273, quoted by Dawson in D'Arcy *et al.* 1930:63)

The pessimism is Jewish: rulers are instituted by God (Dan. 2:37, Wisd. 6:3, Jn 19:11, Rom. 13:1–2); we get wicked ones because we deserve no better.

The City of God

The idea of two cities, one heavenly or of God, the other earthly, has origins as far back as Cicero (*De Legibus* 1.23) and Paul (Phil. 3:20, Eph. 2:19); and the name 'City of God' comes from Ps 86 [Heb. Bib. 87]:3. There is a more immediate source for Augustine's conception in surviving fragments from a lost work by Tyconius, a Donatist theologian whom he much admired (see Dawson in D'Arcy *et al.* 1930:58–9, Bonner in Ackroyd and Evans 1970:554–5, Frend 1952:315–17). Augustine himself had adopted and developed the idea in several works of his middle years, one of which promises the treatise that took shape in his old age as the twenty-two books of the *City of God against the Pagans*. On the earth the two cities, civitates, are two intermingled communities, one consisting of those who belong here, the other of foreigners, peregrini (pilgrims, e.g. *City* 14.19), citizens of a distant place who keep residence away from their true home. The very title, therefore, of the *City of God* announces the guiding theme of Augustine's social philosophy: that the Christian hope of a life after death is hope of a community after death, what the Apostles' Creed calls the communion of saints. Its gathering will be the homecoming of those who, meanwhile, must on earth comport themselves and expect to be treated as aliens, outsiders, unwelcome, and underprivileged, in a place which, though they can help to alleviate its miseries, is not *their* place (cf. *Conf.* 11.29.39).

Augustine's *City of God* divides into two parts, the first of which (books 1–10) seeks to 'refute the enemies of the city of God' (*City* 18.1) by demonstrating the vices and failures of pagan empires, and especially of the existing empire whose chief city had recently succumbed to its first barbarian conqueror.

The second part belongs to the Jewish tradition of apocalypse, but here we have apocalypse rendered coherent, if not convincing, to suit both Augustine's rational mentality and the tastes and demands of the cultured pagan audience to whom he addressed it (see Brown 1967:ch.26). The best-known Christian example of the genre is the book of Revelation, or Apocalypse, of John the Divine, in which visions are vouchsafed of the coming of Christ's kingdom, the destruction of 'Babylon', the binding of Satan, and a general resurrection. Augustine's vision is far more prosaic. He prefaces his description of future events by an account of the creation (see p. 156 above), and a survey of world history such as had been attempted more than once before his time and notably by the Christian bishop and historian Eusebius (*c.*260–*c.*339). According to Augustine the world is destined to persist through six ages between the creation and the final judgement of Christ (e.g. *Gen. Man.* 1.23.35–24.42, *Cat. Rud.* 22.39, *City* 22.30.5, see Markus in Armstrong 1967:407). Five of these ages, each lasting 1,000 years, were complete at the time of Christ's birth; the sixth, which is also spoken of as a millennium but may be of different length (at one point he even envisages 600,000 years, *City* 12.13 (12)), was in progress when Augustine wrote. The termination of this sixth age is described in the last three books of the *City of God*, 20–22. Drawing mainly on Revelation 20 Augustine maintains that when the end arrives the devil, who is now bound and sealed in an abyss, will be released for a period of three and a half years, during which he will persecute the church; this will be a time of terror and chaos. Next Christ will come, to judge both the living and the bodiless dead. The judgement will proceed as in Mt. 25:31–46 (see p. 143 above). Then the whole earth will be consumed by fire, except for human bodies. The bodies of the dead are re-formed from their scattered materials and, together with the bodies of the living, transmuted so as to become incorruptible. Bodily defects may be cured during the process, including perhaps the defects of excessive age or youth, and we are told that it is a consequence of incorruptibility that the body no longer needs food. After the destruction of the earth a new heaven and a new earth are created (this idea comes originally from Isaiah 65:17). The heaven is apparently aloft, up in the sky, since Augustine thinks it necessary to refute the Platonist objection that it is contrary to nature for bodies to rise above the earth (*City* 22.11, cf. 13.8). Thither proceed the souls of the saved reunited with their incorruptible bodies, to enjoy life everlasting.

What sort of life will they lead, or in other words what will they do? Augustine asks the question in the penultimate chapter of the *City of God* (Quid acturi sint?, *City* 22.29). Life in heaven, he answers, will be not so much action as rest and leisure. The saints will live in the peace of God, a peace which passes all understanding (quoting Phil. 4:7). Although there will be time for praising God, he cannot think of anything else that will be done, since where no one is lazy and no one needy there will be neither idleness nor labour. There will be no flattery, no wrongs and – though the saints will vary in status according to their merits – no envy. Life in heaven will be one long holiday, sabbatum non habens vesperam (*City*, 22.30).

It is striking that aside from the reference to worship this description at the end of the *City of God* is wholly negative. The same message emerges from Augustine's more analytical treatment in book 19 where he addresses himself to the traditional pagan philosophical question, 'What is the summum bonum?' To this question the reply given by God's city, he tells us, is 'eternal life' (*City* 19.4) – that is, our good is not to be found in this world but is final in the order of time as well as the order of value. And eternal life differs from the life of saints on earth in possessing 'the reward of victory, eternal peace which no adversary can disturb' (*City* 19.10). We are called happy on earth when we have peace, however small may be the amount of it that can be expected here in a good life. True virtue is

> to subordinate [refert] all the good things of which it makes good use, and all that it does in its good use of good and bad things, and even itself, to that end where our peace shall be of such quality and amount that it cannot be made better or greater. We might therefore say of peace, as we have said of eternal life, that it is the end of all our good. (*City* 19.10–11)

What is this perfect peace, of which peace on earth is no more than a shadow? As the word suggests, it is a state; you do not have to be active in any way to enjoy it. And it is a state of having no enemies, no enemies without but, more especially, none within:

> There is no full peace so long as one is like an occupying power over one's own faults [vitiis imperatur], because the faults that still resist subject one to all the dangers of warfare, while those that have been conquered do not yet allow one to enjoy victory at ease but impose the trouble of keeping them suppressed. (*City* 19.27)

In heaven, by contrast, there will be nothing to govern (imperare), nothing to keep in order, since everything will remain in order of its own accord. As he has said earlier in the book, peace is the tranquillity of order, the condition in which all things remain restfully in their proper place (*City* 19.13).

A later chapter in book 19 repeats the thought that government will not be necessary in heaven ('necessarium non sit officium imperandi mortalibus'), and offers as reason that the requirement of looking after people ('officium consulendi') will disappear when they are happy in their immortality (*City* 19.16). The context is discussion of the duties on earth of heads of households, which perhaps suggests that in speaking of the purpose of government as looking after people Augustine is thinking of provision of services rather than, or at any rate as well as, preservation of order. On the other hand, he may have the particular service of protection chiefly in view, in which case his thought is that governments look after people *by* preserving peace, 'the tranquillity of order'.

In any case it is central to Augustine's conception of heaven that there will be no government in it, no imperium. Saints will not need to keep themselves in order, nor to be kept in order by a governing body of other saints, nor by God. This raises the question why he describes heaven as a city, civitas. One possible answer is that any collection of human beings, however saintly, will get into disagreements; and some of the disagreements will concern the behaviour of members of the collection – for example whether St Columba should still sing psalms in heaven, as he did in Scotland, so loud that he could be heard a mile away. Augustine might also have supposed that even in heaven there will be co-operative activities, such as singing in harmony; and if I am to co-operate with you I must adjust my actions not only to your opinion how I should act but also to your opinion how you should act. These kinds of adjustment need procedures for arriving at agreement and for settling disagreement, and the procedures call for institutions and rules – advisory bodies, executive bodies, appellate bodies, procedures for electing, voting, deputizing, and so on. Institutions and rules of procedure constitute government of a kind, not indeed in the sense of imperium, holding down the disobedient by penalties and threats, but in the sense of administration. That, Augustine might have argued, is why even the communion of saints will rightly be described as a city.

There is little reason to think that Augustine pursued this line of thought. He draws no distinction between penal laws and enabling laws, and he seems to regard the civil power on earth as entirely the product of human depravity. In one passage, admittedly, he may be ascribing decision procedures to the saints, when he says that the earthly city seeks 'a sort of composition of human wills on matters which concern mortal life' (*City* 19.17); and later in the same chapter the same aim is set for the heavenly city during its pilgrimage on earth. But he betrays no awareness that the need for institutions which secure such 'composition' might survive into heaven where the need for threats and penalties on the disobedient will not. The peace of the heavenly city, he says, 'is a completely ordered and completely concordant fellowship [concordissima societas] in the enjoyment of God and of one another in God' (*City* 19.13). A 'concordissima societas' sounds like an association in which there are no disagremeents.

On this implausible foundation Augustine erected his ideal commonwealth of the saints after the Last Judgement. In that consummation the state will wither away, taking with it not only law courts and legislatures, but parish councils and Royal Commissions, working parties and liaison committees, chairpersons, conveners, selection boards, and secretariats. What then will be left that deserves the name of 'city'? His word, 'civitas', had originally meant citizenship, the condition of being a citizen; and Cicero speaks of 'meetings and gatherings of men sharing rights [jure sociati], which are denominated cities' (*De Re Publica* 6.13.13). Besides these common rights (and duties), the notion of citizenship tended also to connote the kind of common loves and loyalties which we have found Augustine importing into his definition of a republic. Thus the Jewish historian Josephus (AD 37–c.100) could be asked about the Jews of Alexandria: 'Why then, if they are citizens (*politai*), do they not worship the same gods as the Alexandrians?' (*Contra Apionem* 2.6.6). It would not be hard for Augustine to give exclusive attention to this latter aspect, applying the word 'civitas' to a collection of men bound together by no institutions or laws but only by fellow feeling and shared values – to anything, therefore, which we would regard as a fellowship or society or community, and which he could synonymously describe as a societas. In the Augustinian view the city of God is not a political association. It has no politics; politics belong with sin.

Further reading

On Donatism see Frend 1952. On the *City of God* see Brown 1967: ch. 16–7.

Bibliography

References in the text are by author and date (in the case of modern works), author and title (in the case of older works), or (in the case of Augustine) abbreviated title; followed by book, chapter, section or page or column number.

Augustine followed the standard ancient practice of dividing his longer works into books; editors have subdivided them into chapters or sections, or usually both. Thus, for example, 'C. Jul. 2.8.23' refers to book 2, chapter 8, section 23 of *Contra Julianum*. I have nearly always given both chapter and section numbers, although it is not uncommon to find one or the other omitted (usually chapters) because in nearly all his works the two number series are concurrent.

In references in the text to modern books, page numbers refer to the source listed first in this bibliography.

General abbreviations

ACW	*Ancient Christian Writers: the Works of the Fathers in Translation*, ed J. Quasten and J. C. Plumpe (Newman Press, 1946–).
AV	Authorized (or 'King James') Version of the English Bible, 1611.
BA	*Oeuvres de Saint Augustin*, with French tr., Bibliothèque Augustinienne (1947–).
BCP	Book of Common Prayer, 1662.
BW	*Basic Writings of Saint Augustine*, tr. with introduction and notes by W. J. Oates, 2 volumes (1948).
CCL	*Corpus Christianorum, Series Latina* (Turnhout, 1953–).
CSEL	*Corpus Scriptorum Ecclesiasticorum Latinorum* (Vienna, 1866–).
Clark	*Augustine of Hippo, Selected Writings* (Classics of Western Spirituality), tr. M. T. Clark (SPCK, 1984).
Denz.	*Enchiridion Symbolorum, Definitionum et Declarationum de Rebus Fidei et Morum*, ed H. Denzinger and A. Schoenmetzer (Herder, 32nd edition, 1963).
FC	*Fathers of the Church*, ed L. Schopp, D. J. Deferrari *et al.* (Catholic University of America, 1947–).
Heb.Bib.	Biblia Hebraica, ed Kittel, 1908.

LCC   *Library of Christian Classics*, SCM.
LF   *A Library of Fathers of the Holy Catholic Church*, translated by members of the English church, ed M. Dods (Parker & Rivington, 1840–57).
LXX   *The Old Testament in Greek, according to the Septuagint*, ed H. B. Swete, 3 volumes (Cambridge, 1909).
NEB   New English Bible: Old Testament and Apocrypha 1970, New Testament 1961.
NPNF   *A Select Library of the Nicene and Post-Nicene Fathers of the Christian Church*, first series (1886–8), ed P. Schaff, reprinted Eerdmans (1971–80).
PG   *Patrologiae Cursus Completus, Series Graeca*, ed J. P. Migne (Paris, 1857–66).
PL   *Patrologiae Cursus Completus, Series Latina*, ed. J. P. Migne (Paris, 1844–55). Augustine is in volumes 32–47, which reprint the Benedictine edition of St Maur, 1679–1700. References are by volume and page number.
SMP   *Selections from Mediaeval Philosophers*, 1929.
Vg   Biblia vulgata, Constantine text, 1592.
WJ   *Augustine, De Natura et Gratia, De Gestis Pelagii, De Spiritu et Littera*, tr. F. H. Woods and J. O. Johnson (London, 1887).

Abbreviated titles of biblical books

For simplicity the list gives abbreviated titles of all biblical books, whether they are mentioned in the text or not. It comprises Augustine's canon in his order (see *De Doctrina Christiana* 2.8.13).

Gen.	Genesis
Exod.	Exodus
Lev.	Leviticus
Num.	Numbers
Deut.	Deuteronomy
Josh.	Joshua
Judg.	Judges
Ruth	
1 Sam.	1 Samuel (= 1 Kings, Vg)
2 Sam.	2 Samuel (= 2 Kings, Vg)
1 Kgs	1 Kings (= 3 Kings, Vg)
2 Kgs	2 Kings (= 4 Kings, Vg)
1 Chron.	1 Chronicles (= 1 Paralipomenon, Vg)
2 Chron.	2 Chronicles (= 2 Paralipomenon, Vg)
Job	
Tob.	Tobias, or Tobit
Est.	Esther
Judith	
1 Macc.	1 Maccabees

2 Macc.	2 Maccabees
Ezra	(= 1 Esdras, Vg; 2 Esdras, LXX)
Neh.	Nehemiah (= 2 Esdras, Vg; 3 Esdras, LXX)
Pss	Psalms
Prov.	Proverbs
S. of S.	Song of Songs (= Canticum, Vg; Song of Solomon, AV)
Eccles	Ecclesiastes
Wisd.	Wisdom of Solomon
Ecclus	Ecclesiasticus (= Sirach, Vg; Wisdom of Ben Sira)
Hos.	Hosea (= Osee, Vg)
Joel	
Am.	Amos
Obad.	Obadiah (= Abdias, Vg)
Jon.	Jonah
Mic.	Micah (= Michaeas, Vg)
Nah.	Nahum
Hab.	Habakkuk
Zeph.	Zephaniah (= Sophonias, Vg)
Hag.	Haggai (= Aggaeus, Vg)
Zech.	Zechariah (= Zacharias, Vg)
Mal.	Malachi
Is.	Isaiah (= Esaias, Vg)
Jer.	Jeremiah
Dan.	Daniel
Ezek.	Ezekiel
Mt.	Gospel according to Matthew
Mk	Gospel according to Mark
Lk.	Gospel according to Luke
Jn	Gospel according to John
Rom.	Epistle of Paul to the Romans
1 Cor.	1st epistle of Paul to the Corinthians
2 Cor.	2nd epistle of Paul to the Corinthians
Gal.	Epistle of Paul to the Galatians
Eph.	Epistle of Paul to the Ephesians
Phil.	Epistle of Paul to the Philippians
1 Thess.	1st epistle of Paul to the Thessalonians
2 Thess.	2nd epistle of Paul to the Thessalonians
Col.	Epistle of Paul to the Colossians
1 Tim.	1st epistle of Paul to Timothy
2 Tim.	2nd epistle of Paul to Timothy
Tit.	Epistle of Paul to Titus
Philem.	Epistle of Paul to Philemon
Heb.	Epistle to the Hebrews
Jas	Epistle of James
1 Pet.	1st epistle of Peter

2 Pet.   2nd epistle of Peter
1 Jn   1st epistle of John
2 Jn   2nd epistle of John
3 Jn   3rd epistle of John
Jude   Epistle of Jude

Acts   Acts of the Apostles
Rev.   Revelation (= Apocalypse, Vg)

Augustine's works

For consistency in ordering the list, abbreviated titles have been given for all Augustine's works, whether or not they are referred to in the text. The dates are sometimes uncertain. Lost works are in square brackets. Among editions, *PL* and *CSEL* are nearly complete, *CCL* and BA still in progress. I have listed all the English translations known to me; these include numerous volumes in four major series of translations from the Church Fathers: *ACW*, *FC*, *LF*, and *NPNF*. H. I. Marrou, *Saint Augustine*, contains a list by J. J. O'Meara of texts and English translations.

[*Admon. Don.*] *Admonitio Donatistarum de Maximianistis*; *c.* AD 406, lost, see *Retract*. 2.29.

Adv. Jud. *Tractatus Adversus Judaeos*; *PL* 42 51–64; *FC* 27; AD 429–30.

Ag. Christ *De Agone Christiano*, 1 book; *PL* 40 289–310, *CSEL* 41, BA 1; *LF* Short Treatises, *FC* 2; AD 396.

An. *De Anima* (A poem); in *Anthologia Latina*, 1st part, fasc. II, 1906, ed A. Riese 43, no. 489.

An. Orig. *De Anima et ejus Origine*, 4 books; *PL* 44 475–548, *CSEL* 60; *NPNF* 5; AD 420–1.

Annot. Job *Annotationes in Job*, 1 book; *PL* 34 825–86, *CSEL* 28.2; AD 399.

Bapt. *De Baptismo Contra Donatistas*, 7 books; *PL* 42 107–244, *CSEL* 51, BA 29; *NPNF* 4; AD 400–1.

Beata Vita *De Beata Vita*, 1 book; *PL* 32 959–76, *CSEL* 63, *CCL* 29, BA 4; *FC* 5; AD 386.

Bon. Conj. *De Bono Conjugali*, 1 book; *PL* 40 373–96, *CSEL* 41, BA 2; *NPNF* 3, *LF* Short Treatises, *FC* 27; AD 401.

Bon. Vid. *De Bono Viduitatis ad Julianam*, 1 book; *PL* 40 429–50, *CSEL* 41, BA 3; *NPNF* 3, *LF* Short Treatises; AD 414.

Brev. Coll. *Breviculus Collationis contra Donatistas*, 1 book; *PL* 43 613–50, *CSEL* 53, BA 32; AD 413.

C. Acad. *Contra Academicos*, 3 books; *PL* 32 905–58, *CSEL* 63, *CCL* 29, BA 4; *ACW* 12, *FC* 5, tr. M. P. Garvey (Marquette, 1957); AD 386.

C. Adim. *Contra Adimandum*, 1 book; *PL* 42 129–72, *CSEL* 25.1, BA 17; AD 394.

C. Adv. *Contra Adversarios Legis et Prophetarum*, 2 books; *PL* 42 603–66; AD 421.

[*C. Cent.*] *Contra quod Attulit Centurius a Donatistis*; *c.* AD 400, lost, see *Retract*. 2.19.

C. Cresc. *Contra Cresconium Grammaticum*, 4 books; *PL* 43 445–594, *CSEL* 52, BA 31; AD 405–6.

C. Du. Ep. Pel. *Contra Duas Epistolas Pelagianorum*, 4 books; *PL* 44 549–638, *CSEL* 60, BA 23; *NPNF* 5; AD 422–3.

[*C. Ep. Don.*] *Contra Epistolam Donati Haeretici*; AD 393, lost, see *Retract.* 1.21.

C. Ep. Man. Fund. *Contra Epistolam Manichaeorum quam Vocant Fundamenti*, 1 book; *PL* 42 173–206, *CSEL* 25.1, BA 17; AD 397.

C. Ep. Parm. *Contra Epistolam Parmeniani*; *PL* 43 33–108, *CSEL* 51, BA 28; AD 400.

C. Faust. *Contra Faustum Manichaeum*, 33 books; *PL* 42 207–518, *CSEL* 25.1; *NPNF* 4; AD 400.

C. Fel. *Contra Felicem Manichaeum*, 2 books; *PL* 42 519–52, *CSEL* 25.2, BA 17; AD 398.

C. Fort. *Contra Fortunatum Manichaeum, Acta seu Disputatio*, 1 book; *PL* 42 111–30, *CSEL* 25.1, BA 17; *NPNF* 4; AD 392.

C. Gaud. *Contra Gaudentium Donatistarum Episcopum*, 2 books; *PL* 43 707–52, *CSEL* 53, BA 32; AD 421–2.

C. Jul. *Contra Julianum*, 6 books; *PL* 44 641–874; *FC* 35; AD 423.

C. Lit. Pet. *Contra litteras Petiliani*, 3 books; *PL* 43 245–388, *CSEL* 52, BA 30; *NPNF* 4; AD 401–5.

C. Max. *Contra Maximinum Arianorum Episcopum*, 2 books; *PL* 42 743–814; AD 428.

C. Mend. *Contra Mendacium ad Consentium*, 1 book; *PL* 40 517–48, *CSEL* 41, BA 2; *NPNF* 3, *LF* Short Treatises; AD 422.

[*C. Nesc. Don.*] *Contra Nescio quem Donatistam*; *c* AD 406, lost, see *Retract.* 2.27.

[*C. Part. Don.*] *Contra Partem Donati*, 2 books; AD 398, lost, see *Retract.* 2.5.

C. Sec. *Contra Secundinum Manichaeum*, 1 book; *PL* 42 577–602, *CSEL* 25.2, BA 17; AD 399.

C. Sec. Jul. *Contra Secundam Juliani Responsionem, Opus Imperfectum*, 6 books; *PL* 45 1049–1608, *CSEL* 85.1 books 1–3; AD 429–30.

C. Serm. Ar. *Contra Sermonem Arianorum*, 1 book; *PL* 42 683–708; AD 419.

Cat. Rud. *De Catechizandis Rudibus*, 1 book; *PL* 40 309–48, *CCL* 46; *ACW* 2, *NPNF* 3, *LF* Short Treatises; AD 399.

City *De Civitate Dei contra Paganos*, 22 books; *PL* 41 13–804, *CSEL* 40.1,2, *CCL* 47–8, ed J. E. C. Welldon (SPCK 1924), Teubner 4th edition 1928/9, BA 33–7; tr. McCracken *et al.* (Heinemann 1966–72) *NPNF* 2, *FC* 8, 14, 24, *BW* (part), tr. Healey (1610, Everyman), tr. Bettenson (1972, Penguin); AD 413–26.

Coll. Max. *Collatio cum Maximino Arianorum Episcopo*; *PL* 42 709–42; AD 427.

Comm. Fort. *Commonitorium ad Fortunatianum*; *PL* 33 622–30, *CSEL* 44; AD 413.

Conf. *Confessiones*, 13 books; *PL* 32 659–868, *CSEL* 33, Teubner (2nd edition 1969), ed. P. de Labriolle (1933–7), Budé 1966, BA 13–14; *LCC* 7, *NPNF* 1, *LF* 1, *BW*, *FC* 21, tr. R. S. Pine-Coffin (Penguin), tr. W. Watts (1631, Heinemann 1912), and many other trs; AD 397–401.

Conj. Adult. *De Conjugiis Adulterinis*, 2 books; *PL* 40 451–86, *CSEL* 41, BA 2; *FC* 27; AD 421.

Cons. Evang. *De Consensu Evangelistarum*, 4 books; *PL* 34 1041–1230, *CSEL* 43; *NPNF* 6; AD 400.

Cont. *De Continentia*, 1 book; *PL* 40 349–72, *CSEL* 41, BA 3; *NPNF* 3, *LF* Short Treatises; AD 395.

Corr. Don. *De Correctione Donatistarum, Liber seu Epistola*, 1 book = *Ep.* 185; *PL* 33 792–815, *CSEL* 57; *NPNF* 4; AD 417.

Corr. Gr. *De Correptione et Gratia*, 1 book; *PL* 44 915–46, BA 24; *NPNF* 5, *FC* 2; AD 426.

Cur. Mort. *De Cura pro Mortuis Gerenda*, 1 book; *PL* 40 591–610, *CSEL* 41, BA 2; *NPNF* 3, *LF* Short Treatises, *FC* 27; AD 424.

Dial. *De Dialectica*; *PL* 32, ed J. Pinborg, with tr. and commentary by B. D. Jackson, Reidel 1975; AD 387. Authenticity disputed.

Disc. Christ. *De Disciplina Christiana sermo*; *PL* 40 669–78, *CCL* 46; AD 397–8.

Div. Daem. *De Divinatione Daemonum*, 1 book; *PL* 40 581–92, *CSEL* 41, BA 10; *FC* 27; AD 406–8.

Divers. Quaest. *De Diversis Quaestionibus LXXXIII*, 1 book; *PL* 40 11–100, *CCL* 44A, BA 10; *FC* 70; AD 388–95.

Doct. Christ. *De Doctrina Christiana*, 4 books; *PL* 34 15–127, *CSEL* 80, *CCL* 32; *FC* 2, tr. D. W. Robertson Jr (*On Christian Doctrine*, Bobbs-Merrill, 1958); AD 396–426.

Don. Persev. *De Dono Perseverantiae*; *PL* 45 993–1034, BA 24; *NPNF* 5; AD 429.

Du. An. *De Duabus Animabus contra Manichaeos*, 1 book; *PL* 42 93–112, *CSEL* 25.1, BA 17; *NPNF* 4; AD 392–3.

Dulc. *De VIII Dulcitii Quaestionibus*, 1 book; *PL* 40 147–70, *CCL* 44A, BA 10; *FC* 16; AD 425–6.

[*Emer.*] *Ad Emeritum Donatistarum Episcopum post Collationem*, 1 book; *c.* AD 417, lost, see *Retract.* 2.46.

Enarr. Ps *Enarrationes in Psalmos*; *PL* 36 67–1028, 37 1033–1968, *CCL* 38–40; *NPNF* 8 (abbr.), *ACW* 29, 30 (on Pss 1–37), Clark (on Pss 119–22), *LF* 21, 25, 30, 32, 37, 39; AD 392–420.

Ench. *Enchiridion de Fide, Spe et Caritate ad Laurentium*, 1 book; *PL* 40 231–90, *CCL* 46, BA 9; *LCC* 7, *NPNF* 3, *LF* Short Treatises, *ACW* 3, *FC* 2, *BW* 1, tr. E. Evans (SPCK, 1953); AD 423.

Ep. *Epistolae*; *PL* 33, *CSEL* 34, 44, 57, 58; tr. J. G. Cunningham (2 volumes), *NPNF* 1 (selection), *FC* 12, 18, 20, 30, 32, tr. J. H. Baxter (Heinemann, 1980, selection); also a recently discovered collection, numbered 1*–29*, *CSEL* 88 (see Chadwick, *Journal of Theological Studies*, 1983).

Ep. Joh. *Tractatus in Epistolam Johannis ad Parthos*, 10 homilies; *PL* 35 1977; *LCC* 8, *LF* 29, Clark (no. 7); AD 407?–415?.

Ep. Rom. *Epistolae ad Romanos Inchoata Expositio*, 1 book; *PL* 35 2087–106; with tr. by P. F. Landes (*Augustine on Romans*, Scholars Press, 1982); AD 394–5.

Ev. Joh. *Tractatus in Johannem Evangelistam*, 124 homilies; *PL* 35 1379–1976, *CCL* 36, BA 71; Clark (nos. 1, 12), *LF* 26, 29; AD *c.*407–*c.*416.

Exp. Gal.   *Expositio Epistolae ad Galatos*, 1 book; *PL* 35 2105–48; AD 394–5.

Exp. Rom.   *Expositio LXXXIV Propositionum Epistolae ad Romanos*, 1 book; *PL* 35 2063–88; with tr. by P. F. Landes (*Augustine on Romans*, Scholars Press, 1982); AD 394–5.

Fid. Op.   *De Fide et Operibus*, 1 book; *PL* 40 197–230, *CSEL* 41, BA 8; *LF* Short Treatises, *FC* 27; AD 413.

Fid. Rer.   *De Fide Rerum quae non Videntur Sermo*; *PL* 40 171–80, *CCL* 46, BA 8; *NPNF* 3, *LF* Short Treatises, *FC* 4; AD 400.

Fid. Symb.   *De Fide et Symbolo Sermo*, 1 book; *PL* 40 181–96, *CSEL* 41, BA 9; *LCC* 6, *NPNF* 3, *LF* Short Treatises, *FC* 27; 3 October AD 393.

Gen. Lit.   *De Genesi ad Litteram*, 12 books; *PL* 34 245–486, *CSEL* 28.1, BA 48–9; *ACW* 41–2; AD 401–14.

Gen. Lit. Imperf.   *De Genesi ad Litteram Imperfectus Liber*, 1 book; *PL* 34 219–46, *CSEL* 28.1; AD 393.

Gen. Man.   *De Genesi contra Manichaeos*, 2 books; *PL* 34 173–220; AD 388–9.

Gest. Emer.   *De Gestis cum Emerito Donatistarum Episcopo*, 1 book; *PL* 43 697–706, *CSEL* 53, BA 32; AD 418.

Gest. Pel.   *De Gestis Pelagii*, 1 book; *PL* 44 319–60, *CSEL* 42, BA 21; *NPNF* 5, WJ; AD 417.

Gr. Christ.   *De Gratia Christi et de Peccato Originali contra Pelagium*, 2 books; *PL* 44 359–410, *CSEL* 42, BA 22; *NPNF* 5, *BW* 1; AD 418.

Gr. Lib. Arb.   *De Gratia et Libero Arbitrio*; *PL* 44 881–912, BA 24; *NPNF* 5, *FC* 59, *BW* 1; AD 426.

Gr. Nov. Test.   *De Gratia Novi Testamenti ad Honoratum*, 1 book; *PL* 33 538–77, *CSEL* 44; AD 412.

Haer.   *De Haeresibus ad Quodvultdeum*, 1 book; *PL* 42 21–50, *CCL* 46; AD 429.

Immort. An.   *De Immortalitate Animae*, 1 book; *PL* 32 1021–34, BA 5, *BW* 1; *FC* 4, tr. G. G. Leckie (Appleton-Century, 1938); AD 387.

Inquis.   *Ad Inquisitiones Januarii*, 2 books; *PL* 33 199–223, *CSEL* 34.2; AD 401.

Lib. Arb.   *De Libero Arbitrio*, 3 books; *PL* 32 1221–1310, *CSEL* 74, *CCL* 29; *ACW* 22, *LCC* 6, *FC* 59, *SMP* 1 (book 2. 1–46); AD 388, 391–5.

Loc. Hept.   *Locutiones in Heptateuchum*, 7 books; *PL* 34 485–546, *CSEL* 28.1, *CCL* 33; AD 419–20.

Mag.   *De Magistro*, 1 book; *PL* 32 1193–1220, *CSEL* 77, *CCL* 29; *LCC* 6, *BW* 1, *ACW* 9, *FC* 59, tr. F. E. Tourscher (*The Philosophy of Teaching*, Villanova, 1924), tr. G. G. Leckie (*Concerning the Teacher*, Appleton-Century, 1938); AD 389.

[*Max.*]   *De Maximianistis contra Donatistas*; c. AD 410, lost, see *Retract.* 2.35.

Mend.   *De Mendacio*, 1 book; *PL* 40 487–578, *CSEL* 41, BA 2; *NPNF* 3, *LF* Short Treatises; AD 396.

Mor. Cath.   *De Moribus Ecclesiae Catholicae*, 1 book; *PL* 32 1309–44, BA 1; *NPNF* 4, *FC* 56, *BW* 1; AD 387/9.

Mor. Man.   *De Moribus Manichaeorum*, 1 book; *PL* 32 1345–78; *NPNF* 4, *FC* 56; AD 388.

Mus.   *De Musica*, 6 books; *PL* 32 1081–194, BA 7; *FC* 4; AD 387–90.

Nat. Bon.   *De Natura Boni contra Manichaeos*, 1 book; *PL* 42 551–72, *CSEL* 25.2, BA 1; *NPNF* 4, *LCC* 6, *BW* 1; AD 399.

Nat. Gr.   *De Natura et Gratia*, 1 book; *PL* 44 247–90, *CSEL* 60, BA 21; *NPNF* 5, *BW* 1, WJ; AD 413–15.

Nupt. Concup.   *De Nuptiis et Concupiscentia*, 2 books; *PL* 44 413–74, *CSEL* 42, BA 23; *NPNF* 5; AD 419–21.

Op. Mon.   *De Opere Monachorum*, 1 book; *PL* 40 547–82, *CSEL* 41, BA 3; *NPNF* 3, *LF* Short Treatises; AD 401.

Ord.   *De Ordine*, 2 books; *PL* 32 977–1020, *CSEL* 63, *CCL* 29, BA 4; *FC* 2; AD 386.

Orig. An.   *De Origine Animi* = ep. 166 to Jerome; AD 415.

Oros.   *Ad Orosium contra Priscillianistas et Origenistas*, 1 book; *PL* 42 669–78; AD 415.

Pat.   *De Patientia*, 1 book; *PL* 40 611–26, *CSEL* 41, BA 2; *NPNF* 3, *LF* Short Treatises; ante AD 418.

Pecc. Mer.   *De Peccatorum Meritis et Remissione, et de Baptismo Parvulorum*, 3 books; *PL* 44 109–200, *CSEL* 60; *NPNF* 5; AD 411.

Pecc. Orig.   see *Gr. Christ.*

Perf. Just.   *De Perfectione Justitiae Hominis*; *PL* 44 291–318, *CSEL* 42, BA 21; *NPNF* 5; AD 415–16.

Post Coll.   *Post Collationem contra Donatistas*, 1 book; *PL* 43 651–90, *CSEL* 53; AD 413.

Praed. Sanct.   *De Praedestinatione Sanctorum*; *PL* 44 959–92, BA 24; *NPNF* 5, *BW* 1; AD 429.

Praes. Dei   *De Praesentia Dei ad Dardanum* = ep. 187, Clark; AD 417.

[*Prob.*]   *Probationes et Testimonia contra Donatistas*; *c.* AD 406, lost, see *Retract.* 2.28.

Ps Don.   *Psalmus contra Partem Donati* (verse); *PL* 43 23–32, *CSEL* 51, ed R. Anastasi (Padua, 1957), BA 28; AD 394.

[*Pulch. Apt.*]   *De Pulchro et Apto*; AD 380, lost, see *Conf.* 4.20,24,27.

Qu. An.   *De Quantitate Animae*, 1 book; *PL* 32 1035–80, BA 5; *ACW* 9, *FC* 4, tr. F. E. Tourscher (*The Measure of the Soul*, Philadelphia, 1933); AD 387/8.

Quaest. Ev.   *Quaestiones Evangeliorum*, 2 books; *PL* 35 1321–64; AD 395–9.

Quaest. Hept.   *Quaestiones in Heptateuchum*, 7 books; *PL* 34 547–824, *CSEL* 28.2, *CCL* 33; AD 420.

Quaest. Pag.   *Quaestiones Expositae contra Paganos*; *PL* 33 370–86, *CSEL* 34.2; AD 408–9.

Regula = ep. 211; Clark; AD 423.

Retract.   *Retractationes*, 2 books; *PL* 32 583–656, *CSEL* 36, BA 12; *FC* 60; AD 426–7.

Sanct. Virg.   *De Sancta Virginitate*, 1 book; *PL* 40 397–428, *CSEL* 41, BA 3; *NPNF* 3, *LF* Short Treatises, *FC* 27; AD 401.

Serm.   *Sermones*; *PL* 38–9, 46 818–940, 945–1004, *CCL* 41 (1961, 50 OT sermons, incl. some not in *PL*); *NPNF* 6 (nos 51–147), *ACW* 15 (Christmas and Epiphany), *LF* 16, 20 (selected NT), *FC* 11, 38 (selected), tr. P. T. Weller (*Selected Easter Sermons*, St Louis, 1959), tr. Q. Howe (*Selected Sermons*, 1967); others not in *PL* ed. Morin (1931).

Serm. Caes. *Sermo ad Caesariensis Ecclesiae Plebem*, PL 43 689–98, CSEL 53, BA 32; 18 September AD 418.

Serm. Dom. Mont. *De Sermone Domini in Monte*, 2 books; PL 34 1229–1308, CCL 35; NPNF 6, ACW 5, FC 11; AD 394.

Simp. *Ad Simplicianum de Diversis Quaestionibus*, 2 books; PL 40 101–48, CCL 44 (1970), BA 10; LCC 6 (bk 1); AD 395.

Sol. *Soliloquia*, 2 books; PL 32 869–904, BA 5; LCC 6, BW 1, FC 5, tr. R. E. Cleveland (Williams & Norgate, 1910); AD 386/7.

Sp. Lit. *De Spiritu et Littera*, 1 book; PL 44 201–46, CSEL 60; NPNF 5, LCC 8, BW 1, WJ; AD 412.

Symb. *De Symbolo ad Catechumenos, Sermo*; CCL 46; NPNF 3, LF Short Treatises, FC 27.

Trin. *De Trinitate*, 15 books; PL 42 817–1098, CCL 50, 50A, ed. L. Arias (Madrid, 1948), BA 15–16; FC 45, LCC 8 (books 8–15), BW 2 (selections), Clark (books 8, 14), NPNF 3; AD 399–419.

Un. Bapt. *De Unico Baptismo contra Petilianum*, 1 book; PL 43 595–614, CSEL 53, BA 31; AD 411.

Un. Eccl. *De Unitate Ecclesiae contra Donatistas*; PL 43 391–446, CSEL 52; AD 405.

Urb. Exc. *De Urbis Excidio*, 1 book; PL 40 715–24; AD 410.

Util. Cred. *De Utilitate Credendi*, 1 book; PL 42 65–92, CSEL 25.1, BA 8; LCC 6, BW 1, NPNF 3, LF Short Treatises, FC 4; AD 392.

Ut. Jej. *De Utilitate Jejunii*, 1 book; PL 40 707–16, CCL 46, BA 2; AD 399–405.

Ver. Rel. *De Vera Religione*, 1 book; PL 34 121–72, CSEL 77, CCL 32, BA 8; LCC 6, tr. D. Robinson (Library of Liberal Arts, 1958); AD 391.

Vet. Test. *De VIII Quaestionibus ex Veteri Testamento*; PL 35 1374–6 (3 only), CCL 33; ante AD 419.

Vid. Deo *De Videndo Deo* = ep. 147 (in Clark); AD 413.

Other books and articles

Ackrill, J. L. (1974) 'Anamnesis in the *Phaedo*' in E. N. Lee, A. P. D. Mourelatos, and R. Rorty eds *Exegesis and Argument* (*Phronesis* supplement 1), van Gorcum, Assen.

Ackroyd, P. R. and Evans, C. F. (eds) (1970) *The Cambridge History of the Bible, volume 1: From the Beginnings to Jerome*, Cambridge, Cambridge University Press.

Alexander of Aphrodisias (fl. *c.*200) (1983 edn) *On Fate*, with tr. and commentary by R. W. Sharples, London, Duckworth.

Ammianus Marcellinus (*c.*330–*c.*391) (1935–40 edn) *Res Gestae*, with tr. by J. C. Rolfe, Loeb Classical Library, London, Heinemann.

Aquinas, T. (*c.*1225–74) (1949 edn) *De Veritate*, ed R. M. Spiazzi *et al.*, Casale Monferrato, Marietti, 8th edition.

—— (1955 edn) *Summa Contra Gentiles* tr. as *On the Truth of the Catholic Faith*, New York, Random House.

—— (1962–75 edn) *Summa Theologiae*, ed with tr. in 60 volumes, London, Eyre & Spottiswoode.

Aristotle (384–22 BC) (1962 edn) *Eudemian Ethics*, ed F. Dirlmeier, Berlin;

books 1,2,8 tr. with commentary by M. J. Woods, Oxford, Oxford University Press, 1982.

—— (1957 edn) *Metaphysics*, ed W. Jaeger, Oxford Classical Texts, Oxford, Oxford University Press tr. by W. D. Ross in *The Complete Works*, ed J. Barnes, Princeton, NJ, Princeton University Press, 1984.

—— (1894 edn) *Nicomachean Ethics*, ed I. Bywater, Oxford Classical Texts, Oxford, Oxford University Press; tr. by W. D. Ross in *The Complete Works*, ed J. Barnes, Princeton, NJ, Princeton University Press, 1984.

—— (1950 edn) *Physics*, ed W. D. Ross, Oxford Classical Texts, Oxford, Oxford University Press; tr. by R. P. Hardie and R. K. Gaye in *The Complete Works*, ed J. Barnes, Princeton, NJ, Princeton University Press, 1984.

Arminius (Harmens, J., 1560–1609) (1629 edn) *Apology against 31 Articles* and *Declarations*, in *Opera Theologica*, Louvain; tr. by J. Nichols *The Works of James Arminius*, London, Longman, 1825.

Armstrong, A. H. (ed) (1967) *The Cambridge History of Later Greek and Early Medieval Philosophy*, Cambridge, Cambridge University Press.

Arnold, M. (1939 edn) 'The Scholar-gipsy', in *Oxford Book of English Verse*, ed A. Quiller-Couch, new edition, Oxford, Oxford University Press, p. 920.

Atherton, C. (1986) *The Stoics on Ambiguity*, Cambridge PhD thesis.

Baker, G. P. and Hacker, P. M. S. (1983) *Wittgenstein: Meaning and Understanding*, Oxford, Blackwell.

Battin, M. P. and Mayo, D. J. (eds) (1980) *Suicide: the Philosophical Issues*, London, Peter Owen.

Bayle, P. (1649–1706) (1697) *Dictionnaire historique et critique*.

Bentham, J. (1748–1832) (1789) *Introduction to the Principles of Morals and Legislation*, ed J. H. Burns and H. L. A. Hart, London, Methuen, 1982.

Bernard of Clairvaux (1090–1153), *Sermons on the Song of Songs*, PL 183 785–1198.

Blackburn, S. W. (1984) *Spreading the Word*, Oxford, Oxford University Press.

Boethius, Anicius Manlius Severinus (*c.*480–*c.*524), *Consolatio Philosophiae*, PL 63 579–862; ed J. O'Donnell, Bristol, Bryn Mawr, 1984; tr. by E. V. Watts, Penguin, Harmondsworth, 1969, tr. by 'I.T.' (1609), Loeb Classical Library, London, Heinemann, 1936.

——, *De Trinitate*, PL 64 1247–1256.

Bok, S. (1979) *Lying*, New York, Random House.

Bonner, G. I. (1963) *St Augustine of Hippo, Life and Controversies*; 2nd edition, Norwich, Canterbury Press, 1986.

Brown, P. R. L. (1967) *Augustine of Hippo, a Biography*, London, Faber.

Burns, J. P. (1980) *The Development of Augustine's Doctrine of Operative Grace*, Paris.

Burnyeat, M. F. (1982) 'Idealism and Greek philosophy: what Descartes saw and Berkeley missed', in *Idealism: Past and Present*, ed G. Vesey, Royal Institute of Philosophy Lectures, volume 13.

—— (1987) 'Wittgenstein and Augustine *de Magistro*' *Proceedings of the Aristotelian Society*, supplementary volume.

—— (1983) (ed.) *The Skeptical Tradition*, Berkeley, California University Press.

Callahan, J. F. (1948) *Four Views of Time in Ancient Philosophy*; new edition, Cambridge, Mass., Harvard University Press, 1978.

Calvin, J. (1509–64) (1536) *Christianae Religionis Institutio* (1st edition); in *Opera* (Braunschweig, 1863–); tr. by F. L. Battles in *LCC* 20, 21.

Cassian, J. (c.360–435) (1955 edn) *Collationes, PL* 49 477–1328; tr. with abridgements by E. C. S. Gibson in *NPNF*, 2nd series, volume 11 (Eerdmans reprint).

Castaneda, H. -N. (1967) 'Omniscience and indexical reference', *Journal of Philosophy*, pp. 203–10.

Chadwick, H. (1986) *Augustine*, Past Masters series, Oxford, Oxford University Press.

—— (1967) *The Early Church*, Harmondsworth, Penguin.

—— (1983) 'New letters of St Augustine', in *Journal of Theological Studies*, pp. 425–52.

Chellas, B. F. (1980) *Modal Logic: an Introduction*, Cambridge, Cambridge University Press.

Chrysostom, J. (c.347–407), *Homilies on Genesis, PG* 53.

Cicero, M. Tullius (106–43 BC) (1946 edn) *De Divinatione*, ed with tr. by W. A. Falconer, Loeb Classical Library, London, Heinemann.

—— (1933 edn) *De Natura Deorum* and *Academica*, ed with tr. by H. Rackham, Loeb Classical Library, London, Heinemann.

—— (1948 edn) *De Re Publica* and *De Legibus*, ed with tr. by C. W. Keyes, Loeb Classical Library, London, Heinemann.

—— (1927 edn) *Tusculan Disputations*, ed with tr. by C. W. Keyes, Loeb Classical Library, London, Heinemann.

Clement of Alexandria (c.150–c.215), *Stromateis (Miscellanies), PG* 8,9.

Codex Theodosianus (438) (1905 edn) ed T. Mommsen and P. M. Meyer, Berlin.

Cross, F. L. and Livingstone, E. A. (eds) (1974) *Oxford Dictionary of the Christian Church*, Oxford, Oxford University Press, 2nd edition.

D'Arcy, M. C. *et al.* (1930) *A Monument to Saint Augustine*, London, Sheed & Ward.

De Ste Croix, G. E. M. (1977) 'Herodotus', in *Greece and Rome* 24.2, pp. 130–48.

Dennett, D. C. (1985) *Elbow Room: the Varieties of Free Will Worth Wanting*, Oxford, Oxford University Press.

Descartes, R. (1596–1650) (1641) *Meditationes* and *Replies*, in *Oeuvres de Descartes*, ed C. Adam and P. Tannery (Cerf, 1897–1913), volume VII; tr. by J. G. Cottingham, R. Stoothof, and D. Murdoch, Cambridge, Cambridge University Press, 1985.

—— (1970 edn) *Philosophical Letters*, ed with tr. by A. J. P. Kenny, Oxford, Oxford University Press.

Diogenes Laertius (fl. c. AD 180) (1959 edn) *Lives of the Philosophers*, ed with tr. by R. D. Hicks, Loeb Classical Library, London, Heinemann.

Donne, J. (1573–1631) (1648) *Biathanatos*, ed. E. W. Sullivan, Delaware, 1984.

—— (1933 edn) *The Poems of John Donne*, cd H. Grierson, Oxford, Oxford University Press.

—— (1959–62 edn) *The Sermons of John Donne*, ed G. R. Potter and E. M. Simpson, 10 volumes, Berkeley, University of California Press.

Duchesne, L. (1903 edn) *Origines du cultes chrétiens*, Paris, 3rd edition.

Dummett, M. A. E. (1964) 'Bringing about the past', *Philosophical Review*;

reprinted in *Truth and Other Enigmas*, London, Duckworth, 1978; also in *The Philosophy of Time*, ed R. M. Gale, Brighton, Harvester, 1968.

Edwards, J. (1703–57) (1754) *Freedom of the Will*, ed. P. Ramsey, New Haven, CT, Yale University Press, 1957.

Erasmus, D. (1469–1536) (1910 edn) *De Libero Arbitrio Diatribe seu Collatio*, ed J. von Walter, Leipzig, 1910; tr. by E. G. Rupp, *LCC* 17.

Eusebius of Caesarea (c.260–c.339), *Chronicon*, surviving in Armenian and Jerome's Latin, *PG* 19 99–598.

Evans, R. F. (1968) *Pelagius, Inquiries and Reappraisals*, London A. & C. Black.

Feinberg, J. (1974) 'Noncomparative justice', *Philosophical Review* 83, pp. 297–338.

Ferguson, J. (1956) *Pelagius, an Historical and Theological Study*, Heffer.

Findlay, J. N. (1964) 'Time: a treatment of some puzzles', in *Problems of Space and Time*, ed J. J. C. Smart, London, Macmillan; also in *Logic and Language*, ed A. G. N. Flew, 1st series, Oxford, Blackwell, 1951; reprinted from *Australasian Journal of Philosophy* (1941).

Frend, W. H. C. (1952) *The Donatist Church*, Oxford, Oxford University Press.

—— (1984) *The Rise of Christianity*, London, Darton, Longman, & Todd.

Geach, P. T. (1958–9) 'Is it right to say or is a conjunction?' *Analysis*, pp. 143–4; reprinted in *Logic Matters*, Oxford, Blackwell, 1972.

—— (1969) 'Praying for things to happen', in *God and the Soul*, London, Routledge.

—— (1969) 'What actually exists', in *God and the Soul*, London, Routledge; reprinted from *Proceedings of the Aristotelian Society*, supplementary volume (1968).

Gibbon, E. (1737–94) (1776–88) *The History of the Decline and Fall of the Roman Empire*, ed J. B. Bury, London, 1896–1902.

Gilson, E. (1951) *Études sur le role de la pensée médiévale dans la formation du système cartésien*, Paris, Vrin.

Grice, H. P. (1957) 'Meaning', *Philosophical Review*; reprinted in *Philosophical Logic*, ed P. F. Strawson, Oxford, Oxford University Press, 1967; also in *Semantics*, ed D. Steinberg and L. Jakobovits, Cambridge, Cambridge University Press, 1971; also in *Readings in Semantics*, ed F. Zabeeh, E. D. Klemke, and A. Jacobson Champaign, Il, Illinois University Press 1974.

—— (1969) 'Vacuous names', in *Words and Objections*, ed D. Davidson and K. J. J. Hintikka, Hingham, MA, Reidel.

Hick, J. (1966) *Evil and the God of Love*; 2nd edition, London, Macmillan, 1977.

Hobbes, T. (1588–1679) (1651) *Leviathan*, ed C. B. Macpherson, Harmondsworth, Penguin, 1968.

Hume, D. (1711–76) (1975 edn) *Enquiry Concerning the Human Understanding* (1748), ed L. A. Selby-Bigge, 3rd edition, Oxford, Oxford University Press, 1975.

—— (1978 edn) *A Treatise of Human Nature* (1739), ed L. A. Selby-Bigge, 3rd edition, Oxford, Oxford University Press, 1978.

—— (1963 edn) 'On suicide' (1777), in *Essays, Moral, Political and Literary*, Oxford, Oxford University Press; also in *Hume on Religion*, ed R. Wollheim, London, Fontana, 1963.

Jackson, B. D. (1972) 'The theory of signs in *De doctrina Christiana*', in *Augustine*, ed R. A. Markus, q.v.; reprinted from *Revue des Etudes Augustiniennes* (1969).

Jansen, C. O. (1585–1638) (1640) *Augustinus*, part 3, *De Gratia Christi Salvatoris*.

Jauncey, E. (1925) *The Doctrine of Grace*, London, SPCK.

Jerome (Hieronymus, Eusebius, ?342–420), *Letter to Demetrias*, no. 130, and *Letter to Eustochium*, no. 22, in *PL* 22, *CSEL* 56, tr. in *NPNF*, 2nd series, volume 6; *De Viris Illustribus*, *PL* 23, tr. in *NPNF*, 2nd series, volume 3; *Commentaries on Jeremiah*, *PL* 24.

Josephus, Flavius (37–*c*.100) (1926 edn) *Contra Apionem*, ed with tr. by H. St J. Thackeray, Loeb Classical Library, London, Heinemann.

Kant, I. (1724–1804) (1787) *Kritik der reinen Vernunft* (2nd edition), tr. as *Critique of Pure Reason* by N. Kemp Smith, London, Macmillan, 1929.

—— (1790) *Kritik der Urteilskraft*, tr. as *Critique of Judgement* by J. C. Meredith, Oxford, Oxford University Press, 1928, 1952.

—— (*c*.1780) 'Suicide', in *Eine Vorlesung über Ethik*, tr. as *Lectures on Ethics* by L. Infield, London, Methuen, 1930.

Kelly, J. N. D. (1975) *Jerome, his Life, Writings and Controversies*, London, Duckworth.

Kenny, A. J. P. (1979) *The God of the Philosophers*, Oxford, Oxford University Press.

—— (1985) *Wyclif*, Past Masters series, Oxford, Oxford University Press.

—— (1969) 'Divine foreknowledge and human freedom', in *Aquinas*, ed Kenny, q.v.

—— (1973) 'Freedom, spontaneity and indifference', in *Essays on Freedom of Action*, ed E. D. R. Honderich, London, Routledge & Kegan Paul.

—— (1969) 'Happiness', in *Moral Concepts*, ed J. Feinberg, Oxford, Oxford University Press; reprinted from *Proceedings of the Aristotelian Society* (1965–6).

—— (ed) (1969) *Aquinas, a Collection of Critical Essays*, London, Macmillan.

Kirwan, C. A. (1978) *Logic and Argument*, London, Duckworth.

Knox, R. A. (1927) *The Three Taps*, Harmondsworth, Penguin, 1960.

Kretzmann, N., Kenny, A. J. P., and Pinborg, J. (eds) (1982) *The Cambridge History of Later Medieval Philosophy*, Cambridge, Cambridge University Press.

Kretzmann, N. (1971) 'Aristotle on spoken sound significant by convention', in *Ancient Logic and its Modern Interpretations*, ed J. Corcoran, Hingham, MA, Reidel.

Lamb, J. W. (1977) 'On a proof of incompatibilism', *Philosophical Review* 86.

Leibniz, G. W. von (1646–1716) (1956) *The Leibniz–Clarke Correspondence*, ed H. G. Alexander, Manchester, Manchester University Press.

—— (1951 edn) 1710 abridgement of the *Theodicy*, tr. in *Selections*, ed P. P. Wiener, New York, Scribner.

Locke, J. (1632–1704) (1690) *An Essay Concerning Human Understanding*, ed P. H. Nidditch, Oxford, Oxford University Press, 1975.

—— (1689) *Epistula de Tolerantia*, tr. by W. Popple (1689), in *Civil Government*, ed J. W. Gough, Oxford, Blackwell, 1948.

Lucas, J. R. (1973) *A Treatise on Time and Space*, London, Methuen.
—— (1970) *The Freedom of the Will*, Oxford, Oxford University Press.
Lucretius (T. Lucretius Carus, 94–55 BC) (1922 edn) *De Rerum Natura*, ed C. Bailey, Oxford Classical Texts, 2nd edn, Oxford, Oxford University Press.
Luther, M. (1483–1546) (1520) *Assertio Omnium Articulorum M. Lutheri, per Bullam Leonis X Novissimam Damnatorum*, Wittenberg.
—— (1526) *De Servo Arbitrio* (1525), Wittenberg, tr. by P. S. Watson in *LCC* 17.
McCloskey, H. J. (1960) 'God and evil', *Philosophical Quarterly*; reprinted in *God and Evil*, ed N. Pike, Englewood Cliffs, NJ, Prentice-Hall, 1964.
Mackie, J. L. (1982) *The Miracle of Theism*, Oxford, Oxford University Press.
Markus, R. A. (1972) 'St Augustine on signs', in *Augustine*, ed Markus, q.v.; reprinted from *Phronesis* 2 (1957).
—— (1972) (ed) *Augustine, a Collection of Critical Essays*, London, Macmillan.
Marrou, H. I. (1957) *Saint Augustine*, New York, Harper & Row.
Matthews, G. B. (1981) 'On being immoral in a dream', *Philosophy*, pp. 47–54.
—— (1972) 'Si fallor, sum', in *Augustine*, ed Markus, q.v.
Melanchthon (Schwarzerd, P., 1497–1560) (1952 edn) *Loci Communes Theologici*, ed R. Stupperich, Gütersloh; tr. by L. J. Satre in *LCC* 19.
Mignucci, M. (1985) 'Logic and omniscience', in *Oxford Studies in Ancient Philosophy*, volume 3, pp. 219–46.
Mill, J. S. (1806–73) (1859) *On Liberty*, Everyman's Library edn, London, Dent, 1910.
Milton, J. (1608–74) (1667) *Paradise Lost*.
Molina, L. de (1535–1600) (1588) *Liberi Arbitrii cum Gratiae Donis, Divina Praescientia, Providentia, Praedestinatione et Reprobatione Concordia*, ed J. Rabeneck, Madrid, 1953.
Moore, G. E. (1873–1958) (1912) *Ethics*, Oxford, Oxford University Press.
Newman, J. H. (1801–90) (1843) 'Sanctity the token of the Christian empire', in *Sermons Bearing on Subjects of the Day*, Rivington.
Newton, I. (1642–1727) (1687) *Principia Mathematica*, tr. by A. Motte, Berkeley, University of California Press, 1962.
Newton-Smith, W. H. (1980) *The Structure of Time*, London, Routledge & Kegan Paul.
O'Daly, G. J. P. (1981) 'Augustine on the measurement of time: some comparisons with Aristotelian and Stoic texts', in *Neoplatonism and Early Christian Thought*, ed H. J. Blumenthal and R. A. Markus, Variorum.
Parmenides (*c*.515–*c*.430 BC) (1951 edn) surviving fragments in *Die Fragmente der Vorsokratiker*, ed H. Diels and W. Krantz, 6th edn, Weidman.
Pelagius (fl. 400), *Letter to Demetrias*, PL 33 1099–1120.
Philo Judaeus (*c*.20 BC–AD *c*.50) (1929–30 edn) *De Opificio Mundi, De Sacrificiis Abelis et Caini, Quod Deus Immutabilis Sit*, ed with tr. by F. H. Colson and G. H. Whitaker, Loeb Classical Library, volumes 1, 2, and 3 respectively, London, Heinemann.
Pike, N. (1970) *God and Timelessness*, London, Routledge & Kegan Paul.
Plantinga, A. (1974) *The Nature of Necessity*, Oxford, Oxford University Press.
—— (1986) 'On Ockham's way out', *Faith and Philosophy*, reprinted in *The Concept of God*, ed T. V. Morris, Oxford, Oxford University Press, 1987.

Plato (427–347 BC) (1900 edn) *Phaedo*, ed J. Burnet, Oxford Classical Texts, volume 1, Oxford, Oxford University Press, tr. with notes by D. Gallop, Oxford, Oxford University Press 1975.

—— (1900 edn) *Sophist*, ed J. Burnet, Oxford Classical Texts, volume 1, Oxford, Oxford University Press.

—— (1900 edn) *Theaetetus*, ed J. Burnet, Oxford Classical Texts, volume 1, Oxford, Oxford University Press, tr. with notes by J. H. McDowell, Oxford, Oxford University Press, 1973.

—— (1902 edn) *Timaeus*, ed J. Burnet, Oxford Classical Texts, volume 4, Oxford, Oxford University Press.

Plotinus (205–270) (1966–84 edn) *Enneads*, ed with tr. by A. H. Armstrong, Loeb Classical Library, London, Heinemann.

Plutarch (*c*.46–*c*.127) (1967 edn) *Adversus Colotem*, in *Moralia*, ed with tr. by B. Einarson and P. H. de Lacy, Loeb Classical Library, volume 14, London, Heinemann.

Possidius (fl. 400) (1919 edn) *Sancti Augustini Vita*, PL 32 33–66; ed with tr. by H. T. Weiskotten, Princeton, NJ, Princeton University Press; also tr. by F. R. Hoare in *The Western Fathers* (1954) and by E. A. Foran in *The Augustinians* (1938).

Price, H. H. (1953) *Thinking and Experience*, London, Hutchinson.

Prior, A. N. (1967) 'Thank goodness that's over', *Philosophy*, reprinted in *Papers in Logic and Ethics*, London, Duckworth, 1976.

—— (1962) 'The formalities of omniscience', *Philosophy*; reprinted in *Papers on Time and Tense*, Oxford, Oxford University Press, 1968; also in *Readings in the Philosophy of Religion*, ed B. A. Brody, Englewood Cliffs, NJ, Prentice-Hall, 1974.

Prosper of Aquitaine (*c*.390–*c*.463), *Ad Rufinum, Contra Vincentium, Responsiones contra Gallos*, PL 51; tr. in ACW 32.

Rowe, W. L. (1972) 'Augustine on foreknowledge and free will', in *Augustine*, ed Markus, q.v.; reprinted from *Review of Metaphysics* (1964).

Russell, B. A. W. (1872–1970) (1930) *The Concept of Happiness* (also London, Unwin Paperbacks, 1975).

Ryle, G. (1900–76) (1971) 'Discussion of Rudolf Carnap: *Meaning and Necessity*' in *Collected Papers* volume I, London, Hutchinson; reprinted from *Philosophy* (1949).

Sage, A. (1964) 'Praeparatur a Deo', *Revue des Etudes Augustiniennes*.

Scruton, R. V. (1986) *Sexual Desire: a Philosophical Investigation*, London, Weidenfeld & Nicolson.

Searle, J. R. (1983) *Intentionality*, Cambridge, Cambridge University Press.

Sedley, D. N. (1982) 'On signs', in *Science and Speculation*, ed J. Barnes, J. Brunschwig, M. F. Burnyeat, and M. Schofield, Cambridge, Cambridge University Press.

—— (1983) 'The motivation of Greek skepticism', in *The Skeptical Tradition*, ed Burnyeat, q.v.

Seneca, L. Annaeus (*c*.5 BC–AD *c*.50) *Epistulae Morales*; ed with tr. by R. M. Gummere, Loeb Classical Library, London, Heinemann, 1917–25.

Sextus Empiricus (fl. *c*.180) (1935 edn) *Outlines of Pyrrhonism* and *Adversus*

Mathematicos, ed with tr. by R. G. Bury, Loeb Classical Library, London, Heinemann.

Shoemaker, S. (1969) 'Time without change', *Journal of Philosophy*, pp. 363–81.

Simplicius (fl. *c.*530) (1882–1909 edn) *Commentaries on Aristotle's De Caelo and Physics*, in *Commentaria in Aristotelem Graeca*, Prussian Academy, volumes 7–11.

Sorabji, R. R. K. (1983) *Time, Creation and the Continuum*, London, Duckworth.

Stump, E. and Kretzmann, N. (1981) 'Eternity', *Journal of Philosophy*, pp. 429–58; reprinted in *The Concept of God*, ed T. V. Morris, Oxford, Oxford University Press, 1987.

Suarez, F. de (1548–1617) (1856–78 edn) *De Gratia*, in *Opera Omnia*, ed D. M. André, Paris, 28 volumes.

Swinburne, R. G. (1977) *The Coherence of Theism*, Oxford, Oxford University Press.

—— (1968) *Space and Time*, 2nd edition, 1981, London, Macmillan.

Taylor, J. (1694–1761) (1740) *The Scripture-Doctrine of Original Sin*, 2nd edition with supplement (1741).

Tichy, P. and Oddie, G. (1983) 'Ability and freedom', *American Philosophical Quarterly*, pp. 135–47.

Von Arnim, H. (1903–5) (ed) *Stoicorum Veterum Fragmenta*, Stuttgart, Teubner.

Waugh, E. (1957) *The Ordeal of Gilbert Pinfold*; also Harmondsworth, Penguin, 1962.

Wesley, J. (1703–91) (1829) *Sermons on Several Occasions*, volume 2, Thomas Tegg.

West, R. (1933), *St Augustine*. London, Peter Davies.

William of Auvergne (c.1180–1249) (1591 edn) *De Meritis*, in *Opera Omnia*, Venice.

Williams, B. A. O. (1978) *Descartes, the Project of Pure Enquiry*, Brighton, Harvester.

Williams, N. P. (1927) *The Ideas of the Fall and of Original Sin*, London, Longman.

Wittgenstein, L. (1889–1951) (1958) *The Blue and Brown Books*, Oxford, Blackwell.

—— (1953) *Philosophische Untersuchungen (Philosophical Investigations)*, with tr. by G. E. M. Anscombe, Oxford, Blackwell.

Wyclif, J. (c. 1330–84) (1984 edn) *De Universalibus*, ed I. Müller, with tr. by A. J. P. Kenny, Oxford, Oxford University Press.

Index

References to Augustine's writings and to the Bible are not listed, except for a few of Augustine's works (see 'Augustine') and the epistle to the Romans (see 'Paul')

910615   15.95